Fruitful Sites:
Garden Culture in Ming Dynasty C.

T0069069

ENVISIONING ASIA

Series Editors: Homi Bhabha, Norman Bryson, Wu Hung

FRUITFUL SITES

Garden Culture in Ming Dynasty China

CRAIG CLUNAS

REAKTION BOOKS

Published by Reaktion Books Ltd
33 Great Sutton Street
London EC1V 0DX
www. reaktionbooks.co.uk

First published 1996
Transferred to digital printing 2013

Designed by Ron Costley
Photoset by Parker Typesetting Service, Leicester

Printed and bound by University of Chicago Press

British Library Cataloguing in Publication Data:
Clunas, Craig
Fruitful sites: garden culture in Ming dynasty China
1.Gardens – China – History   2.China – History – Ming
dynasty, 1368–1644   3.China - Civilization – 960–1644
I.Title
95 1 '.026

ISBN 978 0 94846 288 7

Contents

Photographic Acknowledgements

The author and publishers wish to express their thanks to the following sources of illustrative material and/or permission to reproduce it (excluding those sources credited in the picture captions):

Helen Espir: nos. 34, 35, 36, 38, 39 and 40; John Lee: no. 45; Li Hong: no. 33; Staatliche Museen zu Berlin – Preußischer Kulturbesitz: no. 32; Marie-Hélène and Guy Weill family collection, photo courtesy of Guy Weill: no. 22. The whereabouts of *The Garden of the Unsuccessful Politician* album of 1533 is unknown; it is here reproduced from Kate Kerby's *An Old Chinese Garden: A Three-fold Masterpiece of Poetry, Calligraphy and Painting, by Wen Chen Ming, Famous Landscape Artist of the Ming Dynasty* (Shanghai, 1922), photos courtesy of the Garden Library, Dumbarton Oaks, Washington, DC: nos. 1, 2, 3, 4 and 5.

Acknowledgements

My primary debt is to those in the Victoria and Albert Museum who allowed me the time to work on this book, both in London and in the United States: Elizabeth Esteve-Coll, former Director of the Museum; Charles Saumarez Smith, former Head of Research; and Rose Kerr, Curator of the Far Eastern Collection. I have received help in the Museum also from Rupert Faulkner and Verity Wilson. During my tenure as a Fellow in Landscape Architecture at Dumbarton Oaks, Washington, DC, I was helped above all by Edward Harwood, also by Joachim Wolschke-Bulmahn, Terence Young, Anne Thacher, and many other Fellows and staff of that remarkable institution. In Washington I benefited too from the advice and practical support of Mi-Chu Wiens at the Library of Congress, Lily Keksces at the Sackler Gallery/Freer Gallery, John Dixon Hunt, and Susan Naquin, as well as the staff of the National Agricultural Library, Beltsville, Maryland. The students who took part in my seminar on 'Land and Landscape in Early Modern China', in the Art Department of the University of Chicago, during the winter quarter 1993, taught me a lot, while I was additionally aided in Chicago by Barbara Banks, Elinor Pearlstein, and Thomas Cummins. For other specific pieces of advice, and for the supply of relevant materials, I am very grateful to Peter Burke, James Cahill, Norma Field, Wen Fong, Stanislaus Fung, Joanna Handlin Smith, James Hevia, Joan Hornby, Dana Leibsohn, Patricia McAnany, Joseph McDermott, Charles Mason, Georges Métailié, Helen Saxbee, John Styles, Monika Ubelhör, Shelagh Vainker, Evelyn Welch, and Keith Wilson.

Introduction

This book does not present a history of 'the Chinese garden'. It is written out of a distrust that such a thing exists. What I attempt to do is give an account of some of the discursive practices surrounding the idea of a garden among the ruling society of China, in a restricted geographical area between *c.* 1450 and 1650. These practices are expressed in textual visual representations, in the form of maps, paintings and illustrations to books. They almost entirely emanate from one part of China, the lower Yangtze valley region known as Jiangnan, which by the Ming period (1368–1644), enjoyed pre-eminence both economically and culturally. Some additional evidence comes from accounts of the imperial capital of Peking.

It seems to me useful and necessary to put into circulation in English some small part of the very large quantity of writing about gardens that exists in the Chinese literature of the period. Much of this is in the form of *bi ji* or 'Note-form literature', in which any mention of gardens may be tiny in proportion to the purposes of the total text, and skimming through it to make notes only when the word 'garden' is spotted is an unsound procedure I have found it hard to break away from. However, we have to have a better understanding at the level of who owned what, where, when. I have by no means read all this literature, but I feel I have read enough to sustain an argument about changes in the way the concept of 'garden' was deployable over the period covered in this book, and to make a case that written and pictorial constructions of this category in 1600 were not what they had been in 1500.

My account begins relatively abruptly. There is no examination of the philological roots of the various terms translated as 'garden', nor are there citations of instances of those words in classical Chinese texts of the Bronze Age. This is a conscious strategy of reading, a refusal to make the equation of origins with essences, which is one of the central practices of orientalism. Instead, I have sought to remain alert to what was written about gardens in Ming China as discursive statements in their own right, as 'constituting serious propositions about the world (rather than simply as dead bits of evidence)'.[1] I make an equally conscious attempt to manoeuvre the idea of the garden into proximity with other discourses, such as that of landed property, which have been neglected in the existing English language secondary literature. Although there is a willingness, even an eagerness, to talk about the 'holistic' nature of the Chinese world view, in which things are interconnected and intertwined, in practice there remains a taboo on speaking about the economic implications of cultural practices in China, a reticence that is not entirely explained by the admittedly often scanty evidence. Bringing some of these implications into the foreground in this case is done not in the spirit of revealing the 'true' nature of 'the Chinese garden', of arguing in a reductive way that Chinese gardens are 'really about' the economics of property owning. Rather, this book is offered as a partial 'alternative history', in the spirit of James Cahill's innovative *Three Alternative Histories of Chinese Painting*, and with its viewpoint that 'art history can be validly written in a diversity of ways or modes, depending on which aspects of art and its circumstances we choose as our focus of concentration'.[2]

One incident may foreground the kind of approach this book is written against. In the spring of 1934, the American landscape architect Fletcher Steele (1885–1971) took a three-month trip to the Far East.[3] The modernized itinerary of the Grand Tour, which by the inter-war years was becoming a regular indulgence for wealthy Europeans and Americans, took Steele to a number of sites in North China, and provided him with material that he subsequently presented to his professional peers, in a lecture to the Boston Society of Landscape Architects in 1946. The published version of this lecture bears the uncompromising title 'China Teaches: Ideas and Moods from Landscape of the Celestial Empire'.[4] Its opening section is further titled 'Race and Design – China', and begins with a sentence whose rhetorical crispness allows of no contradiction: 'The Chinese garden is the sanctuary of the introvert.' Steele's purpose, as he insisted in a footnote, was 'not to write about China, but to use China as an illustration for my propaganda for certain ideas and moods of gardens and garden designers. This was my purpose, *not* mere description'. Mere description may be ruled out, but there is no shortage of definition in his writing, as he proceeds by means of statements that circumscribe an entire discourse of what 'the Chinese' do, think and mean, all of it extrapolated from the single site of 'the Chinese garden'.

Steele incorporated the text of this lecture as a chapter of a book published in 1964, though modifying the title, so that China no longer teaches. Now it was simply the case that 'China Knows', just as 'Englishmen Care', 'The French Must Calculate', 'The Italian Feels' and 'Spain Endures'.[5] The text of 'China Knows' contains one significant modification. A sentence that in the earlier version had read 'After seeing everything from Newport mansions to whole cities torn down just to make room for the latest novelty, it is soothing to feel the timelessness of a design idea in China', now substitutes for 'in China' the words 'in a less volatile civilisation'.[6] The thirty years separating these words from Steele's trip might justifiably be considered as years that were in fact quite volatile for the Chinese who lived through them, encompassing as they did civil war, the eight years onslaught of and resistance to Japanese imperialism, another civil war of massive proportions, the upheaval of the socialist transformation of China, the Great Leap Forward and its attendant famine. In 1964, Steele's 'less volatile civilisation' was poised on the brink of the ten years of the Great Proletarian Cultural Revolution.

This may seem like an easy, even a trivial, target – a once fashionable landscape architect's ignorance of international politics. However, it is a blindness which it is now impossible to see as not being a product of the whole complex of ideas we have come to know as 'Orientalism'. Even (I am tempted to say *especially*) a history of gardens that takes no account of this, which asserts the complete separateness of garden writing from other structures of knowing the East, can no longer be seen as self-evidently correct.[7]

Links between 'the Chinese garden' and 'the Chinese character' were being made well back in the nineteenth century, in a context that was explicitly derogatory of both:

Chinese taste in gardening, it thus appears, partakes of the general character of the people, and is characterised by their leading feature, peculiarity. The love of the grotesque and of monstrosities is seldom accompanied in individuals of any country with enlightened views and liberal sentiments, which are almost always combined with simplicity.[8]

An early nineteenth-century author may have disliked Chinese gardens as vigorously as Steele appreciated them, but in both cases it is equally only the authenticating gaze of the Western observer that can authorize statements about them at all. It is not China that 'knows' but 'the West', here embodied in the person of the three-months sojourner Fletcher Steele. He it is who has understood the essential, invariant characteristics that link the formal features of specific landscape sites he has visited to ideas about 'the race'. The race will never change, just as 'the Chinese garden' will never change, and so war, revolution and famine *are* in this scheme trivial events, the narration of which would involve a descent into 'mere description'.

Over the years since Steele wrote, the links between accounts of 'the Chinese garden' and totalizing descriptions of the Chinese race have not necessarily weakened. In fact, the garden has remained throughout this century one of the key exhibits in the account of Chineseness, whether deployed by Chinese authors inside or outside China, or by non-Chinese writers. This was so in the opening sentences of the first English-language monograph on the subject, published in 1938:

In China a garden is more than a place of peace and a projected dream; it is the embodiment of a philosophy of life. The harmonies and subtle rhythms reflect the mutations of a vaster cosmic scheme.[9]

It remains so in more recent studies, which in particular continue to collapse 'the Chinese garden' very rapidly to 'the Chinese idea of nature'. A collection of essays originally published in 1940 includes one (much cited in later writing) on the theme of 'Man and Nature in the Chinese Garden' by an eminent historian of thought, Wing-Tsit Chan. Here 'nature' is rendered as entirely transcendent and unproblematic, with no sense of the role of human agency in its creation and comprehension.[10] Whether in work explicitly focusing on the idea of the garden, or where the garden is adduced as an exhibit in some larger frame of reference, it is easy to assemble a collection of mutually reinforcing statements along the lines that the Chinese garden 'is an expression of artistic ideas and conceptions that have emerged from an intimate feeling for Nature', 'the Chinese garden has retained a more intimate contact with untrammelled Nature', or 'the imperial gardens were an image of Daoist freedom, spontaneity, and humility before "great nature"'.[11] Similarly, there is a sizeable archive of assertions that 'the garden' was a space essentially outside social life, a place of refusal of the ties of the political life and even of kinship, a calm place and a quiet place: 'In gardens, thoughtful Chinese sought release from the irritations, frustrations, discord and cares of life'.[12] The repetition of this image has manifested itself through scholarly work and through popular articles in newspapers. It has taken on tangible form in the creation of a number of 'authentic' Chinese gardens in recent years, including several associated with museums. From the National Palace Museum, Taipei, to the Metropolitan Museum of Art in New York (illus. 37), a 'Chinese garden' is now a key site of 'Chineseness', replacing in America at least the temple interiors that fulfilled the same role sixty or seventy years ago.

I have made the attempt to eschew the comfort of any explanations that rely on ascribed essences intrinsic to the Chinese garden and the Chinese race, but also to the very concept of 'Chinese society' and 'Chinese culture' as historically coherent and stable objects. I am convinced by the argument that 'because our notion of "society" as the main category of analysis itself entails the displacement of agency on to essences, we should replace the notion of society with the idea of a polity'.[13] The idea of an authentic culture as an inherently coherent, self-sufficient affair of essence has not, in my view, survived the critique expressed by James Clifford among others, and now developed by Edward Said in his recent analysis of the articulation of imperialist discourse in cultural forms.[14] I have therefore tried in what follows to challenge the presumption of the essential alterity of something called 'Chinese culture', where differences between historical practices in western Europe and China are maximized and differences between practices in China at different historical or geographical points are minimized. It is my contention that accounts of the garden have been more than usually complicit in the manufacture and sustenance of China's otherness. They have done this through invoking timeless relationships between 'the Chinese' and 'nature', stereotypes that, in the words of Homi Bhabha, are 'a form of knowledge and identification that vacillates between what is always "in place", already known, and something that must be anxiously repeated . . .'.[15] The Chinese garden is, in the accounts of Fletcher Steele, Dorothy Graham and many others, always the same, but we have to keep on saying so.

As a manifestation of material culture, a garden is an artefact of a particular kind. Philosophical arguments over whether a garden is a work of art are not a central concern here, predicated as they are on the concept of a work of art as a type of thing, a pre-existent category, rather than as a fluctuating manner of categorizing that is historically and socially specific and contested.[16] Gardens do not innocently present themselves for examination. This study cannot be situated outside the nascent academic discipline of garden history, a set of practices clustered round the institutional enabling structures of scholarly journals, international conferences and centres of research.

These practices themselves have a history, of the separation of garden history from architectural history, with the concomitant interest in the integrity of individual objects, often focused on their 'original appearance'. This has sometimes acted to privilege early representations of gardens in a rather naïve manner, with less attention given to the problems of representation. Far more sophisticated has been the cultural history approach of John Dixon Hunt, who has sought to ground garden history in the widest possible reading of sources, both within and beyond the traditional canon of 'literature'.[17] An alternative approach has sought to minimize the separateness of the garden from the practices of managing the wider landscape, whether it be the American vernacular landscape studied by J. B. Jackson or the plains of early modern North India, manipulated by the early Mughals in ways that had both aesthetic and economic implications.[18] This 'landscape history' is often practiced by scholars who have a background in historical geography, and who initially at least saw their project in opposition to the architectural and art-historical roots of 'garden history'. In a particularly fine and subtle example of this approach, that of Denis Cosgrove in his recent *The Palladian Landscape*, there is however a recognition that *all* aspects of a complex set of procedures involving Palladio's reshaping of the Venetian *terraferma* for his aristocratic clients must be taken into account if a satisfactorily rich reading is to be achieved.[19] The example of Cosgrove's study is very much in my mind, though I am conscious that the types of material at his disposal are not available for the parts of China and the period of Chinese history about which I write.

Another challenge, since this book, like most books, is written in response to what has already been written, is that posed by Thomas Keirstead's stimulating *Geography of Power in Medieval Japan*, which takes the institution of the 'estate' (*shoen*), long recognized as the central economic formation of medieval Japan, and success-fully reads it as also a 'social space' a *cultural* system capable of organizing meaning for both estate holders and peasants.[20] Keirstead is dealing with an artefact that has been the exclusive province of economic and social historians. I am dealing with one that has been worked on, if at all, only by art historians. I believe Keirstead and I are working towards a common project from different ends, trying to understand the 'basic conditions of possibility' of a given system, rather than providing a typology or a narrative that starts from the premise of the estate's or garden's pre-ordained existence. This has involved a process of trying to make what we all know we know seem less familiar.

In an earlier book, entitled *Superfluous Things: Material Culture and Social Status in Early Modern China*, I essayed a partial account of attitudes to property, and the creation of meaning through those parts of property that were categorizeable as moveable luxuries. However, I excluded the most important kind of property in premodern China, that of property in land. The present work attempts to take up that theme again. The question of the nature of property relations in land is of course far from being an uninvestigated one. Rather the reverse, there is a daunting literature in Chinese, Japanese, English and other languages on systems of land tenure, property rights and tenancy relations, which I should confess at the outset I have in no sense mastered. Similarly, there is an equally extensive literature on 'landscape' as cultural category, focusing on its role as one of the major divisions of subject-matter in Chinese painting. Economic historians and art historians, however, have historically not been very good at taking each other's work seriously. Accounts of land tenure say little about how land was represented as a social fact in writing or in pictures and maps, while histories of painting give correspondingly scanty attention to the fact that the objects represented in landscape painting – be they mountains, gardens or bodies of water – were all of them capable in the Ming and Qing periods of being *owned*, and therefore bought, sold, even gambled away. What makes gardens so interesting is that they are not restricted to a single sphere. They were expensive pieces of real estate, but they were also consciously constructed and aesthetically perceived artefacts. They overlap intriguingly the boundaries of several Chinese categories, and have a power to illuminate the border regions they traverse.

This study therefore begins with discussion of some specific gardens in China, in the major urban centre of Suzhou. It uses this discussion as a way of interpreting less well-documented types of owned landscape, what was said about them, and how they were represented at the time of their creation. I have tried *not* to see visual representations of landscape as constituting the main field of enquiry, or as the main objects requiring explanation, a criticism that has been levelled (rightly in my view), at even the radical 'social art histories' of T. J. Clark and John Barrell.[21] I do not wish to see paintings of gardens discussed as objects, with actual gardens reduced to their 'background', any more than I wish to see the gardens situated 'in their context', be it social or economic. Rather I would like to try to produce an open-ended investigation. The inconsistencies present in this account will serve to emphasize the over-determination of the complex phenomenon that has perhaps been too often subsumed into 'the Chinese garden'.

1 The Fruitful Garden

Some time early in the third quarter of the fifteenth century, a wealthy textiles merchant named Wu Yong (1399–1475) laid out within the walls of his home city of Suzhou an extensive property to which he gave the name 'Eastern Estate' (*Dong zhuang*). For much of the late imperial period, Suzhou, just west of modern Shanghai, was the most populous non-capital city of the empire, housing half a million people by the sixteenth century within an area of at least 14.8 square kilometres.[1] It was a byword for both the production of luxury goods (silks being the most important) and for their consumption by a rich and cultured elite, with a more than usually high proportion of either expectant or retired government officials.

It was in no sense a static urban landscape. Suzhou had been the power base of one of the unsuccessful contenders for power as the Mongol Yuan dynasty (1279–1368) crumbled, and the city had been sacked in October 1367 after enduring a ten-month siege. Large numbers of its elite families were forcibly transported to other parts of the empire, and a new elite loyal to the Ming founder, Zhu Yuanzhang (1328–98), was installed. Suzhou experienced a major flood in 1440, and serious famine in 1454.[2] However, by the end of the fifteenth century, and in particular during the reign of the Hongzhi emperor (1488–1505), there was a sense among contemporaries that Suzhou was regaining some of its former glory.[3] Despite the recovery of urban life, in 1500 it was a city where a considerable amount of productive horticultural land remained within its walls, as was absolutely standard among major Chinese cities at this time.[4] But Suzhou was to start to lose its population from its intra-mural area during the sixteenth century, as the elite abandoned its eastern half (administratively part of Changzhou county) to workers in the textiles industry, moving themselves and their families to the western (Wu county) side, or outside the city walls altogether to suburbs stretching north-west along the canal connecting Suzhou to the resort spot of Tiger Hill (*Hu qiu*).[5]

When Wu Yong was laying out his property, these social and demographic changes lay in the future. An account of the Eastern Estate written by the high official and famous literary figure Li Dongyang (1447–1516; DMB 877–81[6]) gives us some sense of the major dispositions of the landscape it contained:

The land of Su is rich in water-courses. The Eastern Estate of Old Sir Wu within the Fu Gate lies upon [one of] these, with the Chestnut Moat to its east and the West Stream girdling it to the west. Two creeks touch it at the sides, both of which can be reached by boat. Entering from the Bench Bridge you encounter the Rice Plot. Turning and going south, there lies the Mulberry Orchard, going west again is the Fruit Orchard, then to the south is the Vegetable Patch, to the east the Clothes-shaking Terrace, to the south-west the Breaking Cassia Bridge. Entering from the Punt Bank is the Wheat Mound. Entering from the Lotus Flower Bend is the Bamboo Field, laid out in a chequer-board pattern. The whole covers 60 mu.[7] There is a hall called the Hall of the Continuation of Antiquity, a hermitage called the Hermitage of Artless Cultivation, and a studio called the Studio of Rest from Ploughing. He also made a pavilion on the Southern Pond, called the Pavilion for the Appreciation of Delight. With the finishing of the pavilion the affairs of the estate were first completed, with the whole thing being named Eastern Estate, from which he took his secondary name (hao) of 'Old Man of the Eastern Estate' (Dong zhuang weng).[8]

As the text goes on to make clear, the nine acres of the Eastern Estate form a veritable model of rural self-sufficiency, where philosophical ideals of nurturing an antique simplicity and a rustic clumsiness are combined with a complete inventory of the types of land manage-ment necessary for the support of an idealized family of kin and servants: rice, vegetables, fruit, and mulberry trees for silkworm-rearing. It further stresses that this property, unlike so many others in the region, remained in the hands of the same family through Suzhou's turbulent fourteenth century and early fifteenth. Thus the maintenance of property within the Wu family over this violent political transition was a matter worthy of record.

'From the end of the Yuan through to the beginning of our dynasty, eight- or nine-tenths of the neighbours died or migrated, and the Wu alone remained.' Li Dongyang goes on to cite a long statement made to him by Wu Kuan (1436–1504; DMB 1487–9), the son of Wu Yong, creator of the Eastern Estate, in which Wu Kuan praises his father for 'following the Way (dao) and fearing the laws', and for 'preserving his property' (bao qi ye). He continues with an encomium on the notion of 'property' (ye), which is all the more to the point in that what he is describing either is, or is very shortly about to become, his own property. Li Dongyang's prose 'Record' (ji) of the estate is dated 1475, the year in which Wu Yong died. The property would then have been divided equally among his three sons, Wu Kuan being the middle one. It was perfectly possible (though as we shall see, far from inevitable) for sons to keep a property together physically, particularly if it involved a highly visible piece of urban real estate like the Eastern Estate. In view of the stress on the relationship between continuity of property and continuity of family that is contained in the text, it seems plausible that this is what happened in this individual case.

There is, however, an irony embedded in Li Dongyang's account that lies at the heart of the object of this present book. Not only was this synecdoche of rural self-sufficiency physically embedded in one of the most populous cities of the empire, it was embedded in a city which at that very period was beginning to lose the ability to feed itself from the agriculture of its immediate hinterland, and was rather dependent on the products of its manufactures (the real source of Wu Yong's wealth) to support its huge population. The profits made from the silks and other manufactures of the city enabled grain to be purchased from distant areas of the empire, as, for the first time, Suzhou entered a situation where, 'dependent on its markets rather than its fields', it 'could afford to regard nature as an object of aesthetic appreciation'.[9] The Eastern Estate was not a real rural estate, but one of the sights of Suzhou for members of the elite who passed through, taking advantage of the city's reputation as a centre of cultural production and luxury consumption: 'Those court scholars who travelled with Wu Kuan heard of the Aged Sire's virtue, and wrote many poems on the Eastern Estate, which augmented the estate's fame.'

The source from which I have taken the account of the Eastern Estate by Li Dongyang is a gazetteer, a type of local history combining information on the administrative geography, famous sights, typical products and notable inhabitants of a given region. The particular gazetteer in question, the *Gusu zhi* of 1506, was initially compiled by the very Wu Kuan whose contacts in the higher reaches of the bureaucracy ensured the property's fame (though Wu himself died in 1504, and the finished book appeared under the editorship of an even more important member of the Suzhou elite, Wang Ao (1450–1524; DMB 1343–7). Thus it is not entirely surprising that the account of the Eastern Estate is given added prominence within this text by its positioning at the very end of the book's thirty-second chapter, entitled *Yuan chi* ('Gardens and Ponds'). Such a text is not an innocent primary source for the study of Ming dynasty Suzhou (which is the way gazetteers are sometimes read), but a prescriptive text with its own agenda, in this case arguably an agenda for establishing certain families and certain networks of connections as hegemonic within the social landscape of the city. There were gardens in the area that are not mentioned in the text.[10] There were also prominent cultural figures for whom no garden is listed. The Eastern Estate is presented to us as the culmination of a long tradition of the creation of 'Gardens and Ponds' in the Suzhou area, and indeed it bears the name of a much earlier Eastern Estate, the property of the son of Yuan Liao, Prince of Guangling, a magnate active in the area in the fourth century AD.

What is also presented to us is the claim that Wu Yong's actions in building an urban property of this kind are in some sense a novelty. Conventional accounts in Western secondary literature typically see the practice of garden culture as a constant of 'traditional China', but there is a clear sense in contemporary sources of a rhythm of building and decay, of periods when fewer major gardens were constructed and of others when they were relatively more numerous. This was the case with regard particularly to urban garden sites in Suzhou between the twelfth century and the mid-fifteenth, at least in the picture presented by the gazetteer of 1506. It lists fifty-two sites in the chapter on 'Gardens and Ponds', dating from the Eastern Jin dynasty (AD 317–420) down to the Eastern Estate. Each of these sites is accompanied by a varying number of literary citations of prose and verse, enabling us to construct a rough league-table of the fame they enjoyed in the mid-Ming period (remembering that this is as likely to be a factor of the fame of the *authors* involved, as it is of the sites themselves).[11] The famous gardens are associated primarily with the eleventh and twelfth centuries, and their fame is not matched by those of sites created in the subsequent two hundred and fifty years.

One famous urban site of the Song dynasty, the 'Pleasure Patch', was described in the gazetteer as being partially rebuilt in the period 1426–35 by a major figure of the Suzhou elite, Du Qiong (1396–1474; DMB 1321–2), whose father had been one of the victims of the forced population migration initiated by the Ming founder. The garden had been laid out and named in the Song period by Zhu Changwen (1039–98) on the site of a yet more ancient property, the Golden Valley Garden of the Qian family.[12] However, there were only four completely new gardens worthy of inclusion in the gazetteer that had been laid out in Suzhou prefecture in the period from the creation of the dynasty in 1368 to the time of publication, 1506:

The Xia Family Garden was in Kunshan, and was the place of recreation of Xia Chang [1388–1470; DMB 525–6], Chief Minister of the Court of Imperial Sacrifices, on his retirement.
Little Dongting was created by Assistant Censor Liu Jue [1410–72; MRZJ 836] on his return from his post in Shanxi. At his old dwelling outside the Qi gate he piled up stones to make a mountain. There were ten 'views'

(*jing*), with names such as the 'Moustache Fingering Pavilion' (*Nian zi ting*) and the 'Lotus Flower Island' (*Ou hua zhou*). Xu Youzhen [1407-72; DMB 612-5] wrote a preface on it.

The 'Thoughts Hermitage' (*Si an*) is a suburban garden outside the Guo gate at Kunshan, built by the Censor-in-Chief Master Wu. When Zhou Chen [1381-1453; MRZJ 318] was Grand Coordinator he wrote a poem on it.

The fourth, and final, site to be mentioned in the gazetteer is the Eastern Estate itself. Only one of these four properties was therefore within the walls of Suzhou, with another on the city's outskirts, while the other two were, respectively, inside and outside the walls of Kunshan, a smaller and administratively subordinate city to the east. The prose and verse works that mention these four sites allow us to compile a list of twelve men recorded by the gazetteer as being involved in the practice of garden culture in fifteenth-century Suzhou, either as owners or celebrators.

What is striking about this group is the number of connections that bind it together into a cohesive in-group, linked together in numerous ways. Eight of its twelve members had major official careers, almost all of them with Peking connections in the most prestigious parts of the bureaucracy, such as the Hanlin Academy or the Censorate. Furthermore, eight of the twelve (though not the same eight) had major reputations as artists, either as calligraphers or painters or both; Xia Chang, Du Qiong, Xu Youzhen, Liu Jie, Shen Zhou, Wu Kuan, Liu Daxia and Li Dongyang. Some, like Xia Chang and Wu Kuan, combined high office with contemporary and subsequent artistic fame. The number of this group who find a place in the modern, and necessarily highly selective, reference book, the *Dictionary of Ming Biography* of 1976, gives some idea of how prominent they mostly were, a constellation of wealth, culture and political power that placed them close to the very apex of the social order.

To give some examples of the type of networking involved within the members of this group, Du Qiong, the reviver of the Pleasure Patch, was the teacher of both Wu Kuan, who augmented the fame of his father's (and his own) Eastern Estate and who drafted the gazetteer that set the seal on its canonical status, and of Shen Zhou (1427-1509; DMB 1173-7), the wealthy landlord and artist who was particularly close to the Wu family and who is known to have immortalized the Estate both in verse and in an album of paintings. Both Wu Kuan and Shen Zhou were in their turn the teachers of the writer and artist Wen Zhengming (1470-1559; DMB 1471-4), who will be a recurrent presence in my account. Wen's family had links through several generations with the putative group of 'garden founders' outlined above.[13] The retirement from office of Wen Hong, Wen Zhengming's grandfather, was commemorated by a pictorial scroll to which both Li Dongyang and Wu Kuan provided colophons.[14] Wen Zhengming attests to the continuing existence of the Eastern Estate of his teacher, Wu Kuan, and to the continuing vitality of the theme of the celebration of family property, in a poem of 1509 entitled 'Visiting the Wu Family's Eastern Estate and Inscribing a Presentation of Inherited Property'.[15]

There is a clear sense in the sources that what these twelve men considered themselves to be doing involved an element of novelty. The gazetteer's poem on the Eastern Estate by the high official Liu Daxia includes the couplet 'The garden groves of Suzhou once rivalled those of Luoyang,/Over the past hundred years all that can be seen is the Eastern Estate.' The claim that something special, something new, is happening in Suzhou in the attitude to landscape at the end of the fifteenth century is supported by the complaint (written in 1494) of an author who, despite his critical attitude to his contemporaries, was himself within the charmed circle of the Suzhou elite:

Suzhou and Hangzhou are equally renowned as the famous prefectures of Jiangnan. However, the wealthy of Suzhou city and its county cities generally enjoy the splendours of pavilions, lodgings, flowers and trees. Nowadays there are none of these in Hangzhou city. This is because the frugality of customs in Hangzhou is superior to that of Suzhou.[16]

There is a gap here between the rhetoric of the gazetteer account of the Eastern Estate, with its morally enobling rice-fields, mulberry trees, fruits and vegetables, and its encomium on the stability of family property, and the complaint about the 'splendours of pavilions, lodgings, flowers and trees', which violate the equally desirable elite norm of frugality. It is this gap, this area of unease generated in Ming China by the very possibility that land, which both formally and ideally underpinned and stabilized the social order, could potentially enter into the de-stabilizing realm of inappropriately lavish consumption, which forms one of the themes of this book. If we look at the phenomenon of gardens in China from c. 1500 to c. 1600, it is possible to argue that there is a major shift in what is signified by the very concept of a 'garden' at this period, which ultimately tilts the balance of understanding of this particular artefact entirely away from the 'good' realm of production, of natural increase and natural profit through the ownership of land, and towards the problematic realm of consumption, excess, and luxury.

Although I have concentrated so far on the great urban centre of Suzhou, the phenomenon of change in the sixteenth century is one that can be attested in other parts of the empire. John Dardess has shown how the regional elite of the small city of Taihe in Jiangxi province shifted the focus of their interest in land from production to consumption over the same period.[17] Though in no sense renowned for its 'gardens', Taihe was wrapped in an envelope of horticulture, which ranged from small plots of mixed vegetables to large-scale commercial market-gardening. In the fifteenth century it was standard for members of the elite to participate in a little genteel horticulture, a horticulture still directed towards edible crops, and in cognate activities like wood-gathering and fishing. For the Taihe elite, the word *yuan* still maintained the meaning of a productive space which it had held since time immemorial, and which it would continue to have for the majority of China's population throughout the imperial period.

In what I have said so far there is a silent collapse of the Eastern Estate to the category *yuan*, conventionally translated as 'garden', but this should not be allowed to pass without comment. It has been done largely on the strength of its inclusion, indeed its glorification, in the chapter of the gazetteer entitled 'Gardens and Ponds'. This could equally well have been translated as 'Orchards and Ponds'. The total split between the aesthetic and the economic in horticulture is of very recent vintage, as we shall see, but it makes it difficult to employ words in a way that speaks of sites included in completely different fields of discourse. I intend to continue to refuse to provide a definition of 'garden' in the Ming period, preferring to avoid a search for essences in what was a complex, over-determined set of practices. Rather I would seek to draw out some of the ways in which the category *yuan* was deployed in Ming systems of ordering, while accepting that these systems were signifying practices capable of contestation and refusal.

THE GARDEN OF THE UNSUCCESSFUL POLITICIAN

The miniature rice-fields and vegetable patches of the Eastern Estate do not coincide at all with the stereotype of the timeless 'Chinese garden', an excessively aestheticized, asocial space of elaborate rockwork and pavilions. However, its concentration on the mimesis of productive resources was not at all unusual in Suzhou around the turn of the fifteenth century. This can be revealed by an analysis of the contents of an extremely famous Suzhou site called the *Zhuo zheng yuan*, or 'Garden of the Unsuccessful Politician'.[18]

The city of Suzhou today is one of China's most important tourist destinations, and its gardens are one of the main sights on any visitor's itinerary. A modern Chinese survey of 'classical Chinese gardens' describes the currently most famous of them in these terms:

Representative of a traditional Suzhou garden, Zhuo Zheng Yuan, or Garden of the Unsuccessful Politician, is located at the Northeast Street of Lou Men, Suzhou. It was built in the Jia Jing period of the Ming Dynasty by Wang Xianchen, Censor of the Throne. The name comes from a line in the 'Xian Ju (An Idle Life)' rhyme-prose composed by the famous scholar official Pan Yue of the Jin Dynasty. Once when Pan was disappointed in his political life, he retired to live in a farmhouse and led an idle life planting trees and growing vegetables. In the 'Xian Ju' rhyme-prose he writes 'This *is* the way of ruling for an unsuccessful politician.' The garden frequently changed its owners and with each new owner, much reconstruction was done.[19]

If we start to unpack some of the implications of this bland guidebook language, things begin to appear rather more complicated. Wang Xianchen is someone about whom it is possible to know quite a lot, although unfortunately the exact dates of his birth and death are not recorded. He was registered in Wu county, the western of the two counties between which the Suzhou urban area was divided. His early career can be mapped out on the basis of his biography in the standard dynastic history of the Ming, the *Ming shi*,[20] and of two documents relating to his family found in the writings of Wen Zhengming. One of these documents is an epitaph for Wang Xianchen's father, Wang Jin, who died in 1510 holding the position of Investigating Censor (*Jian cha yu shi*), a relatively junior if prestigious post in the supervisory bureaucracy.[21] Wang Xianchen himself entered the bureaucracy at some unspecified date with the post of Messenger (*Xing ren*), subsequently being promoted to the Censorate. In 1490, following an accusation that he had improperly interfered with military affairs on the frontier, he was given a thirty strokes beating and transferred to serve as vice-magistrate of Shanghang county in Fujian province. While passing through his native Suzhou he was warmly treated by the local elite, who provided him with a body of poems consoling him in his misfortune. The preface to this was supplied by Wen Zhengming, then just twenty-one years old by Chinese reckoning, in his first piece of 'public' writing.[22] We do not know on what terms this relationship between the two men was formed, and cannot tease out precisely the nexus of patron–client, elder–younger, official–commoner as it operated in this particular case. We can infer only that Wang Xianchen was older than Wen Zhengming, by at least ten years.[23]

Wan Xianchen obtained the highest level *jinshi* degree in 1493, and at some point over the next decade left the provincial bureaucracy to rejoin the Censorate, since a poem of 1503 by Wen Zhengming addresses him by the title 'censor'.[24] This second career as a 'speaking official' stalled in 1504, when he was again arrested in connection with what his biography refers to as 'the Zhang Tingxiang affair'. This complex imbroglio, which claimed other careers as well as his own, pitted the civilian bureaucracy against the hereditary military elite and the eunuch-run Eastern Depot in a series of claims and counter-claims arising out of an incident in which a peaceful tribal group had been attacked and their attackers then slain in turn by a different faction within the Ming military. Wang Xianchen ended up by being demoted in 1504 to Postal Intendant for Guangdong province. In 1506, on the accession of the Zhengde emperor, he was promoted to be magistrate of Yongjia county in Zhejiang province, a post that again brought him into connection with the Wen family, since Wen Lin had been prefect of Wenzhou (the prefecture in which Yongjia was situated) at the time of his death in 1499. He was still at this post in 1508, when he was the recipient of another poem by Wen Zheng-ming.[25] The death of his father in 1510 necessitated the standard twenty-five months of mourning, however, and it seems to have been at this point that he gave up an official career in favour of the life of a landed proprietor and the persona of a gentleman of leisure.[26] These two aims were completely compatible in the creation of the large garden known by the title *Zhuo zheng yuan*, the Garden of the Unsuccessful Politician.

The site was that of the defunct Dahong Temple, which according to the gazetteer of 1506 had burned down in the Ming conquest of Suzhou, and remained 'a total wasteland' at the time of writing.[27] The exact date of the garden's construction is unknown. The modern garden historian Liu Dunzhen argues for a date somewhere between 1509 and 1513, on the basis of a statement made by Wang Xianchen in 1539 that he had been 'nurturing his lack of success for nearly thirty years', and of Wen Zhengming's reference in 1533 to 'twenty years ago' as the date of Wang's retirement.[28] Wang certainly possessed a garden by 1514, for it is the subject of a Wen Zhengming poem of that year, though it is not until 1517 that one of the same author's poems incorporates the current title – the Garden of the Unsuccessful Politician.[29] This is the earliest absolute proof we have

1 Wen Zhengming, *Many Fragrances Bank* (*Fan xiang wu*).

1-5 Leaves from the album *The Garden of the Unsuccessful Politician* (*Zhuo zheng yuan tu ce*), 1533 version, ink on paper.

2 Wen Zhengming, *Thoughts of Afar Terrace* (*Yi yuan tai*).

3 Wen Zhengming, *Angling Rock* (*Diao zhu*).

4 Wen Zhengming, *Arriving Birds Park* (*Lai qin you*).

5 Wen Zhengming, *Scholar-tree Tent* (*Huai wu*).

of the existence of a garden of this name. Relations between Wang Xianchen and Wen Zhengming, as evidenced by the latter's poems, are steady over the next decade or so. We have poems from 1515 (alluding to time spent in a garden), 1518 (acknowledging a gift of transplanted bamboos) and 1519 (recording a visit to the main architectural structure in the garden, the Tower for Dreaming of Seclusion).[30] There is then a gap of some years (from 1523 to 1527 Wen was away from Suzhou), before poems in 1527 (recording a visit with Wang Xianchen to Tiger Hill) and 1529 (opening with the line 'A lofty scholar in a famous garden among ten thousand bamboos').[31] At some point Wen Zhengming acted as sponsor at the coming-of-age, or 'capping' ceremony for Wang Xianchen's son, a service for which he would receive a gratuity, and not necessarily a purely formalistic one.[32] Then in 1533 came the intervention by Wen Zhengming that has ensured the Garden of the Unsuccessful Politician its place in China's cultural history. This takes the form of an album containing a lengthy prose 'Record' of the garden, which accompanies thirty-one paintings and poems on specific spots within it (illus. 1–5).[33] Wen produced a second album of eight leaves showing sites in the garden in 1551, with different views but the same poems as had appeared in 1533 (illus. 6–11).[34] In addition to these, there are a number of extant or recorded scrolls showing the garden and which are attributed to Wen's brush.[35]

Liu Dunzhen has traced the turbulent history of the garden in later centuries.[36] Several points concerning this tangled history should be noted. The garden has not *survived* from the Ming period in the same sense as Chartres cathedral has survived since the Middle Ages. None of the plant-matter we see today in the Garden of the Unsuccessful Politician has been growing continuously in the same spot for those nearly five centuries.[37] The Garden's very boundaries have not been constant within this century, never mind for over five hundred years. None of the architectural structures we see is of any great antiquity. Perhaps more surprisingly, only a very few of them share the names of features that we know to have been in the garden in 1533. Thirty-two pavilions, towers and other structures can be counted in the garden as it stands today.[38] Of these, only four correspond in name to features on the list of thirty-one given by Wen Zhengming.[39] This is in no way a unique history of transience, but could be repeated for any of the great historic garden sites of modern China. The names now given to individual features in Suzhou's 'Lion Grove' (*Shizi lin*) do not correspond with those known from historic sources.[40]

Modern authors, particularly Liu Dunzhen, have noted the number of changes of owner of the Garden of the Unsuccessful Politician and have stressed the numerous changes in its physical appearance from the time of its creation to the present. Liu for example stresses that the original garden had a very much more natural and open aspect, included none of the artificial hills that are such a striking part of the present layout, and had far fewer structures.[41] His conclusion is modest: the arrangement of the rocks and water in the ponds of the central third may have its origins in the early Qing (over a century and a half after the time of building). The western third retains the late nineteenth-century layout, while the eastern third, totally ruinous by 1949, has been worked over in a modern landscape style suitable for large crowds of visitors, with open lawns and teahouses. Even this seems unreasonably optimistic. Yet there remains a sense in Liu's writing (present yet more strongly in other works of secondary literature), that, despite the vicissitudes of history, there is continuity at the much more important level of essence. Despite changes, there is a certain quintessence of the garden that can survive changes of layout, of planting and of name, never mind the trivial level of ownership, and which can sustain a 'Garden of the Unsuccessful Politician' as some sort of reality behind the temporary veil of 'people's dwellings' or the office of a general (the function of the property in the eighteenth and nineteenth centuries). For the author of the most widely read modern work in English on a Chinese garden, the Garden of the Unsuccessful Politician is 'another garden in Suchow dating from the early Ming period . . .'.[42] This is possible because there has been no challenge to the idea of the 'essence' of a Chinese garden, which privileges continuing fragments of literary discourse over the contingencies of vegetal decay. Why is the Garden of the Unsuccessful Politician a stable presence, rather than a reconstruction? Such an idea would be ludicrous without the conviction that there is something called 'a Chinese garden' that has not significantly changed its patterns of meanings, underlying aesthetic principles and social role from the sixteenth century (or even from well before then) to now.

Whence comes this fame then, that makes the Garden of the Unsuccessful Politician 'the representative type of the Jiangnan classic garden',[43] if it does not stem from enduring intrinsic features of the site? To the acute early nineteenth-century writer Qian Yong, intrinsic features were not important. For him there was another explanation, one that was socially rather than aesthetically grounded:

6 Wen Zhengming, *Many Fragrances Bank* (*Fan xiang wu*).

6–11 Leaves from the album *The Garden of the Unsuccessful Politician*
(*Zhuo zheng yuan tu ce*), version dated 1551, ink on paper. Metropolitan
Museum of Art, New York.

7 Wen Zhengming, *Little Surging Waves* (*Xiao Canglang*).

8 Wen Zhengming, *Xiang Bamboo Bank* (*Xiang yun wu*).

9 Wen Zhengming, *Scholar-tree Rain Pavilion* (*Huai yu ting*).

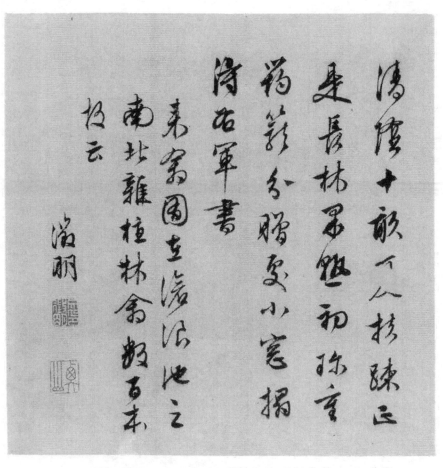

10, 11 Wen Zhengming, *Arriving Birds Park* (*Lai qin you*), with
accompanying inscription.

I would argue that the decay and flourishing of a garden is allied to that of its owner. If the person is remembered, then though it [i.e. the garden] decays it will rise again. If the person is not commemorated, then even though it flourishes it will eventually decay. The literary productions of brush and ink are more lasting than are gardens, since the former cannot decay away. Now when I study Wen Zhengming's paintings, read his record and his poems, I suddenly see the splendours of the towers and terraces, the flowers and trees, and more than three hundred years of decay and restoration, recovery and loss, scattered like cloud and blown by the wind, seems to appear before my astonished eyes.[44]

Yet the biographical literature is silent about the identity or activities of the great majority of the individual owners of portions of the site in the Qing period.[45] By and large they were not famous as writers or painters, or as actors on the political scene. Although Qian pays obeisance to the idea of the famous owner, in this particular instance it is in fact the much more famous figure of Wen Zhengming who creates the garden anew for him. The garden now exists as an adjunct to the works of art that surrounded its early existence; to a degree it is they that produce the garden, not the other way around. This is done so with particular potency in that the person doing the recording and depicting is Wen Zhengming, by Qian Yong's day in the Qing period the unassailable epitome of the scholar–amateur ideal.

THE FRUITFUL GARDEN

The paradigm of the garden as essentially an object of pure aesthetic significance is hard to escape, but we may make the effort to break free of its gravitational field and by doing so prise the Garden of the Unsuccessful Politician from its exclusively pictorial associations. One way of complicating the picture, and of introducing a dimension that is rigorously excluded from most modern discussion of Chinese garden history, is to read Wen Zhengming's 'Record of the Garden of the Unsuccessful Politician' in a naïve and simplistic manner for the information it contains on the agronomy of the garden in 1533. Let us pretend we have never heard of the rich associative aesthetics of 'the Chinese garden'. To do so involves a risky reading strategy that privileges agronomic texts as neutral descriptions, instead of the prescriptive and socially rooted phenomena they were.[46] They were a phenomenon whose production expanded greatly in the Ming period, particularly after the mid-sixteenth century, as part of a larger picture of the commodification of knowledge at this period.[47] It is not suggested that a purely agronomic reading is a justifiable way of getting at the truth about 'the Chinese garden'. However, in an attempt to de-centre the primacy of aesthetic discourse in writing about garden culture, a reductive, even crass, reading against the grain of a highly contrived literary text may serve well enough.

What does Wen Zhengming say was growing in the Garden of the Unsuccessful Politician in 1533? In the order in which the plants are encountered in the 'Record', the list is as follows: lotus, bamboo, willow, oranges, pines, juniper, peaches, sophora, elms, flowering plum, tree peony, herbaceous peony, orange osmanthus, crab apples, *ziyao*, apples, rugosa roses, plum, roses, cypress, calamus, privet, plantain and hibiscus. Of course, a bald recital like this gives no sense of the degree of impact the various species might have had on a visitor to the Garden. Fortunately the 'Record' does contain a certain number of more or less impressionistic quantifications of at least some of them. Bamboos are mentioned as being present at six specific sites in the garden. There are 'many' pines, while sophora, cypress and elm trees are 'numerous'. There are 'several tens' of orange trees, and what may also be a significant number of peach trees, the blossom being described as 'like a red cloud'. We know that there is only one plum (*li: Prunus domestica*), brought specifically from Peking, in whose climate it flourished more readily. By contrast, the number of flowering plum trees (*mei; Prunus mume*) is described as 'a hundred' in the 'Record', and as 'several hundred' in the relevant accompanying poem.[48] The number of apple trees is also given as 'several hundred', which according to the accompanying poem covered an area of ten *mu*. Arbitrarily assuming that 'several hundred' flowering plums take up about the same space as 'several hundred' apple trees (i.e. ten *mu*), we arrive at the figure of twenty *mu*, or very nearly three acres, devoted to two compact groves of fruit-bearing trees. This is a fairly high proportion of the total of sixty-two *mu* that Liu Dunzhen assigns to the original, as well as to the present, layout of the garden, particularly when it is remembered that ponds make up about one-third of the total land area. Even allowing for the difference between a Ming *mu* and a modern one, this puts practically half the land area of the garden under a combination of flowering plums and apples in 1533. Trees, and in particular fruit trees, must also have been the dominating presence in the other half, since the majority of the more ornamental shrubs were concentrated at only one site in the garden, on *Fan xiang wu*, 'Many Fragrances Bank' (illus. 1, 6), which bore both kinds of peony, the orange osmanthus, crab apple and *ziyao*.[49] This is very different visually from any garden visible in China today.

Let us look in more detail at the role played by fruit in the world of goods in Ming Suzhou, and in particular at the fruit trees specified in the Garden of the Unsuccessful Politician. By the Ming, all major cities and even county seats were surrounded by zones of horticulture.[50] In terms of the total land area of the Jiangnan region the amount under fruit trees was probably not very large, but in such a fertile area with a benign climate a relatively small plot could be enough to supply the needs of a household. A fourteenth-century agronomic treatise, 'Wang Zhen's Book of Agriculture' (*Wang Zhen nong shu*), begins its section on horticulture thus:

Plot fields (*pu tian*) are fields for planting vegetables or fruit. The 'Rites of Zhou' says 'Employ horticultural land (*yuan di*) in plot fields (*pu tian*).' The annotation reads 'A plot is such things as tree fruits and vine fruits.' Such fields are surrounded by a wall and bounded by a hedge and ditch. Only 10 *mu* with its back to a city wall is sufficient to feed several mouths. If it is rather farther from the city then the amount of fields can be increased up to a maximum of half a *qing* [50 *mu*].[51]

We are dealing here with a context where the average size of landholdings was not of itself very large. Really large estates were not common in Ming Jiangnan. Another agronomic writer of the late Ming, this time a small landlord from Jiaxing, asserted that ten *mu* was the upper limit which a 'top-class farmer' could manage on his own, while in the early Qing a retired grandee could boast of living comfortably on twenty *mu*, and supporting a household of ten persons to boot.[52] The climate and fertility of Europe and North America encourage perceptions of landed wealth as being inseparable from the idea of 'broad acres', of lots of land, but there are a number of other historical contexts where the input of skill is a much more important variable than sheer quantity of land. Sixteenth-century China was in this respect less like contemporary Europe than it was like sixteenth-century Mexico, where it was calculated that one man could work between 0.5 and 0.75 hectares of the highly fertile lakeside *chinampa* land, only one hectare of which was sufficient to feed fifteen to twenty people.[53] The notion of wealth in land being dependent on quantity is not always applicable in a context where inputs of skilled labour to very productive soils may be a more decisive factor.

Viewed in this light, Wang Xianchen's 62 *mu*, the majority of which was under fruit trees, comes to look potentially like a powerful economic resource, a piece of real estate that was not only relatively large by contemporary standards but which was planted with lucrative, market oriented cash crops. The profitability of citrus fruit trees, of which Wang had 'several tens', in particular was proverbial. They had been grown commercially since the Warring States period (475–221 BC), from when the term 'wooden slaves' (mu nu) dates.[54] By the Song period (960–1279) the Lake Tai region was the centre of the orange industry, from where oranges were widely exported (unlike, say, apples, oranges will travel well, and retain their value over a considerable distance).[55]

The largest single blocks of trees were those I have been translating as 'apple' and 'flowering plum'. In Chinese the former are laiqin, 'bringing birds', or linqin, 'wood birds', after the supposed attractiveness of the fruit to bird life. This is really a small, sour-sweet apple, mentioned in literature as early as the Han period rhyme-proses on the imperial parks, and identified by one modern scholar as identical to the small sha guo apples sold candied on sticks across north China (illus. 12).[56] They were never eaten raw off the tree, but always after further treatment (which presumably could only enhance their market value). According to the early seventeenth-century 'Complete Book of the Administration of Agriculture' (Nong zheng quan shu), the linqin flowered (the blossom was red) in the second month, the fruit being ripe in the sixth or seventh month. The fruits were often dried and ground to make linqin flour, a food similar to the Tibetan tsamba, which could be reconstituted in water. They were also candied in honey, in which form they were particularly recommended to be eaten as an accompaniment to wine, and preserved with their original colour by a process of pickling in vinegar and alum.[57]

The flowering plum (Prunus mume Sieb. et Zucc.) is a plant with even more possibilities (illus. 13). Here, however, the historically attested Chinese aesthetic appreciation of the plant's blossom has rather crowded out the fact that it produces fruit. There can be no disputing the fact of the ubiquity of the flowering plum (botanically closer to Prunus armeniaca, the apricot, than it is to Prunus domestica, the plum) as symbol and metaphor in Chinese poetry, painting and in the decoration of luxury artefacts. This usage has been excellently catalogued in the recent publication Bones of Jade, Soul of Ice: The Flowering Plum in Chinese Art.[58] Here we learn that as early as the Song period flowering plum blossoms were a cash crop, sold door to door by vendors who used elaborate forcing techniques to get their produce on the market first. We learn too that the grove of ten mu of the trees (a grove the same size as that of Wang Xianchen) planted on the shores of the West Lake by Zhang Xi was one of the sights of Southern Song Hangzhou. Be we are also firmly told, in 'Mei Hua: a Botanical Note' by the distinguished Chinese botanist Hui-lin

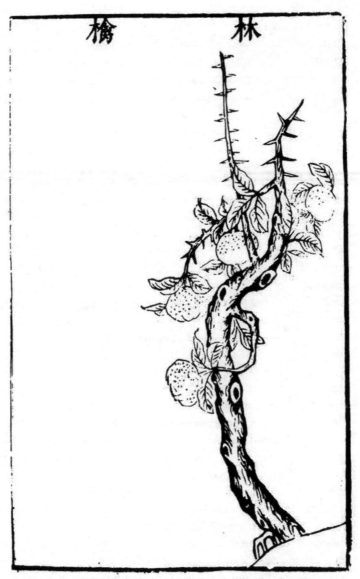

檳 林

12 Linqin tree (*Malus asiatica Nakai*), woodblock print, from Wang Qi's encyclopaedia *Illustrated Compendium of the Three Powers* (*San cai tu hui*), c. 1609.

Li, that 'the fruit is scarcely edible'.[59] We are left with the clear impression that aesthetic consideration alone could lead to the planting of large groves of a tree with scarcely edible fruit. Such an assertion becomes puzzling if one takes even a cursory look at the agronomic literature, where the fruit of the flowering plum is presented as a highly significant item of the Ming diet. Certainly the fruit is unpalatable in its raw state, but it had been for millenia one of the principal forms of relish making the consumption of bulk carbohydrate in the form of rice, millet or wheat breads palatable. The *Nong zheng quan shu* again gives a number of specific recipes for dealing with the fruit, which ripened in the fifth month (the very month of Wen Zhengming's description of the Garden of the Unsuccessful Politician). Flowering plums pickled in brine were called *bai mei*, but they were also candied, dried, honeyed and used to make a sour plum sauce that was diluted with water and drunk as a refreshing summer beverage. One of the most popular ways of treating them was by making *tang cui mei*, 'Sugar crispy flowering plums', pickled in sugar and vinegar. Flowering plums were also picked when half-yellow and smoked to form *wu mei*, or 'black plums'. *Nong zheng quan shu* asserts that these are to be eaten as a medicine, rather than as a foodstuff, though the distinction between these two categories was in the Ming period scarcely a meaningful one.[60] Early Western observers of Chinese life remarked in general on the riches of the orchards of China available in the market-place. Gaspar da Cruz, writing in 1556, mentioned 'another kind of plum which we have not, with long, wide stones, sharp at both ends, and of these they make prunes'.[61] Nor have the fruits of *Prunus mume* vanished entirely from the Chinese diet to the present day, something that can be empirically verified by a trip to any Chinese supermarket, where a jar of *suan mei*, or flowering plums pickled in brine, is always available at the relish shelf.[62]

How then have we come to a situation where the fruit of the flowering plum has become 'scarcely edible'? One explanation is that fruit-based side relishes are much less prominent in the Chinese diet now than they were before the adoption of New World food plants, a process which began with the introduction of the peanut some time before the first reliable reference to it, in 1538.[63] One has only to imagine eating millet or rice porridge for breakfast without salted peanuts, or imagine Chinese cuisine in general without the equally American chilli pepper, to realize that early Ming food must have relied much more heavily on highly flavoured relishes from indigenous sources. Significantly, in Japan, where American food crops made no significant inroads until this century, the *umeboshi*, or salted flowering plum, remains to this day a mainstay of the table. Even so, I would prefer to see the oblivion of the flowering plum's edibility as being at least as much grounded in the larger trend towards an exclusively aestheticized understanding of Chinese garden culture. Salted flowering plums become unthinkable, on the way to becoming 'uneatable'.

To press home this point, let us look at the economic value of the other plants in the Garden of the Unsuccessful Politician. A single plum tree is unlikely to have made much impact on its owner's wealth. However crab apples (*hai tang*) were eaten after various types of preparation, while the peach trees (their blossom 'like a red cloud') gave fruit that had from very ancient times been used to make a luxury fruit vinegar.[64] Other foodstuffs were provided by trees that we might not immediately associate with the kitchen. Of course there are bamboo shoots, but pine kernels were also eaten in the Ming, as were the young shoots of elm trees: 'elm sauce' was used as medicine for chest complaints. The soft shoots of the sophora tree were boiled in water to rid them of bitterness, then dipped in vinegar and ginger as an aperitif. They were also dried and used to make a herbal tea. The same trees had numerous other economic uses, which are prominent in the agronomic literature. Elm is described as only worth planting by those who live near cities, where its high-value timber can be cut for sale only ten years after planting. This quick growth cycle led to the saying that if you planted twenty elms at the birth of a child then the value of the timber would pay for that child's wedding. The Garden of the Unsuccessful Politician contained 'numerous' elms. Pines, described by the great botanist Li Shizhen (1518–93; DMB 859–65) as 'the chief of all trees', did not provide good timber, but the resin was used in all kinds of aromatics, while the soot from burned pine wood was the chief ingredient in the manufacture of ink (illus. 14). The garden contained 'many' pines. The timber of willows was used in building, and *Nong zheng quan shu* gives the same kind of calculations of the rate of return on investment as it does in the case of elms. Cypress and juniper were grown commercially, their branches cut and marketed for use in flower arrangements. Finally, there were trees in the garden that played a major role in the textiles industry, the industry on which the wealth of Suzhou as an urban centre largely rested. The flowers of the crab apple were used in the creation of dyestuffs, while it was the flowers of the sophora tree (once more, 'numerous') that were the main source of yellow dye for silk textiles (illus. 15).[65]

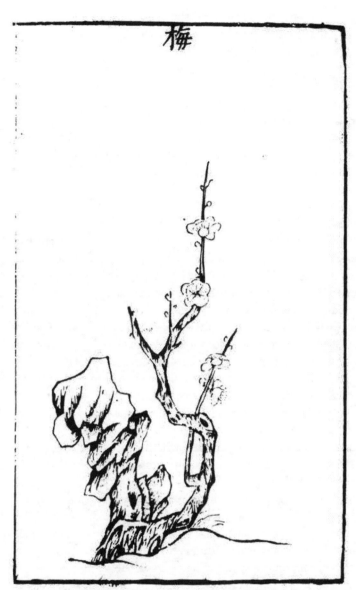

13 Flowering plum tree (*Prunus mume*), woodblock print,
from Wang Qi's *Illustrated Compendium*.

There is yet one more feature of the Garden of the Unsuccessful Politician that at the very least has the possibility of playing an economic role, and that is the large area of water that currently takes up about a third of the area, and which was clearly an equally prominent part of the total scene in 1533. The raising of fish for the market was not only an activity with a long pedigree, it was an activity seen as extremely profitable. In *Nong zheng quan shu* the author quotes an ancient adage to the effect that 'There are five methods of livelihood, and water livestock is the best'. 'Water livestock' means *fish*. He cites calculations of the rate of return on investment, and gives a great deal of conventional wisdom, some of it of great antiquity, on fish rearing. The ponds must not be too deep, as this makes the water too cold and inhibits growth. Some of these saws have a surprising bearing on what might look at first sight like purely aesthetic decisions regarding ponds. For example, the placing of islands in the middle of ponds will encourage the fish to exercise, causing them to grow. Lotuses should be planted around the edge of ponds as a means of discouraging predatory otters.[66] While we cannot be sure, there is certainly an implication that the pond in the Garden of the Unsuccessful Politician contained fish. The tenth painting and poem in the Wen Zhengming sequence together cover 'The Angling Rock' (illus. 3), and while the former shows an individual desultorily dangling a rod in the water, the poem proclaims that 'You must know that the one who now casts the line/Is not a true lover of fishing'.[67] The suggestion is not that there are no fish in the pond, rather that the disinterested angler does not care whether he catches one or not. Ming fish-management procedures did not in fact rely on gentlemen with rods, but rather on periodic emptying of the ponds, something that the record suggests would have been perfectly possible given the hydrology of the garden's water supplies. If the pond did contain fish, it was all the more valuable in that it was a pond protected by a wall. Song estate management literature is full of anecdotes stressing the importance of maintaining surveillance on valuable property, even to the point of going out and camping in a hut by the side of the pond to prevent the fish being poached.[68]

At one level, then, what we have in the Garden of the Unsuccessful Politician can be read as productive capacity behind a wall. It was also a particular kind of productive capacity, and one not available to all, in that a great deal of initial investment was required. Land reclamation, and in particular the digging and dredging of large-scale ponds, was very expensive.[69] Similarly, the planting of trees implied a willingness to see capital tied up in productive capacity that might

14 Pine tree, woodblock print, from Wang Qi's *Illustrated Compendium*.

槐

15 Sophora tree (*Sophora japonica*), woodblock print, from Wang Qi's *Illustrated Compendium*.

not see a return for a number of years. However, there is evidence that, prior to the tax reforms associated with the name of Zhang Juzheng (1525–82; DMB 53–61), which began to be put in place from the 1560s, many members of the Jiangnan elite preferred to invest in almost any form of productive capacity rather than fields producing staple grains. Francesca Bray has pointed out, in a long overview of the post-Song situation, that

One did not make a fortune through being a landlord, one became a landlord through making a fortune. Land was safe, land was respectable, but profits on trade, moneylending, or commercial plantations of sugar, fruit or timber, were all much higher, and many wealthy families preferred to invest in these other sources of income.[70]

She cites a study of the tenure by Hai Rui (1513–87; DMB 474–9) of the magistracy of Chun'an, which supports the view that the fiscal regime of the early and mid-Ming penalized ownership of rice-fields in a manner that increased the attractiveness of the exploitation of marginal land.[71] Joseph McDermott has made the same point, remarking that 'very heavy land taxes drove many gentry landlords to invest their wealth outside of agriculture'.[72] While it may seem strange to consider a sixty-two *mu* block of real estate set within the walls of the richest city in Jiangnan as in any way relating to the category of 'marginal land', it probably was so in that it was marginal to the main categories of taxable land. It is even worth speculating at this point whether the contemporary association of Suzhou with gardens was in some way due to the existence within the walls of large quantities of unused or under-used land, the result of a shrinkage of the urban population. In this respect Suzhou around 1500 resembled contemporary Rome, where there were large amounts of productive horticultural space within the walls. In Rome too, this productive space was becoming a subject of an aesthetic discourse, as the *vigne*, real working vineyards, of the fifteenth century gave way to the self-consciously non-productive practice of *villeggiatura*.[73]

In laying so much stress on the productive *potential* of the garden landscape, I may be overstating the case, as a way of correcting an equally imbalanced concentration on aesthetics in the study of Chinese garden practices. However, I do so in the knowledge that scholars of early modern Europe are also engaged in a process of unbundling from seemingly serene and highly finished artefacts like the 'Renaissance garden' and the 'English landscape garden' a much more complex nexus of interactions of the aesthetic, the social and the economic. Claudia Lazzaro has observed that no Italian garden, up to and including the Villa d'Este, which was famous for its grapes and salad greens, failed to produce foodstuffs, and has in fact found most of the material for her large-scale study of the Italian Renaissance garden in the literature of agriculture and estate management.[74] Robert Williams has focused specifically on the intertwining of moral and economic discourses in the eighteenth-century English landscape park. He has shown that it makes no sense to oppose 'the garden' to productive agricultural land as 'mutually exclusive environments', arguing instead that

the economic framework in reality underpinning such estates... suggests that histories of the landscape garden have paid insufficient attention to their economic base, preferring instead to share the pastoral perspective.[75]

He shows in particular the political and commercial considerations underlying the increased attention paid to estate silviculture in the early eighteenth century. This was not just 'a cultural manifestation almost wholly aesthetic and intellectual in purpose' (which is how it has generally been described), rather it was a reaction close to panic to the depletion of timber stocks, on which the British navy, and hence the nation's very existence, was believed to depend. Private woodlands were massive investments, and had been explicitly so viewed since Elizabethan times; they were 'stored capital to be axed and realized at some future date'. Williams shows too how the cutting of rides through woodlands, something which began to appear in the eighteenth century, is a practice determined by the needs of hunting. The park was for English aristocrats what it had been for their Anglo-Saxon predecessors – a store of living, huntable, edible animals. Similarly, and despite the strictures of landscape architecture theorists, productive fishponds remained in England as an important part of decorative schemes at least until the early nineteenth century.[76]

There are many points in Lazzaro's and in Williams's analyses (which have not seriously been disputed) of the economic aspects of the early modern European garden that are suggestive for students of China. At this point I would like to follow up just one of them, the idea of the garden as a place not simply of economic resources but of *stored* economic resources, realizable at some point in the future. Modern scholarship agrees that Ming China was rather poorly supplied with mechanisms for accumulating economic resources, and for transferring them easily as the demands of individual or family strategy dictated. I have argued elsewhere that, at least by the sixteenth century, antiquities and works of art functioned partly in this way. A bronze vessel or a scroll – easy to store, to protect and to transport – could yet embody large sums of cash, realizable at short notice on the open art market (at least in major urban centres).[77] The other major way of storing economic capital was in the form of land, but this was subject to claims of the wider kin group with regard to its disposal, and so had distinct drawbacks. As we shall see, fewer such constraints seem to have existed with regard to gardens. A piece of urban or suburban real estate, covered with fruit trees and with valuable timber clustering around a pond stocked with fish, was a piece of disposable wealth on a grand scale. At one level of reading, this is what the Garden of the Unsuccessful Politician was.

How legitimate is it, in fact, to read Wang Xianchen's property in this agronomic light, against the grain of almost everything that has been written about it? Two additional points give me confidence in doing so. One is an argument *a silentio*, and correspondingly weaker for that. This revolves around the exclusion of the category *yuan*, 'garden', from the purview of the otherwise very extensive pattern of Ming sumptuary legislation.[78] This sumptuary legislation encompassed every aspect of material culture that it was possible to view as an object of consumption, from garments and dwellings to furniture and tableware. Its prescriptions are detailed and specific. For example, an edict of Hongwu 26 (1393) laid down that the houses of commoners were to be no more than three spans (*jian*) wide, a rule that was repealed in 1447. Nowhere do we see any reference to the category of 'gardens', which suggests that the early Ming legislators viewed a garden as being something *conceptually* allied to production, rather than as an object of luxury consumption, like silver tableware or vermilion lacquered gateways. Here again we have the attractive liminality of the concept, in an artefact that was too much an object of consumption to be taxed like a rice-field, and too much of a productive space to be subject to the control of the sumptuary legislation.

My second point about the legitimacy of reading the Garden of the Unsuccessful Politician as part of a broader economic framework is rather more firmly grounded, and revolves around the literary allusions giving rise to the very name *Zhuo zheng yuan*. In his 'Record' of 1533 of the garden, Wen Zhengming puts these words into the mouth of its owner, Wang Xianchen:

Of old, Master Pan Yue's official career did not advance, therefore he built living-rooms and planted trees, irrigated a garden and sold vegetables, claiming that this was also administration (*zheng*), but of the unsuccessful (*zhuo*). From the time I was first appointed an official down to the present, forty years have passed. Some of my contemporaries have raised their status to the highest offices, climbed to the topmost ranks, while I have retired in old age as a Sub-prefect. My administration is even more unsuccessful than that of Yue, and the garden is an acknowledgement of this.

Wen Zhengming actually goes on to quibble with Wang's choice of Pan Yue as a role-model, on the grounds that this third-century magnate was an arch-hypocrite, whose poetry might invoke the delights of 'Dwelling at Leisure' (the title of the poem from which the allusion comes), but who spent his entire life in the practice of court infighting, 'fawning on the influential of his day . . .'. Wen goes on to praise by contrast the sterling moral qualities of Wang Xianchen, 'who has cast aside office and been living among his family, so to speak, building living-rooms and planting trees, irrigating a garden and selling vegetables, unfettered and at ease, enjoying the delights of dwelling at leisure in this place for twenty years'.

It is always far easier to find the *locus classicus* of a Chinese literary allusion than it is to map the way that allusion may have been used across a long period of time. However, the allusion to Pan Yue's poem 'Dwelling at Leisure' does surface in one very intriguing context not previously noted, and that is precisely the context of the agronomic treatise. The section on *pu tian*, 'plot fields', the basic unit of horticulture, in the 'Book of Agriculture' (*Nong shu*) of the fourteenth-century writer Wang Zhen, immediately following the claim that horticulture can of itself provide 'an annual profit' several times that of ordinary fields, says this:

As for those gentlemen nurturing the original constitution, it can act as a site of retirement while also providing sustenance. Or again, persons seeking an official post, if they have no detached villa, can base themselves there temporarily. Just as the man of Hanyang watered his beds with his own strength, or Heyang lived at leisure and peddled vegetables, what obstruction is there here to fulfilling the Dao?[79]

The first allusion, to the 'man of Hanyang', refers to the 'Heaven and Earth' chapter of the classic work *Zhuangzi*, and to the tale of the man who refused to use a well-sweep to water his fields for fear of the 'machine heart' such a mechanical contrivance would bring with it. However, 'Heyang' here refers to Pan Yue. We therefore have the situation that the very classical allusion explicitly employed by Wang Xianchen in naming his garden is one found prominently in an agronomic context, and specifically in a discussion of the advantages of horticulture in terms of its ability to unify profitability with 'fulfilling the Dao'. It is of course impossible to prove a direct influence of the agronomic treatise on Wang Xianchen's choice of name for his garden. But it can be shown by its subsequent publishing history that Wang Zhen's 'Book of Agriculture' was in circulation in the Ming period. The earliest surviving edition is one of 1530, just three years prior to the 'Record of the Garden of the Unsuccessful Politician'. And the prestige of the text is shown by the fact that Xu Guangqi chose to copy the passage verbatim into his 'Complete Book of the Regulation of Agriculture' in the early seventeenth century (illus. 16).[80]

It would be wrong to argue that this reference exhausts, or even approaches exhausting, everything that is signified by the choice of name *Zhuo zheng yuan*. It has within it numerous other connotations, most of which centre on the word *zhuo* – 'unsuccessful', 'clumsy', 'artless'. It was at one level an everyday word of polite language in the Ming period, used in a deprecatory way to mean little more than 'my'.[81] It was a common element in the 'styles' (*zi*) or 'by-names' (*hao*) of Ming gentlemen. But there was a whole area of moral reference as well, by which *zhuo* came to mean 'artless', 'guileless' and 'unsophisticated' in the sense of free from any hint of trickery or deceit. The opposite of *zhuo* in the standard classical dictionaries was *qiao* – 'skilful', 'intricate', 'tricksy', a word with very dubious moral overtones.[82] A *Qiao zheng yuan* ('Garden of the Cunning Politician') would have clearly been an anathema. The phrase *shou zhuo*, 'preserving one's artlessness', was forever associated in the educated mind with the figure of Tao Yuanming (365–427), the archetype of the man of noble mind who abandons office for a life of self-sufficiency and reclusion. One of the pavilions in the Wu family's Eastern Estate, established some fifty years before Wang Xianchen built his garden, is named *Zhuo xiu*, 'Artless Cultivation' (in the Confucian sense of cultivation of the self, not of the soil).[83]

Although this type of connection seems to have been lost sight of, there is really nothing surprising in the transference of allusions from the texts of agronomy to those of horticulture, conceived as an aesthetic object. The overlap is present in some of the earliest texts that praise the ordered and owned landscape. One of these is the *Jin gu yuan shi xu*, 'Preface to the Poems on the Golden Valley Garden', by the third-century magnate Shi Chong. Shi was an extremely close associate of Pan Yue (originator of the *zhuo zheng* allusion), and the two perished on the same execution block in AD 300. Pan's is the only

16 Plot fields (*Pu tian*) from Xu Guangqi, *The Complete Book of the Regulation of Agriculture* (*Nong zheng quan shu*), 1640.

poem to survive, along with Shi's own prose preface, from those written at a literary gathering at the latter's Golden Valley Garden in AD 296.[84] Shi's description of his property (in Richard Wilhelm's translation) stresses its bucolic charms, which arise from its clearly productive capacities:

Both high and low ground had clear springs, and an abundance of fruit trees, bamboos and pines. There were medical herbs, ten *ch'ing* [= 1,000 *mu*] of cultivated land, 200 head of sheep, and chickens, pigs, geese and ducks were also provided. Furthermore there were water-mills, fish ponds and caves and everything that would delight the eye and satisfy the mind.

While the idea that sheep and water-wheels could 'delight the eye and satisfy the mind' might be alien to the modern stereotype of the Chinese garden, it would have posed no problems, once again, for Wang Xianchen's European contemporaries. Here too there was a continuous seepage of ideas from the discourse of agronomy to that of aesthetics. In fifteenth-century Italy the Vigna di Napoli (later better known as the Villa Carafa) was decorated with quotations from the Roman agricultural writers Columella and Varro. A hundred years later, the landscapes that Andrea Palladio modelled for his wealthy clients in the Veneto drew their force from the prestige accorded to 'holy agriculture'; purely decorative gardens were of little import.[85] Ralph Austen's seventeenth-century treatise, *The Spirituall Use of an Orchard*, is saturated with the idea that 'pleasure' and 'profit' are conjoined in the raising of fruit trees.[86]

One could go further and demonstrate overlaps of language and theme between the sequence of Wen Zhengming poems on this site and the long poem that takes up half of the section on 'plot fields' in Wang's 'Book of Agriculture'. The overwhelming moral authority accorded to agricultural production as the *ben*, the 'roots', of society in the traditional order of political economy is too widely recognized to need further discussion. I will instead go on to argue that it is this ability to act as a hinge between profit and purity, between economic power and cultural/moral authority within the Confucian cosmic order, which gives the practice of garden culture its force in Ming society. To try to understand one without the other, beguiled by the very explicit nature of one part of the total meaning set against the occluded, even deliberately obfuscated, meaning of the other, is to impoverish our understanding. I shall further go on to argue that the creation of the garden as a pure object of luxury consumption, a process I would associate with the latter half of the sixteenth century and the opening decades of the seventeenth, is incomprehensible without an awareness of the practices involved in the aesthetic consumption of still essentially productive landscape. Distinction, as Pierre Bourdieu has demonstrated, must be exercised most rigorously against that thing which an artefact or a practice is closest to, and hence in greatest danger of being mistaken for. If we accept that any Ming garden was in constant peril of being mistaken for a wealth-producing and wealth-reproducing chunk of high-value real estate, this gives us a way of apprehending some of the necessity of stressing its 'otherness'. The garden must, in Foucault's terms, be made into a 'heterotopia',

a kind of effectively enacted utopia in which the real sites, all the other real sites that can be found within the culture, are simultaneously represented, contested and inverted. Places of this kind are to be found outside of all places, even though it may be possible to indicate their location in reality.[87]

The 'Orchard of the Unsuccessful Politician' would not be a heterotopia.[88] The 'Garden of the Unsuccessful Politician', as recreated in verse and painted image by Wen Zhengming, is well on the way to becoming one.

The Garden of the Unsuccessful Politician's balancing act between economic riches and cultural wealth could be signified by its major cash crop, fruit. I have already pointed out the high market value there was for fruit, and the economic attractiveness of growing it. A slightly facetious explanation for the aesthetic attractiveness of fruit, as opposed to other crops, may lie in the fact that (unlike vegetables or rice) Ming fruit trees were not extensively manured with human excrement, and that when they were manured it was in the winter, when even in Jiangnan less time is spent outside.[89] Fruit, however, had in addition rich, old and still vigorous symbolic associations:

Vegetables and fruit were not only an essential part of the Chinese diet, they also symbolised purity and sobriety. They were the food not only of the common people unable to afford meat, but also of pious Buddhists, hermits with magical powers, and scholars living in rustic seclusion; they signalled the renouncement of worldly values.[90]

An important but very rare Ming text that deals with the same sort of juxtaposition of the philosophical and spiritual delights of eremitism with the practical details of agronomy, is the *Qu xian shen yin shu*, 'Book of Divine Eremitism of the Emaciated Immortal', by the aristocrat Zhu Quan, Prince of Ning (1378–1448; DMB 305–7), seventeenth son of the founder of the Ming dynasty. This polymathic author had a wide range of interests in the spiritual dimension of what are to us, though they were not in the Ming, technical subjects – astronomy, medicine, agronomy, the pharmacopoeia. He was also a poet and dramatist, a writer on geomancy and alchemy, as well as being involved in the overtly religious traditions of Daoism and Buddhism. This did not of itself prevent him from having a wide array of friends and connections in the scholarly and bureaucratic elite, which was at this date much more sympathetic to Daoism than it was to be later in the dynasty. His undated 'Book of Divine Eremitism', in four chapters, is described by a modern bibliographer as being 'concerned with the trivia of daily life for so-called "recluses cultivating the Way"'. Its chapter on 'Strategies for Returning to the Fields' includes a calendar of monthly tasks in the area of cultivating trees, flowers, fruits and vegetables, largely abstracted from an earlier agronomic treatise of the Yuan dynasty.[91] It was this kind of highly prestigious linkage of the eremitic tradition with the practicalities of raising certain kinds of crops (note that it contains nothing about staple grain crops like rice) which provided part of the background familiar to educated readers of the landscape management practices in the Garden of the Unsuccessful Politician.

The emic concept operative here is that of *qing gao*, 'pure and lofty'. It is a concept that links man with the natural world, and is equally applicable to both, though not to manufactured artefacts of any kind. The *Nong zheng quan shu*, quoting a much earlier source, describes the fruits of the 'green calyx flowering plum' as 'particularly pure and lofty'.[92] Many of the mentions of fruit in the literature surrounding Ming horticulture are to do with establishing it as a commodity somehow distant from the market. Partly this is done by associating fruit with the idea of religious sacrifice, and with the obligation of mutual gift-giving as a crucial cement of elite sociability. The classical statement of this set of ideas is in the *Rites of Zhou*, where fruit trees are said to 'provide for sacrifices, and for entertaining guests and relatives'.[93] In the case of the Garden of the Unsuccessful Politician, Wen Zhengming's preface to his poem on 'Awaiting the Frost Pavilion' makes allusion to the text of the famous 'Offering Oranges Letter' (*Feng ju tie*) by Wang Xizhi (321–79), not only one of the most famous calligraphic masterpieces in Chinese history, but a document, known to every educated person, embodying the ideals of upper-class reciprocity through the presentation of gifts of fruit. The poem (illus. 10) accompanying the 'Arriving Birds Park' (i.e. the grove of ten *mu* of apple trees) makes similar reference to this set of ideas:

Summer boughs give pure (*qing*) shade to ten *mu*.
In this extensive grove the fruit are just beginning to ripen.
In the place where the precious, heavy panniers are divided up as gifts,
At a small window he personally copies the writing of the General of the Right [i.e. Wang Xizhi].

This 'enclaving' of fruit as a commodity discussed as if it were withdrawn from the market-place is similar to some of the ways of talking about works of art in the Ming period, and can also bear comparison with the role of fresh-water fish as a high-status gift in early modern England: along with meat from game animals, the ability to distribute gifts of these high-ranking foodstuffs acted to signify a place in the English social hierarchy that was far greater than that conferred by the mere commercial value of the present.[94] My reading of the Garden of the Unsuccessful Politician here is not designed to prove that Wang Xianchen was a major figure in the pickled plum industry. It is very unlikely that he derived any major part of his income from this property. And it is likely that all sorts of other allusions could be read by his guests into the name of his garden, and of the features within it. The names of features, explicated in Wen Zhengming's prose introductions to the poems, allude to the Tang owner of the site, Lu Luwang, as well as to Su Shunqin (1008–48), builder of the Surging Waves Pavilion (*Canglang ting*) in Suzhou, and to the Tang poet Du Fu (712–70). Clearly there are references to the owner's political career, to the stereotype of the righteous official wronged by malicious enemies. There are allusions to Peking, the seat of imperial power, in the form of the plum tree transplanted from that northern climate, and in the shape of the 'Jade Spring', *Yu quan*.[95] This well is described thus in Wen Zhengming's prose introduction to the relevant poem:

In the capital, at Xiangshan, there is a Jade Spring, and the owner [Wang Xianchen] often dipped and enjoyed it, hence his style of Jade Spring Hermit. Here he has obtained a spring in the garden's south-east corner, the sweetness and coldness of which is suitable for tea. It is not inferior to the Jade Spring, and so he gave it this name to show he had not forgotten.[96]

No one type of allusion is sufficient to explain the programme of the garden. But the agronomic references of the Garden of the Unsuccessful Politician, like those of the Eastern Estate, are both numerous and obvious, perhaps so obvious to contemporaries that they escaped comment. No one, in 1500, supposed that a *yuan*, whether translated as 'garden' or as 'orchard', could be anything other than a space for growing things. The 'natural' increase of horticulture was a sanctioned, even sanctified, form of profit, at a time when the notion of profit derived from trade was becoming an increasingly problematic one. Just as with contemporary Europe, the actual configurations of land and labour, and in particular the practices of tenancy and rent, were generally expressed 'in conceptions of the land itself as the producer of commodities; rent is, as a consequence, not treated as the payment made on the basis of organised social production using land, but rather as a natural product, a "gift of Nature"'.[97] In the sixteenth century as the years passed, this problem would develop to the degree where the aesthetic consumption of productive space was too easily confused with simple raising of crops for profit. At that point, the orange trees would have to go, and the garden be refocused in a more purely aesthetic direction.

2 The Aesthetic Garden

GARDENS OF THE EMPEROR

If, as I have argued in the preceding chapter, there was a significant revival of garden culture in Suzhou towards the end of the fifteenth century, what possible sources did its practitioners and commentators have for their ideas? Obviously there was the literary record of Suzhou's own past splendours in this field. Although a site like that of the Surging Waves Pavilion (*Canglang ting*) might be a total ruin in the mid-Ming, it was available, even down to details of its topography, to a writer like Wen Zhengming through records of it in verse and prose.[1] However, there was another currently existing model available, in the form of the imperial garden complex in Peking. There is a presumption that any borrowings either of broad landscape concepts or of detailed formal features of layout that took place between Suzhou and Peking must have been from the former to the latter, and that in general Peking enjoyed relatively little prestige as a centre of culture and taste. This may not, in fact, have been the case. It can certainly be demonstrated that borrowings took place in a northwards direction in the eighteenth century, when emperors returning from tours of inspection to the south deliberately recreated the sights of that region in several imperial parks to the north-west of the capital.[2] But the possibility exists that in the fifteenth and sixteenth centuries the borrowing flowed the other way. In this tentative chronology, the revitalization of the imperial gardens in Peking acted as an inspiration to a relatively small but very prestigious group of the Suzhou elite, whose activities as garden creators, picturers and describers were then imitated more widely in the immediate Jiangnan area, and then through the wider empire as the sixteenth century went on.

Parks and gardens had long been associated with the dwelling complexes of rulers, and were an expected adjunct to them.[3] A Directorate of the Imperial Forest Park (*Shang lin yuan jian*) was set up by the first Ming emperor at some unspecified point in the Hongwu era (1368–98), but abolished in the same reign on the grounds that it had harmed the people's property (or livelihood, *fang min ye*).[4] This establishment was initially at Nanjing, the first Ming capital. The Directorate was refounded in 1407 (before the move of the capital to the north), and had its establishment trimmed somewhat in 1425, by which time it was presumably established at Peking (although it was not until 1441 that offices to accommodate it were completed there).[5] It originally had ten sections. Six of these were responsible respectively for the rearing of large livestock (cattle, sheep, goats and pigs), for fowl (geese, ducks and chickens), for vegetables, for fruit and flowers (note the linkage), for fish and for ponds, and for ice. The remaining four had accounting and supervisory functions. In this original establishment, the role of supplying foodstuffs for the huge needs of the imperial court was prominent, something that was carried out by extensive estates on the outskirts of the capital. However, it did from the start go hand in hand with aesthetic endeavours, centred around the Western Park (*Xi yuan*), situated to the west of the palace buildings.[6] This was the subject of building works in the Xuande reign (1426–35), and again in the Tianshun reign (1457–64). The throne was informed in 1460 that the small-scale pavilions were completed, and the larger palaces were extensively restored in 1530. There was a flurry of further building work over the next decade: the Jiajing emperor used the garden as a setting for Daoist religious observances, and new structures were built to accommodate them.[7] Most of the work took place on the Island of Jasper Flowers (*Qiong hua dao*), in the centre of the long lake, stretching north to south, which was the garden's main feature.[8] The fame of these great precincts was announced to sixteenth-century European readers in the writing of Gaspar da Cruz, who had never set eyes on them himself, but presumably had absorbed from Chinese opinion the idea that

Within his gates he [the emperor] hath very great enclosures with very great lodgings, great kitchen and pleasure gardens, orchards, and many fish-ponds in which are great stores of fish.[9]

The imperial gardens were an important site of ideas about the good landscape in the Ming. One of the important early texts here is the 'Record of the Grant of an Excursion in the Western Park' (*Ci you Xi yuan ji*) by Li Xian (1408–67; DMB 819–22), detailing a visit that took place during his tenure as Grand Secretary between 1464 and 1467, i.e. shortly after the gardens were first completely renovated. Such a visit was received as a special mark of imperial favour, worthy of permanent record in elaborate prose. There are similar accounts in the collected writings of a number of high Ming officials, including Yang Shiqi (1365–1444; DMB 1535–8) and Han Yong (1422–68: DMB 498–502). Li's 'Record' lists the features of the garden in a manner that was to become standard for garden descriptions in the Ming and was employed by Wen Zhengming in his 'Record of the Garden of the

Unsuccessful Politician'. In its descriptions of thick stands of timber and dense groves of fruit trees, interspersed with relatively few structures, it also provides a model for some of the formal features of that and other Suzhou gardens. For example, the source of the ponds in the north-east corner of the site is explicitly compared to 'the Jade Spring in the Western Hills', a beauty spot that was to be replicated at least once in Suzhou.[10] Several of the pavilion names draw on the same sort of corpus of allusions as would be employed in the southern gardens around fifty years later, and some at this period were still roofed with thatch, giving a rustic air even to these imperial precincts. Wheat fields provided grains for sacrifices, as well as a link with an agronomic garden like Wu Kuan's Eastern Estate.[11] There were also some distinctive features, such as enclosures for birds and beasts.

Li Xian, the author of the 'Record of the Grant of an Excursion in the Western Park', was a particular friend of Wang Ao, a man also of high rank and with similarly privileged access, who forms a plausible link between the gardens of the imperial capital and those of his native Suzhou. Although as we have seen, Wang did not include his own properties in the Suzhou gazetteer of 1506 which he edited, there is no doubt he owned some of the most celebrated gardens in the Lake Tai region. His own 'Western Garden' (Xi yuan, but with a different character from the yuan of the imperial 'Western Park') was at Xiajia Lake, while his even grander 'Truly Apt Garden' (Zhen shi yuan) was at East Dongtingshan, the scenic peninsula (famed for its oranges) that juts out into Lake Tai to the west of the city.[12] Here it was adjacent to the property of his younger brother. Both sites were celebrated in verse by his client, Wen Zhengming. The Truly Apt Garden is the subject of a set of poems by Wen dated 1511 and entitled 'Sixteen Odes on the Truly Apt Garden of Master Wang, Pillar of State' (Zhu guo Wang xian sheng Zhen shi yuan shi liu yong).[13] These poems memorialize individual features of the garden, some of which are very close in name to features in the Garden of the Unsuccessful Politician he was later to write about. While Wang Ao had a 'Lotus Bank' (Furong an) and an 'Apple Patch' (Laiqin pu), Wang Xianchen had a 'Lotus Bend' (Furong wei) and an 'Apple Park' (Laiqin you). The names may simply have been generic, with no specific individual reference intended. In the following year, 1512, Wen provided a poem recording his attendance on Wang Ao at an outing and party in his other property, the Western Garden.[14]

In addition to literary records, Wang probably commissioned pictorial memorials of his property from the Suzhou artist Tang

Yin (1470–1524; DMB 1256–9), an exact contemporary of Wen Zhengming and like him very much in the orbit of the now-retired grandee. Although the original in neither case survives, Anne de Coursey Clapp has identified two Tang Yin compositions as being essentially topographical studies of Wang Ao's properties at Dongtingshan.[15]

The imperial gardens seem to have become rather more accessible to low-ranking members of the Peking bureaucracy by the early sixteenth century. They were certainly visited on more than one occasion during 1525 by Wen Zhengming himself, in the course of his brief career as an official of the Hanlin Academy. His collected works contain poems entitled 'Touring the Western Park', 'Again Visiting the Western Park on an Autumn Day', and a sequence with a prose postface called 'Ten Poems on the Western Park'.[16] He was accompanied on the last occasion (which in fact took place in the spring) by three friends and colleagues, Chen Yi (1469–1538; MRZJ 578), Ma Ruji (1493–1543: MRZJ 410) and Wang Tongzu (1497–1551; MRZJ 30). According to his own account, this was no signal mark of imperial favour – indeed the emperor would have had no idea they were in his garden.[17] Chen Yi had taught in the palace school, and had come to know a certain Wang Man, an official of the Directorate of the Imperial Forest Park, who conducted the four of them on a tour. According to Wen: 'On my return, and following what I had noted and remembered, I made these ten poems.' The imperial park is compared to a heavenly realm, 'something which could not be spied in the world of men'. (It is still a piece of great good fortune to be admitted to this closely guarded precinct.) As with the earlier account of Wang Ao's garden, the whole is dealt with in discrete units, listed as ten 'views' (jing). These are: Longevity Hill (Wan sui shan), the Great Pond (Tai ye chi), the Island of Jasper Flowers (Qiong hua dao), the Hall of Radiance Received (Cheng guang dian), Dragon Boat Harbour (Long zhou pu), the Plantain Garden (Ba jiao yuan), the Hall of Joy Received (Le cheng dian), the Southern Terrace (Nan tai), Hare Garden (Tu yuan) and the Level Terrace (Ping tai). A short prose preface is provided for each poem, the one on Longevity Hill reading:

Longevity Hill is to the north-east of the imperial city beyond the Xuanwu Gate, and is the protecting hill (zhen shan) of the Great Within. On it groves of trees extend their shade. It is particularly rich in rare fruits, another name of it being Garden of a Hundred Fruits.[18]

Wen's visit to the garden may have been fortuitous, but it was not necessarily unique. It seems plausible that, just as Wen had visited the imperial park, and written about it a sequence of poems with topographical prose comments *before* he did the same for Wang Xianchen's Garden of the Unsuccessful Politician, so grander personages like Wu Kuan, Wang Ao and Wang Xianchen himself may well have had the model of the imperial gardens before them when they set out to remodel or build from scratch their own properties.

THE ROLE OF THE ARISTOCRACY

The gardens of Peking, other than those of the imperial court, had played a role as centres of elite sociability in the fifteenth century. The most renowned gathering of this type is the 'Elegant Gathering in the Apricot Garden' (*Xing yuan ya ji*) held on the property of Grand Secretary Yang Rong (1371–1440; DMB 1519–21) in April 1437. Nine men, all of high rank, were present, including Grand Secretary Yang Shiqi, who as we have seen was familiar with the imperial gardens, and who provided the prose 'Record' of this particular get-together. It was further commemorated by a painting from the brush of the court painter Xie Huan (illus. 20).[19] A second famous gathering of this type was held in the Bamboo Garden of Zhou Jing (1440–1510; DMB 267–9) in 1499, the participants this time including Wu Kuan, owner of the Suzhou Eastern Estate. It was recorded too by painters who were present, and both this and the earlier painting were reproduced around 1560 in a book entitled *Er yuan ji*, 'Two Garden Records' (illus. 17,18).[20] This published version of the poems and pictures relating to these two celebrated Peking events coincided with a great expansion of interest in garden culture and its history among a wider elite across the empire. However, in Peking itself it was not the bureaucratic elite that was to dominate the landscape as the sixteenth century wore on, but the aristocracy of imperial relatives, and the descendants of those military supporters of the early emperors who had been rewarded with hereditary titles and the large estates necessary to support them in style.[21]

THE EXPANSION OF GARDEN CULTURE

In the southern capital of Nanjing, at the heart of Jiangnan, where 'literati' ideals were most fully realized, the aristocracy too dominated the social landscape of the city, and it was their gardens that were celebrated. This is shown in the list of properties in the city contained in a famous essay by Wang Shizhen, his 'Record of Visiting the Gardens of Jinling' (*You Jinling zhu yuan ji*; Jinling is an alternative name for Nanjing).[22] He lists fifteen sites, no fewer than

17 After Xie Huan, *The Elegant Gathering in the Apricot Garden* (*Xing yuan ya ji tu*) (1437), woodblock print, from *Two Garden Gatherings* (*Er yuan ji*), *c.* 1560. Library of Congress, Washington, DC. This section of the print shows Grand Secretary Yang Shiqi (1365–1444) and Wang Zhi (1379–1462).

18 After Lü Ji and Lü Wenying, *Birthday Gathering in the Bamboo Garden* (*Zhu yuan shou ji tu*) (1499), woodblock print, from *Two Garden Gatherings* (*Er yuan ji*), *c.* 1560. Library of Congress, Washington, DC. This section of the print shows Wu Kuan (1435–1504), owner of the Eastern Estate in Suzhou.

ten of which are attached to the residences of various members of the family of the dukes of Weiguo, the descendants of Xu Da (1332–85; DMB 602–8), original companion in arms of the founder of the dynasty. None of these sites predates the beginning of the sixteenth century. Of the remaining five gardens Wang records, two are the creation of other members of the imperial aristocracy (the marquises of Wuding, resident in Peking, and the decayed clan of the princes of Qi), with only three being ascribed to the class of scholar bureaucrats to which Wang himself belonged.

Wang's essay is paraphrased in a work on the history, topography and customs of Nanjing published in 1617 by a native of the city, Gu Qiyuan (1565–1628). In a subsequent passage on 'Ancient Gardens', he lists a number of long-lost parks and gardens, mostly dating from the period of the Northern and Southern Dynasties, when Nanjing was a capital almost continuously. He comments that Nanjing was in the past rather poorly provided with the private gardens of the scholar-gentry (shi da fu), and explains this fact in the following way:

At the beginning of the dynasty, regulations were established on the basis of ancient precedents, and orders forbade the civil and military officials from occupying too much marginal land, thus obstructing the dwellings of the people. Nor were they allowed to dig ponds for rearing fish, lest they damage the vital breath (qi) of the earth. Thus at that time the great families rarely constructed gardens and parks, and those gardens recorded by Wang Shizhen were mostly created since the Zhengde (1506–21) and Jiajing (1522–66) eras.[23]

Contemporary sources are unanimous in seeing this period from about 1520 as one in which the category of gardens divorced from ideas about productive property expanded greatly, and one in which the number of people involved in the practices of aesthetic horti- culture greatly increased. The situation in Suzhou itself will be looked at in greater detail below, but the same time frame can be extended to other areas. The garden of the Qin family at Wuxi, known originally as Feng gu xing wo, and surviving to receive imperial visits in the eighteenth century under the name Qichang Garden, was laid out in the Zhengde period.[24] Almost all the references to gardens brought to light by a trawl through the Dictionary of Ming Biography (admittedly an unscientific process) are to new building campaigns in the sixteenth century. For example, Wu Guolun (1524–93; DMB 1490) is described as constructing the first garden to be seen in his native district of Xingguo, in Huguang province, after he was cashiered in the 1570s. It cannot have been the case that horticulture was unknown in the area, but rather that the structure of learned references and aesthetic and social practices with which Wu chose to surround his property was new to the region, and may well have been done in conscious imitation of what was already becoming fairly widespread in somewhere like Suzhou. Qi Biaojia's listing of 191 gardens in his native region of Zhejiang contains only sites recently created.[25] A modern collection of written 'Records' of famous gardens contains fifty-seven such prose pieces, of which four date from the Tang period (618–906), ten from the Song (960–1279), and twenty-two and twenty-one from the Ming (1368–1644) and Qing (1644-1911) dynasties respectively.[26] Of the Ming pieces, the earliest is Wen Zhengming's 'Record of the Garden of the Unsuccessful Politician' of 1533. While this is not a statistically rigorous sample, its inclusion of more texts for the last 110 years of the Ming than for the 267 years of the entire Qing is suggestive of the intense degree of attention paid to gardens at this period. Modern Chinese scholars all concur in seeing an absolute increase in the number of aesthetically construed gardens as being a phenomenon of the sixteenth century.[27]

SUZHOU IN THE LATER MING

A less impressionistic look at what the elite chose to record about Suzhou and its gardens in the latter half of the Ming period shows the degree of expansion in garden culture that was taking place. The Surging Waves Pavilion (*Cang lang ting*) at Suzhou, which had been only a name from the distant past in the 1530s, when it was used by Wang Xianchen as the name of one feature in his own garden, was rebuilt from scratch in the Jiajing period by Hu Zuanzong, prefect of the city.[28] It is the gazetteers that give the clearest picture of how the elite perceived expansion in this type of activity to have taken place.

Administratively, the city of Suzhou was part of two different counties, Changzhou county covering the eastern half, and Wu county comprising the western half of the city and the belt of territory to the shores of Lake Tai.[29] The former was provided with a gazetteer in 1571, subsequently revised and published in 1598.[30] It is a relatively modest affair as Ming gazetteers go, perhaps reflecting the status of Changzhou as the less affluent side of the city, and as such has no separate chapter devoted to gardens. Instead, chapter Thirteen combines 'Famous Sites' (*Gu ji*), 'Graves' (*Zhong mu*), 'Residences' (*Di zhai*) and 'Garden Pavilions' (*Yuan ting*). The first of these categories does include a certain number of historic garden sites, but the 'Garden Pavilions' category lists seventeen properties altogether, mingling vanished historic ones with extant gardens in a way which is less systematic than that of the gazetteer *Gusu zhi* of 1506, where the purely literary gardens are listed first before the actual ones.[31] Four of the seventeen in this case are records of gardens definitely no longer extant, leaving thirteen possibly real ones to be listed, a figure far higher than the five contemporary gardens listed in the gazetteer of 1506 for a far larger geographical area. In most cases only a bare listing is given, for example 'The Awakening Heart Pavilion (*Xing xin ting*) is by the Fu Gate'. More extensive notice is given to two gardens already encountered, Wu Yong's Eastern Estate and Wang Xianchen's Garden of the Unsuccessful Politician:

The Eastern Estate was made by Mengyong, father of Wu Kuan, [posthumously titled] Wending gong. In all it has/had twenty-two views (*jing*). There is a 'Record' by Grand Secretary Li Dongyang, and a painting by the recluse Shen Zhou.
The Garden of the Unsuccessful Politician is/was within the Lou Gate, west of the Dahong Temple. It was opened up and enlarged by Censor Wang Xianchen, to over 200 *mu*. The splendour of its flourishing trees and curving waters was first in Suzhou. There is a 'Record' by the Expectant Official Wen Zhengming.

What is deemed worthy of record here are principally the distinguished literary and artistic figures who have celebrated the gardens, rather than the gardens' intrinsic features. Also noteworthy is the way the Eastern Estate is now reduced to a series of 'views'. A garden is now something to be looked at, and something where individual features take precedence over the integrative mix of land management types (fruit, vegetables, rice, mulberries) that were described by Li Dongyang in the 1470s.

   The other Suzhou gazetteer, that for Wu county published in 1642, has much more material on gardens, to which it devotes an entire chapter. This is entitled 'Garden Groves' (*Yuan lin*), the term that has won out in modern Chinese as the regular word for 'garden', though as we have seen in the Ming period it existed side by side with alternatives such as 'garden pavilion' (*yuan ting*) and 'garden ponds' (*yuan chi*) as the name for the whole category. The Wu county gazetteer lists fifty-five sites, a massive expansion since 1506 and still a considerably greater number than that seen in the 1598 gazetteer of the other Suzhou county. Twenty-seven of these predate the Ming dynasty, the remaining twenty-eight, beginning with the 'Pleasure Patch' of Du Qiong, being Ming foundations. Several of these early Ming gardens were no longer extant at the time of writing. For example the 'Just-so Patch' (*Shi shi pu*) of retired Grand Secretary Shen Shixing (1535–1614; DMB 1187–90), described as 'the most splendid of the garden groves in the western part of the city', was built on the site of the defunct Pleasure Patch.[32] The accounts of individual gardens are considerably more extensive than the bare listing in the Changzhou gazetteer, often incorporating samples of prose or verse. In the majority of cases the identity of the garden's owner is given along with its location, and there are occasional editorial judgements on the quality of the result, on the lines of that given for Shen Shixing's property. Thus we are told about the 'Cold Mountain Detached Villa' of Zhao Huanguang (1559–1625) at Mount Zhixing, where the poet lives in retirement with his wife (Zhao's wife was herself a noted writer, and the daughter of Wen Zhengming's great friend Lu Shidao). This is a 'spring of the immortals and a world apart', where even all the furniture is 'such as is not seen in the world of men'.[33] Prominence is given to the 'Fragrant Grasses Hillock' (*Xiang cao cha*) of Wen Zhenheng (1585–1645), great-great grandson of Wen Zhengming, aspirant arbiter of taste, and author of the 'Treatise on Superfluous Things' (*Zhang wu zhi*, written *c.* 1615–20), a guide to appropriate consumption behaviour for the Suzhou elite, for which Zhao Huanguang had acted as an honorary editor.[34] It is described in this way:

Tall trunks and rare rocks, square ponds and sinuous streams, towers of cranes and enclosures for deer, 'fishskin couches and swallow-tail curtains', as well as delicate bamboo shoots and fine grasses, great peaks and potted flowers; all splendour and luxury was prepared for this noble name.[35]

The word used for 'luxury' (*chi*) is rich in negative connotations of lavish wastefulness and inappropriate excess. By 1642 it was terms such as this one that, rather than references to the morally ennobling sphere of productive resources, pervaded writing about gardens.

The period that saw the quickening of interest in the creation of new gardens, first of all in Suzhou, then in the other cities of the economically crucial lower Yangtze area, then in the wider empire, was one that witnessed an increase in all forms of luxury consumption behaviour by the elite. This was followed by an increase in the number of complaints that such behaviour was disruptive, wasteful and ultimately subversive of the right ordering of society. Two quotations will have to stand in for what was in fact a whole genre of such social criticism aimed directly at Suzhou:

As for the customs of the populace, in general those south of the Yangtze are more extravagant than those north of it, and no extravagance south of the Yangtze surpasses that of Suzhou. From of old the customs of Suzhou have been habituated to excess and splendour and a delight in the rare and strange, to which the sentiments of the people are invariably drawn. . . . . To turn people's inclination from moderation to excess is easy, but to return them from excess to moderation is difficult.[36]

And again:

Although Suzhou has hegemony in leisure activities, and enjoys the rich profits of rivers and seas, the people are flighty and cunning, and their customs are luxurious and extravagant. . . . Everyone else considers them as stupid and laughable, but they flaunt themselves as famed for superior cleverness. They do not realize it is their very cleverness which makes them foolish.[37]

These complaints about 'extravagance' and 'excess' are to a large extent topoi, though topoi which were to become increasingly shrill as the sixteenth century wore on. Such terms began in the course of this period to be applied to the gardens of the wealthy. As we have seen in the previous chapter, as early as 1494 it was being argued that the prominence of gardens in Suzhou was due to a lack of 'frugality'. Gardens were seen by the end of the century as a natural part of the expansion and intensification of luxury consumption behaviour that had taken place during the previous fifty years. Shen Defu writes:

At the end of the Jiajing period (1522–66) the empire was at peace, and prosperous members of the official classes, in intervals between the construction of gardens and the training of singers and dancers, turned to the enjoyment of antiquities.[38]

These connections with luxury and with consumption were topoi that it was not possible to apply to productive land, the essentially moral category to which I have argued the hegemonic early Ming great gardens such as the Eastern Estate and the Garden of the Unsuccessful Politician belonged. How had gardens changed from sites signifying 'production' to sites referring to the more problematic category of 'consumption'?

PLANTS, ROCKS, LUXURIES

Gardens had certainly changed physically in a number of ways. Groves of fruit trees gradually became less prominent in the garden landscape, to be replaced by rare flowering shrubs of no possible economic value, including types imported from south-east Asia.[39] One author notes that 'The glory of a garden lies in the number and sizes of its trees', and goes on to give a hypothetical complete list of desirable species:

The most precious are the Tianmu pine, the *guazi* pine, the *poluo* tree, the magnolia, the 'Western Palace' crab apple, the 'hanging threads' crab apple, the *qiu tong*, the gingko, the 'dragon's claw' sophora, the *pinpo*, the quince, the citron, the pear flower, the hydrangea, the luohan pine, the Guanyin pine, the green calyx flowering plum, the 'jade butterfly' flowering plum, the prasine peach, the indian coral tree and the cycas. Today, the various renowned gardens of Nanjing are rich in famous flowers and precious trees, but those which have all of the above are rare indeed.[40]

This list is dominated not by 'oranges' or 'flowering plums' in general, but by specific rare varieties. The only plants on it that also appear in the contemporary 'Complete Book of the Administration of Agriculture' are the gingko and the quince, as well as the generic 'pine' and 'sophora', demonstrating the degree to which there has been a move away from an interest in economic species. There was an interest in rare species from beyond the borders of the empire, for, as in eighteenth-century Europe, the assimilation of the overseas Other to the natural world was easily made. The same author writes of the 'great embroidered red ball flower' (*da hong xiu qiu hua*), described as not native to China, but brought in an ocean-going ship from Thailand to Jinjiang, 'when Shen Shengyu was governor there'. The crab apples in the courtyards of one Nanjing temple were said to have been brought from the Western Ocean by the great eunuch admiral Zheng He (1371–1433). New varieties were being developed, or transplanted at this time, as we see in the discussion of camellias:

There are two types of camellia in this region; one has single petals and a yellow heart in the middle, while one is the 'Precious Pearl', where in the middle of the single petals, fragments of little red petals cluster like pearls, hence the name. Recently there has been another white variety, with flowers rather like the 'Precious Pearl', but the colour has a tinge of light yellow, and it has a very strong perfume. It is far superior to the red one.

Another novelty was the red-rose azalea of Suzhou, which appeared for the first time in the gardens of Nanjing in the second half of the sixteenth century, transplanted with great difficulty.[41] The Peking garden of Zhang, Earl of Hui'an, was noted for its 'tens of thousands' of herbaceous peonies, while on a much smaller scale a garden could still be renowned and attract attention in the early seventeenth century for its 'several hundred plants from different places, and of different varieties; so [many that] even the gardeners could not identify them' (illus. 38).[42] Such exotica played the same role in the great sixteenth-century gardens of China as they did in those of contemporary Europe, where the effect was that they 'widened the gulf between an aristocratic or a connoisseur's garden and one whose planting was available to a much wider range of incomes and social situations'.[43] They served to differentiate the practice of aesthetic horticulture from the continuing existence of other types of land use.[44]

As well as rare plants, rocks played an increasingly important part in garden design.[45] Here it is necessary to keep in mind the distinction between single rocks, whether sited in the ground or in movable tubs, and agglomerations of rock. The two did not have an equally long, nor a continuous history. The connoisseurship of stones goes back to the Song period and beyond, and is exemplified by a text like Du Wan's 'Stone Catalogue of Cloudy Forest' (Yun lin shi pu), which has a preface dated 1133 although, significantly, it was not printed until the late Ming.[46] Single rocks, in particular the naturally pierced and foraminate boulders known as 'Great Lake Rocks' (Taihu shi), after the body of water near Suzhou where they originated, were a particular focus of interest of the Song aesthete emperor Huizong, who formed an infamous 'Flower and Rock Network' (or Mafia?) to supply his capital with the finest examples.[47] However, these rocks seem not to have as yet been seen as an indispensable part of garden design in every area of China in the Song period. Wang Shizhen, in the late Ming, noted that the Song 'Record of the Gardens of Luoyang' by Li Gefei makes no mention of rocks at all.[48] It is possible that the vogue for these rocks owes something to their presence in temple gardens, where they were deemed to impart an other-worldly appearance redolent of the Western Paradise. A Japanese visitor to eleventh-century Suzhou was particularly struck by the rockwork in the garden of the Baoen Temple there,[49] and rocks may have remained a Suzhou speciality until a later date. The Suzhou writer Huang Xingzeng (1490–1540: DMB 661–5) certainly thought so. In his Wu feng lu ('Record of the Customs of Suzhou'), he dates the fashion for Taihu rocks from the notorious figure of Zhu Mian, impresario of the 'Flower and Rock Network'. In his own day 'the wealthy and powerful of Suzhou compete for these rocks', the chief artificers of which were Zhu Mian's descendants, now established at Tiger Hill (illus. 35, 36).[50] One of the most famous ensembles of rockwork in the city in the Ming period belonged to a Buddhist temple, and was known as the Lion Grove, Shizi lin (illus. 41).

Established in the Yuan dynasty, and painted by the great Yuan painter Ni Zan (who, despite later legend, played no part in the design of the rocks), this site was completely ruined by the early Qing, was built over for housing, and had to be rebuilt from scratch for a southern tour of the Qianlong emperor in 1762.[51] Its present appearance is therefore no guide to its arrangements in the Ming, and the intriguing possibility of a central role for Buddhist symbolism in the popularization of garden rocks must remain no more than speculation. Rocks are not mentioned in the 'Record of the Garden of the Unsuccessful Politician', and Wen's paintings show only a single example of Taihu rock (illus. 9).

The elaborate 'artificial mountains' (jia shan), a type of composite rockwork that was also a speciality of Suzhou, began to be one of the visually dominant features of the fashionable garden elsewhere in China after about 1550 (illus. 26, 36). They were seen as something of a novelty to the Hangzhou writer Lang Ying (1487-c. 1566; DMB 791-3), writing about the middle of the century, and one which was not without its negative side:

Recently rich and noble families have taken to piling up artificial mountains, and though they get their mountains, they naturally do not have the vital air of real mountains. Moreover, in spring and summer they are infested with snakes, which means that moonlit nights cannot be enjoyed [outdoors].[52]

The artificiality and 'perverseness' of building artificial mountains when real mountains are all around, and the inevitable inferiority of elaborate gardens (associated with the taste of wealthy eunuchs) to the natural scenery they supposedly imitate, is a theme in the writing of the culturally conservative Fujian author Xie Zhaozhe (1567-1624; DMB 546-50). These structures are rarely mentioned without some reference to the great expense of making them, as Lang Ying and Xie Zhaozhe make clear. The single pitted and pierced 'Great Lake Rocks' could be dear enough:

A fine one is worth a hundred gold pieces [= 100 ounces of silver, 3,750 g.], and even a poor one is never less than ten or twenty. A garden (yuan chi, 'garden pond') cannot be without one of these pieces, but they are very hard to obtain in my native Fujian. For they are stopped by the mountain ranges, and cannot reach here unless transported by sea. Kunshan rocks resemble carved jade, but they do not exceed two or three feet, and are only objects for the table. Lingbi rocks make a sound if struck, but fine ones are even harder to obtain. Ye Shaolin of the Song period tells how he once passed through Lingbi, and obtained a rock a little over four feet, for which he paid eight hundred gold pieces. This is excessively dear.

Nowadays there are no Lingbi rocks of four feet in height, nor are there any rocks costing eight hundred gold pieces.[53]

However, a good artificial mountain could cost ten times that in Suzhou. The same Fujian writer, Xie Zhaozhe, laid down what constituted 'a good one' in terms that suggest a sophisticated audience deploying a specialist vocabulary of connoisseurship:

A skilful maker will take pains over the details, so that the scene is not piled and folded, the rocks are not reversed and turned, sparseness and looseness are appropriate, proportions are harmonious. Thus the natural (*zi ran*) is not lost in the midst of human craft (*ren gong*), and a marginal piece of land preserves the flavour of the wilderness. Eschew a fractured fussiness, which is distasteful. Eschew a formal order, which approaches vulgarity. Do not have an excess that strives after splendour. Do not have too much cleverness, which buries the real. Thus people will wander among them for a whole year without wearying. As for obtaining these things, in general rocks are easy to get, water is harder to get, and large and ancient trees are even harder to get.[54]

Xie here provides another explanation for the greater prominence of rocks in late Ming gardens, the ease with which they could be purchased and the speed with which they could be installed. A rock garden was an instant garden, desirable for those who did not have a continuous involvement with land ownership dating back to the Yuan dynasty.

Although modern writers have often concentrated on the cosmological connections of rocks, and their links with deeply held views about the nature of the universe, Ming writers are as likely to associate them with the luxury consumption of the age. Thus Xie Zhaozhe:

The Yizhou Garden of Master Wang Shizhen has a rock over 30 feet high, such that the city gate was demolished to effect its entry. This is very close to excess. . . . The constructions of the men of old can be known by their extreme naturalness (*zi ran*). This is not like the rich and noble families of today, who do no more than contest for massive splendours.

Foppish great merchants do not fail to enjoy the delights of terraces and torrents, but these are not preserved because they do not deserve to be preserved. Narrow-minded vulgar officials devote themselves to building and ornamenting in order to amuse themselves, yet most of what they do is hateful – there are no hills and valleys in their breasts . . .[55]

This concern with 'hills and valleys in the breast' was, as we shall see, to become one of the key responses to the enmeshing of garden landscape in the restless, competitive social world of the late Ming state. The role of gardens in this competition is brought out very forcefully in a survey of the sites of Suzhou by the great essayist and poet Yuan Hongdao (1568–1610):

A Brief Account of Gardens and Pavilions (Yuan ting ji lüe)
The gardens and pavilions of Suzhou known by name in olden days were the Southern Garden (*Nan yuan*) of the Qian Family, Su Zimei's Surging Waves Pavilion, Zhu Changwen's Pleasure Patch and Fan Chengda's Old Hermitage at Stone Lake (*Shi hu jiu yin.*) Nowadays they are all in ruins, and their vaunted lofty ridges and clear pools, secluded monticules and verdant stands of bamboo have become places where herdboys and woodcutters chop fodder and gather stones. In recent days, within the city walls, the garden of Assistant Administration Commissioner Xu inside the Feng Gate has been the most splendid. Its painted walls assemble their tints, flying streams encircle it. Water passes between rocks, people pierce the depths of caverns, and the ingenuity (*qiao*) surpasses that of the natural world, to become as magical as the work of demons. There are a thousand streams and myriad ravines, so that the visitor almost becomes confused as to his directions. It is in competition for pre-eminence with Wang Shizhen's little Garden of the Earth Spirit (*Qi yuan*). The Garden of the Earth Spirit is spacious and open, with every flower and rock having the flavour of retirement. Xu's garden is rather harmed by its cleverness and splendour. Wang Ao's garden was within the Chang and Xu Gates, by the side of Xiajia Lake. Its water and rocks are also beautiful, but there are several dilapidated spots, and it would be lovelier with some restoration. Xu Qiongqing's garden is at Lower Pond (*Xia tang*), outside the Chang Gate. It is spacious and grand, wide and imposing, with towers to the front and dwellings to the rear, enough to intoxicate the visitor. The stone screen was erected by Zhou Shichen, and is thirty feet high, and perhaps two hundred feet in width, foraminate and jaggedly sheer, like a broad landscape painting. There is not the least trace of any cutting, truly a miraculous piece of work! By the side of the hall is a very high earth mound, with many ancient trees. On the mound is a single Taihu rock, called the Auspicious Clouds Peak (*Rui yun feng*), which is some thirty feet high, of an intricacy unsurpassed in Jiangnan. The story goes that it was bored by Zhu Mian,[56] who was just transporting it in a boat when the rock and its container suddenly sank to the bottom of the lake. He could not retrieve it, and went on his way without achieving his ends. Later it was bought by a Mister Dong of Wucheng, who got it as far as mid-stream when the boat sank again. Mister Dong then ruined himself in hiring expert divers to get it, who retrieved it in an instant, both container and rock appearing from beneath the water. Now it has eventually come into the possession of Mister Xu. Fan Changbai told me that this rock has lights gleaming within its cavities every night, and there can be no doubt that this rock is a divine object (*shen wu*). The Garden of the Unsuccessful Politician is within the Qi Gate, but I have never managed to see it. Tao Zhouwang

praised it effusively, for its fine trees and luxuriant groves, its clear waters and green stems. It is about a *li* or more in circumference, and is the most unique of all the famous gardens.[57]

THE SURVIVAL OF THE AGRONOMIC TRADITION

In Yuan's essay (datable by internal evidence to before 1602) there are above all no more references to the great gardens of Suzhou as containing rice-fields, vegetable patches or groves of mulberry trees. The early seventeenth-century writer Wen Zhenheng (1585–1645) is aware of the impeccable moral credentials of such features on a gentleman's property, but would rather they were well out of sight:

As for arbours of beans, vegetable patches or the wild herbs of the mountains, they are of course not odious, but they should form a separate area of several *qing* [a *qing* was 100 *mu*]; it is not an elegant thing to have them planted in a courtyard.[58]

And he further writes with regard to green vegetables:

. . .it is suitable to order the gardeners to plant a lot of them to provide side dishes, but this must be done without thoughts of commercial profit, which makes you no more than a vegetable peddler.[59]

Wen's great-great-grandfather, Wen Zhengming, almost a century earlier, had been happy to accept the patronage of, and depict and describe the garden of, Wang Xianchen, a man who could happily quote a literary allusion that described him precisely as 'irrigating a garden and peddling vegetables'. By 1620, even to play at being a vegetable peddler was problematic for some members of the elite.

Why should this have been so? One explanation is that the great expansion in the numbers of those engaging in hitherto very restricted elite practices of garden culture meant that it was no longer safe to say who was a gentleman recluse alluding to the delights of bucolic self-sufficiency with his groves of orange trees, and who was an oranges magnate. For despite the changes made in the gardens of the very great, there was no doubt that the practice of economic horticulture continued, or even intensified during the sixteenth century. A foreign observer like Gaspar da Cruz, who saw China in the 1560s but had no contacts in the higher reaches of the elite, was struck by the qualities and variety of vegetables, nuts and fruits available in Chinese cities. He saw little in the way of 'gardens', though he did remark that in the houses of the 'common people' in Canton, 'It hath after the house that is at the entry a court with solaces of small trees and bowers with a very fair little fountain'.[60]

The economic referents of the garden did not disappear all at once, nor did they ever disappear completely. The early seventeenth-century garden of Qi Biaojia, at Shanyin county in Zhejiang province, still contained mulberry trees, and another which he merely visited contained a massive grove of over one thousand orange trees.[61] Oranges, referred to by their nickname of 'wooden slaves' (from their profitability) were present in the 'Returning to the Fields Garden' (*Gui tian yuan*) laid out between 1631 and 1633 on part of the site of the by then derelict Garden of the Unsuccessful Politician in Suzhou, along with a quantity of peaches, plums and flowering plums. But by this date the garden's owner, Wang Xinyi, devotes considerably more attention in his account to his rockwork.[62]

Agronomic literature flourished in the sixteenth century and early seventeenth, and books were written that addressed varying levels of the social hierarchy. Relatively lowly were the 'householder's manuals', works containing a wide range of information aimed ostensibly at small-scale landowners. Much of this was eminently practical, and much of it had to do with the successful practice of economic horticulture. One of the most widely circulated works of this genre was *Bian min tu zuan* ('An Illustrated Epitome to Benefit the People'; illus. 19), printed at least six times in various parts of the empire from the Chenghua (1465–87) reign to the Wanli (1573–1620). This is a composite, slowly accumulated work with no individual author. Like other works in the genre, such as *Ju jia bi yong shi lei quan ji* ('Complete and Categorized Essentials for the Householder') and *Duo neng bi shi* ('Generalized Competence in Humble Affairs'), it combines information on household tasks (in which horticulture is prominent) with information on imitating the luxury lifestyle of the urban rich. The 'Illustrated Epitome' contains basic information on what is needed for painting and calligraphy, and the care of the *qin* zither, the indispensable musical companion of the gentleman scholar.[63] Other works contain information on how to create a 'study', how to create a fake patina in antique bronzes, and how to care for bronzes in one's own collection.[64] But it is significant that none of these works contain any information on purely aesthetic horticulture (they never, for instance, discuss rocks). For the relatively humble audience at which they were aimed, raising plants purely for pleasure was a luxury too far. The same is true of the readership for a widely circulated work entitled *Bu nong shu* ('Enlarged Book of Agriculture') by Shen Lianchuan, a small land-owner from Jiaxing in Jiangsu province, who wrote in 1639. Here economic considerations are firmly to the fore:

收割

竹枝詞

無雨無風
斫稻天斫
歸場上便
心寬收成
須趁晴明
好榮也乾
時米也乾

19 Reaping, a woodblock print, from *An Illustrated Epitome to Benefit the People* (*Bian min tu zuan*), 1593 edition.

Though one often talks about the burdensome nature of heavy taxes, dwelling sites and graves are both suitable for consideration as sources of income. At grave sites plant *gan ge* [not identified], which is suitable for firewood. If your dwelling site is spacious and broad then in front plant elm, sophora, paulonia and catalpa, at the rear plant bamboos, at the side set up a plot, and in the central courtyard plant fruit trees. All of these can provide for the expenses engendered by sacrifices, guests and relatives, and can save you spending money in the marketplace. For an inner courtyard, no trees are better than those such as flowering plum, jujube, citron, orange and ailanthus. None are worse than those such as peach, plum, apricot and persimmon, for the fruit bursts easily and cannot be stored, hence no profit.[65]

This was the sort of attitude which a fastidious upper-class writer such as Wen Zhenheng had to take pains to distance himself from.

THE TRIUMPH OF AESTHETICS

At a higher social level, the split between economic and aesthetic horticulture began to be marked. Texts published or republished in late Ming *congshu* (collectanea: uniform editions of originally disparate works) confine themselves largely to technical matters. A number of works of this type are collected in the *Ge zhi cong shu* ('Collectanea of the Investigation of the World'), edited by the great bibliophile Hu Wenhuan and published in 1603.[66] There is *Nong sang ji yao* ('Essentials of Agriculture and Sericulture'; preface dated 1592), and *Zhong shu shu* ('Book of Planting Trees') by Yu Zongben. The latter text does contain some of what might be called 'cultural background' to its technical prescriptions. The whole question of 'planting trees' is said in the preface to be an affair of 'a scholar in reclusion living in retirement'. The 'sacrifices and guests' topos is invoked as a justification, before the author goes on to discuss flowers:

Flowers can form part of a prospect, and thereby give pleasure to the senses and delight to the eyes; furthermore they have a personal meaning to those scholars who are practising reclusion and searching for the Way of regulation of life. Thus it is well known that their presence in a garden is enough to provide for self-sufficiency and self-delectation.[67]

The form of this text is to set out month by month the various horticultural tasks, then to go through various plants systematically: grains, mulberry, bamboo, trees (for timber), flowers, fruit and vegetables. The picture it paints is of a relatively small plot where decorative and economic species are freely intermingled. It specifically says 'Plant tree peonies and peonies in a vegetable garden (*cai*

20 Xie Huan, *The Elegant Gathering in the Apricot Garden* (*Xing yuan ya ji tu*), dated 1437, section of a hand scroll, ink and colour on silk. Metropolitan Museum of Art, New York, The Dillon Fund Gift.

21 Wen Zhengming (1470–1559), *The Yingcui Studio*
(*Yingcui xuan tu*), hanging scroll, ink and colour on paper.
National Palace Museum, Taipei, Taiwan.

22 Wen Zhengming, *Living Aloft* (*Lou ju tu*), 1543, hanging scroll, ink and light colour on paper. Private collection.

Top: 23 Du Qiong (1397–1474), *Befriending the Pines (You song tu)*,
hand scroll, ink and colour on paper. Palace Museum, Beijing.

24 Qiu Ying (c. 1494–1552), *Dwelling in a Garden (Yuan ju tu)*, hand scroll, ink and colour on paper. National Palace Museum, Taipei, Taiwan. Note the grove of fruit trees in flower at the left of the picture.

25 Dish, carved red lacquer on a wooden core, early 15th century.
British Museum, London.

26 Qian Gu (1508–78), *The Small and Tranquil Garden* (*Xiao zhi yuan*),
album leaf, ink and colour on paper, from the album *Travel Sketches* (*Ji
xing tu ce*). National Palace Museum, Taipei, Taiwan.

27 Qiu Ying (c. 1494–1552), *The Garden of Solitary Delight* (*Du le yuan tu*), closing section of a hand scroll, ink and colour on silk. Cleveland Museum of Art.

28 Shen Zhou (1427–1509), *The Thousand Buddha Hall and the Pagoda of Cloudy Cliff Monastery*, leaf from the album *Twelve Views of Tiger Hill* (*Huqui shi er jing tu ce*), ink and colour on paper. Cleveland Museum of Art.

29 Ma Yuan (c 1190–1230), *Egrets on a Snowy Bank*, hanging scroll, ink
and light colour on silk. National Palace Museum, Taipei, Taiwan.
Trees in paintings provided patterns for the appreciation of dwarfed
specimens.

yuan) and they will flourish particularly well', and 'Beside beautiful flowers and trees you must plant things like onions and shallots, for the stimulation of their musky smell'.[68] Again, such reminders of the existence of edible vegetables would have been anathema to Wen Zhenheng, who ordered them removed to a distance.

Such a separation was not a one-way process, with the discourse of aesthetics banishing any hint of the economic. It happened in the other direction too. The most important agronomic treatise of the late Ming is the 'Complete Book of the Regulation of Agriculture' by Xu Guangqi (1562–1633), left incomplete at his death.[69] Xu takes over more or less unaltered the section on 'plot fields' from the *Nong shu* of Wang Zhen, written in the Yuan period and cited in the previous chapter.[70] However, Xu omits all of Wang's poems on horticulture, which actually make up the majority of the entry in the earlier book. If onions have no place in gentlemen's gardens, poems now have no place in agronomic treatises. Two entirely separate discursive fields, with different patterns of authorization of statements, have now been created.

Given the existence of this vast body of horticulture that retained earlier concerns, the wealthy of the later Ming period were forced to differentiate themselves more rigorously from practices they had once (when gardens were rarer) been prepared to embrace, albeit at a symbolic level. Differentiation has to be deployed most rigorously, and most stringently, against those practices or commodities that are closest to the thing being defended, and hence where the degree of confusion is potentially greatest.[71] It was the ubiquitousness of 'orchards' that made the proponents of 'gardens' so vehement.

The withdrawal from engagement with the economic landscape in the latter part of the Ming is a phenomenon that occurred widely across the empire. In his study of Taihe county, John Dardess notes that 'After the sixteenth century, interest in workaday landscapes faded away. Enthusiasm for landscape shifted from the actual to the ethereal and artificial.'[72] He shows how patronage of local topographical painters, and involvement in horticultural activities, was replaced with a concern for gardens full of imported exotic flowers, laid out in conscious imitation of the gardens of Suzhou. Contemporary descriptions of the 'Spring Floating Garden' (*Chun fou yuan*) of Xiao Shiwei, built in the 1620s in the western suburbs of Taihe city, are at pains to point out that it is *not* a productive space. Dardess points out that 'although these gardens happened to have been built in T'ai-ho they had no special connection with it', and concludes:

From the early Ming discovery of beauty and value in the real world of nature and life on the land, one ends in the late Ming and early Ch'ing determination to ignore and avoid that world, with the creation of toy fantasies in artificial lakes and landscaped gardens, and a preference for moonlit surrealisms to the daylight world of work, settlement and subsistence.[73]

Dardess here may be idealizing the actual as opposed to symbolic involvement of the early Ming elite with 'work, settlement and subsistence', but the broad picture he paints is a convincing one. It is supported by Joanna Handlin Smith's reading of the property of a single owner, in a context where it was the taste of that owner that defined the quality and renown of a garden. With the commodification of absolutely everything in the late Ming, and no barriers other than wealth to the possession of attributes formally limited to a relatively small elite, that elite began to fear a collapse of the social and wealth hierarchies into each other. There is ample evidence that gardens were not exempt from this general trend, and that they were either being created by, or were coming into the possession of, merchants who could not claim any connection with the sanctifying form of wealth derived from landholding. An account of the 'Mysterious Plot' (Xuan pu) of the Wu family of Xiuning, in Anhui province, makes it clear that a full kit of rare plants, fabulous rocks and Daoist religious attributes could be assembled by anyone who had the wealth to do so. Such anecdotes become a standard part of the half-admiring, half-appalled accounts of the rise of the Anhui plutocracy at this period.[74] Gardens were now clearly commodities. Individual elements of gardens were equally commodities that could change hands with some frequency. The immensely wealthy family of the Chancellor Chen Zan lived at East Dongtingshan outside Suzhou, where they built a dwelling 'resembling a palace' with a 'flower garden' (hua yuan – the term is a relatively rare one in Ming texts) of 100 mu. They purchased at great expense a 'master peak' of a rock, and tried to ship it home in a raft, which sank in Lake Tai. They then took a month to build a coffer dam, but dredged up the 'wrong' rock, which subsequently turned out, when the first stone was recovered, to be an exact pair. These miraculous menhirs had pride of place in Chen's garden, but were sold by a descendant, passing very quickly through the hands of two separate owners.[75]

Here rocks and even whole gardens were no different from other forms of luxury cultural property, for example paintings, which could change hands with surprising rapidity.[76] In such a commercially fluid situation, it came to be the case that less attention was paid to what was owned (since anyone could achieve that), and more to the *way* it was owned, in particular to the structure of references within which the possession was enmeshed. Hence the size of a garden became less important; indeed it was rather praiseworthy to have a small garden if this was compensated for by aesthetic excellence, and there is a burgeoning in the seventeenth century of names on the lines of 'Half-Acre Garden' and 'Mustard Seed Garden'.[77] The miniature here fulfils Susan Stewart's definition of the 'overly cultural'.[78] What distinguishes the aesthetic garden from the productive one is not simply a different series of crops (flowers instead of fruit), since the former continued in many cases to include plants that had a market value. Rather, it is the manner of possessing that becomes important. This had always been the case for a few, but now in the latter part of the Ming it was to become a strategy that was much more widely available and much more widely practised. In Stewart's trenchant phrase, 'only "taste", the code word for class varieties of consumption, articulates the difference here'.[79]

ACCESS AND RECLUSION

With the invention of taste as the central mechanism regulating the social dimension of consumption, and more importance granted to the manner of possessing, the question of access to gardens played a crucial part. Early western writers on Chinese gardens make great play of their inaccessibility, their role as a haven for their owners far from the cares of office or of family, as essentially a-social spaces. Certainly the concept of 'reclusion', *yin*, is foremost in Ming writing about gardens, and particularly in the names given to gardens or to features within them.[80] There is an equally long tradition of the acceptance of the fact that *real* reclusion in the remote depths of the countryside is not a real option for those possessed of social obligations. This acceptance appears as early as the apologia for landscape painting by the Northern Song painter Guo Xi.[81] It was a commonplace of almost proverbial status that 'The first choice of a location for making a home is the countryside, then the suburb, and lastly the city',[82] but this did not mean that it was the location most frequently chosen. The symbolic dissociation of the elite from celebration of the productive landscape was matched by a growing tendency for landlords to abandon the countryside in favour of the city as the sixteenth century progressed. Ming writers employed a term, first coined in the Southern Song, which contained within itself the oxymoron of simultaneous withdrawal and social engagement, the term *shi yin*, 'city recluse' (illus. 30). On one level, this

城南高隱

僧牛伊昔區堵原何如南郭張家隱此歌
恨不驚人句行草炒八臨池工衡門柳色和
煙碧小院荷花映日紅浮雲世事異朝夕
水調高卦全眞風　萬曆戊子之夏保逸
仰泉足賣踽相與高論終日家和有贈

楊李友弟宏也初鳴甫記

30 Song Xu, *Lofty Hermitage South of the City* (*Cheng nan gao yin*),
1588, hanging scroll. Palace Museum, Beijing.

meant no more than the man to whom it was applied was not an office holder, but one who pursued his own private interests.[83] It could also be applied to gardens, as in the name *Shi yin yuan*, 'Reclusion in the City Garden', given to the property of Yao Zhe (zi Yuanbai) at Nanjing. The builder asked advice from Gu Lin (1467–1545), a figure from Suzhou who was part of the circle of Wen Zhengming, achieved the *jinshi* degree in 1496, and was a famous arbiter of literary taste in the southern capital. Gu's advice was to 'Plant many trees, build a few structures'.[84] The idea of a hermitage in the city came to the fore with the Ming period, and it quickly became hackneyed. Xie Zhaozhe's complaint directed at the vulgarity and crassness of the names given to contemporary gardens and garden features cites *shi yin* as the very worst of all, prevalent in his native Fujian and in Zhejiang, eschewed in the more sophisticated circles of Suzhou.[85] It made use of long available ideas (ideas with Buddhist connotations) that remoteness from the world was not a matter of physical distance but of inner mental state. The fourth century emperor Jianwen di (r. 371–2) had observed that 'The place where one is mentally alive need not be remote. . . '.[86] The term 'place where one is mentally alive', or 'place where the mind is concentrated', *hui xin chu*, is one frequently alluded to in Ming writing on gardens. An early Ming text, the 'Record of the Deep Purple Studio', records that

The ancients had a saying that the place where one is mentally alive need not be remote. With a thick grove of trees, the fish and birds will imperceptibly approach of their own accord. . . . Now this studio is sited in the city, but will cause people to think of the hills and woods; is this not beautiful?[87]

The convenient effect of the deployment of these ideas was to allow the upper reaches of the Ming elite to eat their cake and have it, to enjoy the kudos of eremitism without actually eschewing the cultural, social and security benefits of life in or near to a major urban centre. As Wang Shizhen put it in the late sixteenth century: 'The character of dwelling in the mountains is silence, the character of dwelling in the city is clamour; only dwelling in a garden enjoys the happy medium'.[88] Wen Zhenheng is even more explicit about the sheer impossibility of abandoning the convenience of his native Suzhou for some remote, if scenic spot:

Dwelling among mountains and waters is best; next comes dwelling in a village, then dwelling in the suburbs. Even if our sort of people cannot rest in caves or sojourn in gullies, following the tracks of famous hermits, but are admired in the city, it is essential that gates and courtyards be elegant and clean, that dwellings and cottages be pure and clear. Thus pavilions and terraces have feelings of the untrammelled scholar, chapels and belvederes the charms of the recluse. One must plant fine trees and rare bamboos, display epigraphic specimens, books and pictures. Thus the dweller will forget his aging, the sojourner there will forget to go home, the wanderer there will forget his weariness. In hot weather there will be cooling zephyrs; in freezing times there will be cheering warmth. If one indulges in extravagant earthmoving and planting, valuing colourful effects, then it becomes like a fetter, a mere cage.[89]

One could argue on the basis of this a broadly three-stage model of the development of concerns in the garden culture of the self-conscious Ming elite: from a focus on its agronomic references, and to the morally good life of self-sufficiency, through a concern for a wide variety of rare and splendid plants, to a final engagement with the more slippery mechanism of taste. Though undeniably crude, this model as a heuristic device does have the benefit of introducing some sense of change over time into what is too often seen as a static phenomenon.

Both ostentation and taste can only be deployed in a social arena, and both are meaningless without an audience. Timothy Brook has put this well:

Possessions hidden away or gardens to which outside entry was forbidden were of no value in the stressful competition for status in late-Ming gentry society. Their consumption had to be conspicuous, and that conspicuousness invariably imparted to every social interaction a public significance. The gentry related to each other in public as a public elite.[90]

The orientalist fantasy of the sequestered scholar will not survive a reading of the copious Ming sources that make it plain that great gardens were generally accessible, if not to absolutely everyone, then to those of the respectable classes who could afford to tip the doorkeeper. This was a practice with a long pedigree. The first private gardens, those of southern aristocrats of the period after the fall of the Han dynasty in AD 220, were by and large not available to anyone other than inmates of the owner. The earliest Suzhou private garden (listed as such in all the Ming gazetteers) was the fourth-century garden of Gu Bijiang, who famously chased the great calligrapher Wang Xizhi from the premises when the latter incautiously attempted an uninvited visit. This changed over time. A former imperial hunting park known as the Qujiang Park, situated south of the Tang capital

Chang'an, was effectively a public park from the early eighth century. The imperial gardens of the Northern Song dynasty (960–1127), the 'Golden Lustre Pond' (Jin ming chi) and the 'Grove of Jasper Trees', were ritually opened in the second month 'for the officials and the people' (fishing permits could be purchased), while the private aristocratic gardens of Luoyang at the same period were also open to visitors, and not merely at festival times. Fan Zhongyan in the Song justified his frugal decision *not* to build a garden in Luoyang, and instead to spend the money on charity, on the grounds that he could easily visit all the gardens he wanted to. A Song poem by the author Shao Yong, entitled 'Visiting the Gardens of Luoyang', runs: 'The gardens of Luoyang do not close their gates . . . who needs to know the owner in order to enter?'[91] The famous 'Garden of Solitary Delight' (Du le yuan) of the retired statesman Sima Guang was certainly accessible to his peer group, and even to a wider public. In the Ming period the imperial gardens in the late 1400s and early 1500s were not indiscriminately open, but the 'grant' of a visit to them was relatively easy to come by. By the end of the sixteenth century access was even freer, and a trip to see the tigers and leopards of the imperial menagerie being fed with live dogs was one of the sights of the capital for gentleman visitors.[92] The gardens of the hereditary imperial aristocracy were open to visitors, as is clear from Shen Defu's listing of them under the heading of 'gardens which can be visited, and which I myself have seen', and his statement that 'at peony time' everyone visits the Earl of Hui'an's garden.[93] The Italian Jesuit Matteo Ricci was taken by friends in 1598 to see the Duke of Weiguo's garden in Nanjing. He describes it as 'il piu bello di questa citta', and praises its towers, terraces and 'altri edeficij magnifichi, as well as a hill of artifically made rocks, full of many caves, loggias, steps, pavilions, shelters, fishing places and other galanteries'. He describes the labyrinthine nature of the garden, 'requiring two or three hours' to traverse it all, but his account makes it plain that he had no prior social connection with the owner, who was not present during the tour.[94] Gardens were prominently listed in guidebooks, with the clear implication that they could be visited. Most Ming writing on gardens is placed within a context of relatively easy access. Qi Biaojia had visited nearly two hundred properties in his native Shanyin county, and received a stream of visitors (not all of whom can have been personally known to him) in his own garden.[95] A garden where guests were absolutely not admitted was a rarity, and one worth recording, as in 'A Record of Avoiding Guests in the Apt Garden' (Shi yuan bu ke ji) by a native of Huating, Lu Shusheng (1509–1606).[96] Lu argues that most people spend only one day out of ten in their gardens, and are not true owners but guests on their own property. On his modest plot of only two *mu* he is a true owner, since guests are never admitted. Lu, however, was out of step with the behaviour of the majority of his peers. The occasionally mass nature of garden visiting, even in gardens owned by the bureaucratic scholar elite, is seen in one source describing Suzhou in the late sixteenth century:

Xu Shaopu, by name Tinglu, was a man of Taicang in Suzhou prefecture, who later dwelled in Suzhou city, and served as Assistant Administrative Commissioner of Zhejiang province. His family dwelling was in a garden within the Feng Gate, and reached one to two hundred *mu* [15 to 30 acres] of rare rocks and sinuous ponds, splendid halls and high towers, all extremely majestic and grand. In springtime the visitors were like ants, and the gardeners admitted them for coins. Many of his neighbours set up wine shops to serve the visitors. A few of those who entered the garden did not behave themselves, but picked the flowers and shouted; they were all prosecuted, and for this reason people did not care to enter lightly. The household servants in his employ all took extreme care of his property, and lorded it over the district, the people of which feared them like tigers.

The same source goes on to tell how an unseemly wrangle between Xu's servants and a mourning party in 1602 led to his garden being sacked by an angry mob and 'over half of it' being destroyed. It continues:

Mr Xu is no longer prominent, though the garden still exists, but commended to the name of some other official as owner, to avoid misfortune. The space between its halls and belvederes is already clogged with thick weeds.[97]

Now seen as a locus of conspicuous consumption, the garden of a rich man was an obvious focus for attack in the increasingly numerous social uprisings that swept across the Suzhou region in the closing decades of the Ming period.

The accessibility of the gardens of the rich in Ming Jiangnan has several implications. It clearly identifies them as spaces of social competition, as fully involved in the search for status and power. Far from being an unseen refuge, a garden was a way of proclaiming its owner's wealth *and* taste to a wide audience. The garden of the Grand Preceptor in Peking announced itself to passers-by with its prominent inscription and red gateway. That gardens fulfilled this role runs counter to the received wisdom about the relatively private nature of luxury consumption in early modern China. In a recent essay distinguished for the breadth of its comparative approach, Peter Burke has written of China: 'It was not the facade (as in Italy) but the interior of the house which was decorated on a lavish scale. The display was intended for the family and its friends.'[98] A consideration of the evidence reviewed above may, on the contrary, support the view that Ming gardens (together with the commemorative arches to be discussed in chapter Three) played very much the same social role as did conspicuous expenditure on building in Italy at the same period. At the very least, they played the same part as did the great Italian gardens of the day, access to which has been studied by David Coffin. The garden of Cardinal Andrea della Valla, installed in the 1520s, had an inscription explicitly extending the right of access 'for the delights of citizens and strangers', while Giovanni Pontano, in his *I trattati delle virtù sociali*, openly associates the *virtù* of 'Splendour' with gardens made accessible to one's peers and to a wider public. Foreigners in the sixteenth century frequently remarked on the right of access to great Roman gardens, from the 1560s often achieved by a street door that gave onto the garden without passing through the *palazzo*.[99] The current debate among historians of early modern China regarding the aptness or otherwise of Jürgen Habermas's concept of the 'public sphere' might do well to at least take account of the fact that at the time there may have been rather more 'public space', in a narrowly materialistic sense, than has been presented in standard accounts of Chinese cities.

By the late Ming, the construction of gardens had become an obsession celebrated among the upper classes. The gardens of this tiny minority were now fully established as objects of luxury consumption. In describing how he ruined himself through this means, Wang Shimin (1592–1680) is careful to stress the lack of any commercial acumen on his part. Gentlemen were supposed to know how to spend money, not make it:

Having been amply provided for by my forefathers, I am ignorant of anything to do with a livelihood: I do not even know how to use a scale or handle an abacus. Yet I was fatally addicted to gardens. Wherever I lived I set up rock arrangements and planted trees so as to express my sentiments and amuse my eyes. During the prime of my life I was bent on constructing and planting in heroic proportions. Once I gave in to my extravagant fancy I no longer thought about the consequences.

Wang's autobiographical account, translated in full by Pei-yi Wu, goes on to describe the simultaneous creation of two great tracts of peonies, rocks and sculptured earthworks in a suburban setting.

97

When economic stringencies forced the sale of one of them to a Buddhist community it vanished back into the wider productive landscape almost immediately, its ornamental species cut down for firewood. The other garden is described as in full decay, 'trampled underfoot by yokels and swains' (suggesting again a degree of access even in despite of the owner's wishes).[100]

The word *pi*, here translated as 'addiction' but also meaning 'obsession' or 'craving', was important in Ming theories of the personality. The 'craving' was what formed the individual, distinguishing the man of taste from the common herd.[101] The same word is used by Wang Xinyi in describing the impetus that led him to build his Returning to the Fields Garden on part of the site of the ruined Garden of the Unsuccessful Politician in the years 1631-5:

My nature has a craving for hills and mountains, and whenever I encounter a place of fine mountains and water I wander back and forth indecisively, scarcely able to bear to leave, gazing at it for a long time till my heart pounds and my fingers itch – there is indeed enlightenment in painting.[102]

The context he lays out for the garden, far from being in any sense the productive landscape, is natural uncultivated scenery, 'mountains and water' (*shan shui*), a term seldom if ever without a cosmological tinge, as we shall see. Despite the allusion to rural self-sufficiency in the title of the garden, there is nothing in its layout to allude to productivity at all. The family fields of glutinous rice may be visible in the distance from one of its towers, but they are kept well beyond its walls. The other context provided for the garden is the representation of 'mountains and water' in painting, an area of practice that came to dominate the terminology of garden making, as gardens were seen as exclusively aestheticized spaces. This type of reference is never made in earlier Ming texts, such as Wen Zhengming's 'Record of the Garden of the Unsuccessful Politician'. By the time Wang Xinyi got his hands on the same tract of land one hundred years later, it was very clear that the land was a surface to be manipulated in the way a painter manipulates the blank spaces of paper or silk:

The land was suitable for a pond, so I made a pond there. I removed the soil from the pond and piled it up high. It was suitable for hills, so I made hills. By the pond and between the hills it was suitable for a dwelling, so I made a dwelling.

Wang finishes his 'Record of Dwelling in the Returning to the Fields Garden' with an encomium on different types of rocks, which are

31 Zhao Mengfu (1254–1322), *Bamboo, Rocks and Lonely Orchids* (*Zhu shi you lan*), section of a hand scroll, ink on paper. Cleveland Museum of Art. The kind of painting which was supposed to act as a model for the disposition of elements within the aestheticized Ming garden.

discussed entirely in terms of how they approximate to the styles of two of the most prestigious old masters of Yuan dynasty painting. Thus intricate rocks are in the style of Zhao Mengfu (1254–1322; illus. 26), while 'clumsy' (zhuo, as in Zhuo zheng yuan) ones are like the brushwork of Huang Gongwang (1269–1354). These luminaries provide the inspiration for the garden's design:

I disposed their [the rocks] perspective and proportions according to the style of these two, and entrusted the work to the skilled hand Chen Siyun, who took three years to complete it.

Paintings, as infinitely more prestigious cultural artefacts, might provide the models by which the forms of the land could be manipulated. Dong Qichang (1555-1636) owned several paintings on the subject of the 'Peach Blossom Spring' by the Yuan artist Wang Meng (1308–85), and it was his ownership of these scrolls that led him to attempt to buy the actual landscape depicted in them.[103] Dong also owned two scrolls, the 'Thatched Cottage' and the 'Wangchuan Villa', attributed to the Tang poet and painter Wang Wei (701–61), and makes it clear that he expected them to be used in the disposition of property:

Fortunately I possessed the copies of the 'Thatched Cottage' and the 'Wangchuan Villa'. . .some gentlemen's gardens can be painted, but my paintings can be gardened (ke yuan).[104]

Another major result of the trend towards the ascendancy of a miniaturized and pictorialized aesthetic of gardens in the sixteenth century was the growing practice of raising pot plants, and the dwarfing of trees and other large shrubs to create the miniature landscapes usually known in English by their Japanese name of bonsai (Chinese, pan zai, 'pot planting', or pan jing, 'pot landscapes'). Although there is a pictorial and textual evidence that some of the necessary techniques were practised as far back as the Tang dynasty,[105] it also seems plausible that such things were a speciality of Suzhou and one that spread extensively through China only in the course of the sixteenth century, as part of a wave of expansion of garden culture that also has Suzhou as a key point of origin. In 1506 the author of the Suzhou gazetteer seemed to feel the need to explain the term, as if it might be unfamiliar:

The people of Tiger Hill are excellent at planting strange flowers and rare blossoms in a dish. A dish with pine or antique flowering plum, when placed on a table, is pure, elegant and delightful.[106]

Huang Xingzeng, writing before 1540, tells how, in the Suzhou region, 'even humble families in rural hamlets decorate small dishes with island [landscapes] as a pastime'.[107] Writers at mid-century, like Tian Rucheng, whose *Xi hu you lan zhi yu* has a preface dated 1547, are already imbued with the idea that it is the aesthetics of painting that provide a system of discrimination for dwarfed trees:

As for the growing of pine, cypress and *hai tong* in dishes, they mostly imitate a pictorial idea (*hua yi*). Aslant and supine ones are in the Ma Yuan (fl. *c.* 1190–1260) technique [illus. 29], those with erect trunks and spreading foliage in the Guo Xi (*c.* 1001–90) technique. Other forms, such as 'phoenix and crane on pavilion and pagoda' are variously refined and marvellous, and can be laid out for pure enjoyment.[108]

At the end of the century, the Nanjing writer Gu Qiyuan continues to stress the importance of a 'pictorial idea', as well as providing evidence that Suzhou was still considered to be the source of the finest exponents of the art:

Of old, dish landscapes to be placed on a table consisted of no more than one or two types of Damnacanthus.[109] Recently, flower gardeners (*hua yuanzi*) have moved here from Suzhou, and the number of varieties has increased, so that apart from Damnacanthus there are things like Tianmu pines, *yingluo* pines, crab apples, prasine peaches, little-leaf boxwood, carnations, Xiangfei bamboo, *shuidongqing*, narcissus, small plantains, wolfberry, gingko and flowering plum. These must have roots and trunks, with a pictorial idea to the branches and leaves, and must be installed in an antique porcelain dish with fine stones. The price of the expensive ones can go as high as several thousand cash.[110]

That gardens were now pure objects of luxury is shown clearly by their inclusion in morality books of the late Ming, texts that listed among other types of transgression to be avoided those of excessive consumption. The most influential and widely circulated of these was Liu Zongzhou's *Ren pu* ('Chart of Humanity') of 1634, where a 'Warning against attachment to flowers and rocks' appears sandwiched between similar warnings against love of leisure, gambling, accumulating too many antiques, and lust.[111] The warning takes the form of a number of anecdotes about the refusal of noted gentlemen of the past to allow the great expense of garden construction.

In a recent essay, Joanna Handlin Smith has foregrounded the issue of garden building as conspicuous consumption in the late Ming, and of explicit criticism directed against this practice by contemporaries like Liu Zongzhou. One early sixteenth-century garden builder avoided this criticism by having the construction work carried out as part of a famine relief effort, to give wages to the displaced.[112] In the case of the figure she studies, Qi Biaojia (1602–45), a defence against this criticism involved arguing for the garden as a site of elite solidarity, of shared social engagement, rather than as part of a brute struggle for prestige through the display of wealth. It must have been a defence of some weight since, as Handlin Smith points out, Qi remained on perfectly good terms with Liu Zongzhou, with whom he shared the connection of passing the examinations in the same year.[113] Accessibility was a crucial part of this defence, for only access by the owner's peer group in the elite (and their recording of the garden in prose, verse and pictorial compositions), only their shared consumption could serve to make wealth *qing*, or 'pure'. 'Access' was here a practice that formed the aesthetic garden and differentiated it from economic horticulture, since the access denied was the very point of horticultural *property*. Access at one and the same time reinforced ownership, while submerging and disguising it in an aesthetic discourse of nature. 'The garden' was a way of making money look natural. The paradox was that in creating access to the site an owner also risked the resentment of those who felt that he was unreasonably flaunting the great wealth necessary to create one of these purely aestheticized landscapes. He risked allowing access to those who would break the flowers and shout, and he risked ultimately providing an easily identifiable symbolic concentration of his wealth that could be wrecked relatively easily in a time of social unrest. There was to be no resolution of this paradox. The late Ming garden was not a set of meanings but a site of contested meanings: readable differentially as a pure space of aesthetics or as a luxury object *par excellence*, a battery of wealth. In this respect it is similar to the concept of 'luxury' itself, also a site of contest that is historically generated in specific social circumstances, and which also can reach no resolved and stable meaning as long as those social circumstances endure. A luxury is not a type of artefact, but a type of transaction. In the Ming period it was inseparable from the idea of the market, or more precisely of the commodity, which can float free of ideas such as social reciprocity. A Ming painting became a luxury when it 'came loose' from the context of social relations it was created to serve. The possibility of inappropriate excess in the consumption of painting came along with this free-floating commodity state. In Confucian social theory, no property, and most certainly no property in land, should float free of social categories and the discourse of kinship.[114] By the sixteenth century it most certainly did, as famous gardens, like the paintings they increasingly resembled, frequently changed hands anything up to once a decade. This instability in what was meant to be most stable, property in land, was embodied in a particularly disquieting degree in the distinctive artefact of the garden, the oxymoron of 'land' as 'luxury'.

3 The Gardens of the Wen Family

THE PERSON OF WEN ZHENGMING

One way of introducing a closer focus into our reading of changes in attitudes to garden culture and to landscapes in the Ming period is to follow over a period of time the members of one family, their engagement with property in land, and their aesthetic responses to that land. One Suzhou elite family for which the sources available for such a diachronic study are particularly rich is that of Wen Zhengming (1470–1559), already encountered several times in the previous chapters. Over the course of the Ming dynasty, and on into the early Qing, the members of the Wen family owned land from which they derived their income, they governed and collected taxes on land on behalf of the state, they owned gardens and wrote about them in prose and verse, they wrote about the gardens of others, and they represented both gardens and other types of landscape in pictorial form. One wrote a treatise on elegant living that incorporates extensive prescriptive material on how a gentleman's garden should be, while another was even an official of the Office of the Imperial Forest Park. A look at these individuals, at the transmission of property within the family, and at the verbal and visual representation of the gardens and landscape they created, opens the possibility for a reintegration of aesthetics and economics at the level of family and individual practice. Instead of a simple chronological progression through the family's involvement with gardens and landscape, I intend to plunge in at the middle, with the almost iconic figure of Wen Zhengming himself, the perfect 'Chinese scholar'. In giving a degree of scrutiny to questions of the construction of his persona, both in and after his lifetime, I hope to bring into play some of the understanding of self that was to be so important in the Ming ideal of the garden as a potential model of the good society. Here all the sources need to be treated with a particular degree of respect. In addition to Wen's own writings (as edited anonymously after his death), we have various contemporary and near-contemporary necrologies of him.[1] These are all texts that exist to serve the aim of 'fixing' the commemorated individual in his social and familial context, and which, not surprisingly, are distinguished by their tone of filial praise for the recently deceased. They are not 'raw data'. No more is the seemingly blander and more matter-of-fact family genealogy, the *Wen shi zu pu*, compiled in the early eighteenth century by a descendant, Wen Han.[2] Like the gazetteers, whose parameters are spatial rather than being those of a kin-group, the genealogy is not an innocent 'primary source' but a discursive text in its own right, with which we must engage. There is nothing else to read.

There can be no doubt of Wen Zhengming's importance to his descendants. The preface to the 'Treatise on Superfluous Things' by his great-grandson Wen Zhenheng (1585–1645), written by Shen Chunze, resounds with pride in a name that achieved an empire-wide fame:

I said to Wen Zhenheng: Your late great-grandfather, the Grand Scribe Wen Zhengming, was the very nonpareil in the Suzhou region of sincere antique virtue and lofty rectitude, and lived to be nearly a hundred years old. The family's transmitted renown has been fragrant and widespread. Its 'paintings in poems' and 'poems in paintings' have been the very high point among the ingenious minds and marvellous hands of Suzhou, who are all members of your lineage.[3]

Wen Zhengming's fame in the Qing dynasty was augmented by the esteem for his painting felt by the Qianlong emperor (r. 1736–95). A poem written by the emperor in 1765, during the course of a southern trip, compares Wen Zhengming to the current imperial favourite Shen Deqian (1673–1769), both being Suzhou literati of ancient family. The conclusion is that Shen is the finer poet, but Wen had the more accomplished hand as painter and calligrapher. When the ruined Surging Waves Pavilion was rebuilt in Suzhou by Song Lao (1634–1713; ECCP 689–90) during his governorship of Jiangsu between 1692 and 1706, it seemed a natural choice that the new name-board for the property should be in Wen Zhengming's calligraphy.[4] It is as 'painter and calligrapher' that Wen Zhengming has been celebrated down to the present day, and it might seem reasonable to situate him in relation to gardens primarily through the medium of painted representations, such as his two separate sets of views of the Garden of the Unsuccessful Politician described in chapter One.

This, however, is a reasonable act, but one that I wish to resist for the moment.[5] Ming dynasty texts tend to invert the priorities of modern biographies of Wen, giving less space to his artistic accomplishments than they do to his writings (chiefly to his poetry), his moral character, and his admirable unworldly detachment from the sordid details of life. We learn from the necrology written on his death by his son that he was well-read on points of law and government regulation, and was often called on to settle points of ritual. Unlike the standard Ming landowner, he took no concern for the management of his property:

His nature was to detest mundane matters, and all family affairs were entrusted to Madame Wu [his wife], who managed everything to do with funerals and mournings, the marriages of sons and daughters, the building of houses and purchase of real estate, all without bothering my father one jot.[6]

This ideal of 'pure and lofty', so particularly associated with Wen Zhengming (and also with the fruit crops of some of Suzhou's gardens) conjures up an effortless withdrawal, a disinterested disengagement from the mundane. However, it is a disengagement that functions to create opportunities for re-engagement, for reintervention in the mundane sphere, which are thereby granted much greater force and cohesiveness than would otherwise be available to them. Hence the emphasis on qing gao, 'pure and lofty', a manner of behaviour that operated as a series of refusals to acknowledge, among other things, the existence of economic facts of life. In Ming dynasty terms, the economic facts of life were overwhelmingly facts derived from the realm of land and of property in land. The concept of qing gao, the defining characteristic of the recluse, might (by stretching a point) be read as a sort of secular, non-transcendent 'holiness'. Peter Brown has written of this phenomenon in the Eastern Roman Empire in Late Antiquity:

The life of the holy man . . . is marked by so many histrionic feats of self-mortification that it is easy, at first sight, to miss the deep social significance of asceticism as a long drawn-out, solemn ritual of dissociation – of becoming the total stranger. For the society around him, the holy man is the one man who can stand outside the ties of family, and of economic interest; whose attitude to food itself rejected all the ties of solidarity to kin and village that, in the peasant societies of the Near East, had always been expressed by the gesture of eating.[7]

Mortification was distasteful, and the severing of family ties theoretically repugnant, to the Ming elite but there are helpful ideas here, particularly in Brown's understanding of holiness as something intimately related to power of a non-coercive type, as a slowly accumulated reservoir of prestige and influence that could be dispensed in small individual acts or in one major intervention in the secular sphere. It was his disengagement from the everyday that gave the 'lofty recluse' his moral leverage: 'it [the descriptive terminology of reclusion] describes a self-conscious, highly moral, well-educated elite that actively participated in the most engaging activities of the times.'[8] No one exemplified the Ming practice of *qing gao* more fully than Wen Zhengming, the man who did more than any other to 'create' the Garden of the Unsuccessful Politician we have today.

Wen, on his return to Suzhou from an abortive political career in Peking at the end of the 1520s, set about acquiring that fund of moral authority for which he was to be renowned, by a process of refusal of social engagement. This is exactly the kind of authority to intervene, acquired through a series of social refusals, that Brown has discerned in the hermits of the early Christian empire. The garden, through its associations with eremitism, provided the site for the acting out of those refusals. Mimicking the state of total withdrawal through the deployment of the, in fact, socially engaged artefact of the *yuan* allowed members of the elite to accumulate desired moral and social leverage without the distasteful stigma of asceticism.

A Ming garden could be a site of power in that society because it was above all a site of storage, a site of accumulation in a society that was poorly served by alternative mechanisms of accumulation. The very etymology of the word, as made explicit by early commentators, lay in the notion of enclosure, of keeping things in and keeping out those who would illicitly appropriate the desirable things of a legitimate proprietor. In the words of one Tang commentator: 'That which has a hedge is called a *yuan*.'[9] Here there is a very close comparison with the family of etymologies relating to gardens in the principal Indo-European languages, all of which also revolve around the notions of enclosure and separation.[10] I revealed in chapter One how a piece of real estate like the Garden of the Unsuccessful Politician could, through the use of specific land management practices, and in particular through silviculture, be legible as a sort of battery of wealth, storing and preserving the large amounts of economic capital invested in it at the time of its creation. I have also attempted to show how the same space could in the Ming serve to store up cultural and moral capital on behalf of its owner, by giving him a place to be in the world that was at the same time intimately bound up with ideas of refusal and withdrawal. It also gave to its owner a place to be with other equally, or more highly-charged, personalities engaged in the 'pure and lofty' practice of eremitism. Instead of seeing 'withdrawal', and the figure of the hermit, as timeless constants of 'traditional Chinese culture', endlessly repeating patterns established by earlier writers such as Tao Yuanming, I would prefer to see their meaning as imbricated with the specifics of social and cultural power, and in changes taking place in the balance of these over Wen Zhengming's lifetime. Mori Masao, summarizing the work of other Japanese scholars, has shown how from the late fifteenth century, success in the examinations began to play an ever larger part in sustaining elite status, while locally, often rurally, based elites declined in relative importance:

To sum up, there were two types of landowning gentry with a Confucian educational background in the fifteenth century: the ch'u-shih-type tax chiefs residing in local districts, who could not remain mere passive spectators towards the interests of local society, and the chin-shen residing in cities who indulged themselves in luxury without worrying about anything else.[11]

The division into altruistic rural squires and selfish urbanites is perhaps overdrawn, but it can be dramatized in the histories of two men with whom Wen Zhengming was himself intimately involved. His painting tutor, Shen Zhou, personified the older style of rurally based, non-degree-holding tax chief, while Wu Kuan, he of the Eastern Estate, held high status based on success in the examination system, joined to wealth derived at least initially from commercial sources in the textiles industry. Wang Xianchen too, proprietor of the equally urban Garden of the Unsuccessful Politician, was a member of an official family, a status he shared with Wen himself, the son of a Prefect and the nephew of an Assistant Censor-in-chief. The gardens celebrated in the 1506 Suzhou gazetteer, with its group of inter-related degree-holders, and the gardens celebrated by Wen, are, by and large, the property of people for whom the truly rural – while celebrated at the imaginary level – was becoming less immediate as an everyday experience. Withdrawal was celebrated precisely among those who had been exposed to the wider world of politics, who had something to withdraw from, if only symbolically.

THE WRITINGS OF WEN ZHENGMING

The specific acts of involvement of the Wen family, and of Wen Zhengming himself, with garden culture can be traced in several ways, and here this will be attempted by means of an examination of their collected writings. In the case of Wen Zhengming himself, this almost certainly underestimates the amount of contact, since as we shall see not every piece of social verse was deemed worthy of anthologizing after his death, and it is likely that only a portion of his oeuvre survives. Similarly, the terminology of gardens in the Ming was a fluid one, not always employing any of the words we would expect. This means that I have almost certainly missed 'garden' poems in a trawl through the collected verse of Wen and his relatives.

What follows can be considered as a sample only. It omits the series of works on the Garden of the Unsuccessful Politician listed in chapter One.

In the 'Collected Works of Five Masters of the Wen Family' (Wen shi wu jia ji) are the poems of Wen Hong (1426–79), his grandson Wen Zhengming himself, his sons Wen Peng (1497–1553) and Wen Jia (1499–1582), and the former's son (and compiler of the anthology) Wen Zhaozhi (1520–after 1588). Wen Hong is represented solely by a set of poems entitled 'Twenty-eight Poems on the Returning-to-Possession Garden' (Gui de yuan ershiba yong),[12] which refer to a site I have not as yet managed to identify. Their existence should remind us that there were gardens prior to the early sixteenth-century expansion, but they cannot compare with the quantity of material bequeathed by later members of the same family. A painting by Yao Shou (1423–95), with an essay by Li Dongyang and poems by Wu Kuan, depicts the rural retreat to which Wen Hong is supposed to have withdrawn on his retirement, though this may be a purely conventionalized rendering, as no dwelling of Hong's is recorded as a site of aesthetic note in the family genealogy.[13]

Wen Zhengming's poem of 1490, 'An Old Garden'[14] written when he was twenty years old, seems to be a purely poetic exercise, but one of 1493 entitled 'Thanking Master Zhuang of Jiangpu for a Lodging at the Dingshan Thatched Hall'[15] is an early example of the type of occasion-specific verse that is so prominent in Wen's collected works, as in those of his peer group. Master Zhuang is unidentified, but this is not the case for the dedicatee of a poem of 1504 entitled 'A Small Party at Kongzhou's Pond Pavilion',[16] where Kongzhou is Qian Tongai (1475–1549; MRZJ 876), a slightly younger contemporary who became a close friend and the father-in-law of Wen's second son, Wen Peng.[17] The property of relatives is celebrated in another composition of 1504, entitled 'In the Gu Clan's Xiangying Hall there is a Flowering Plum planted by my Grandmother's Hand'.[18] In the following year came poems on 'Drinking on a Summer's Day at Yike's Pond Pavilion' and 'The Chen Clan Jiaxi Hermitage', which may refer to the same property, or at least the same family, quite possibly that of his father's mother.[19] It seems likely that the poem of 1506 called 'Enjoying the Cool at the Chen Clan Pond Pavilion' and the set of 'Eight Compositions on Chen Guinan showing me his Autumn Garden, and in Appreciation of a Feast'[20] refer to the same family. In 1509 came the first poem clearly related to a patronage rather than a familial connection, with 'Visiting the Wu Clan Eastern Estate and Offering a Poem on the Inheritance of Property',[21] and the same year saw 'Following the Rhymes of Writing on the Matter of Wang Bing's New Estate', describing a bucolic idyll of 'a thousand orange trees and ten *mu* of fish'.[22] The decade closed with 'The Ancient Rocks at Daofu's Western Chapel', celebrating his friend Chen Daofu (1483–1544; DMB 179–80).[23]

Wen provided in 1511 the already mentioned 'Sixteen Odes on the Truly Apt Garden of Master Wang, Pillar of State'[24] celebrating the great Wang Ao, and also (for a much less stellar official contact) 'Drinking on a Summer's Day at Tang Zizhong's Garden Pavilion'.[25] The same friend received in 1512 'A Small Party in Tang Zizhong's Describing Garden Pavilion at the Beginning of Summer' and 'Drinking on a Rainy Evening at Zizhong's Garden Pavilion'.[26] The year 1512 also saw another poem for Wang Ao, 'Attending Master Shouxi at an Outing and Party in the Western Garden', and one on 'The Stone Wall in the Xiao Clan Garden'.[27] In 1513 Wen wrote 'The Surging Waves Pond' and 'Passing the Eastern Estate of Wu, Master Wending',[28] then in 1516 a lone poem on the property of his close friend Tang Yin entitled 'A Small Party on the Ninth Day at Ziwei's Northern Estate'.[29] 'Two Poems on Visiting the Garden of Minister of Justice Bai' were written in 1518, and 'Thirteen Poems on the Garden Ponds of Xu Zirong' in 1519.[30] A visit to Nanjing in 1523 produced 'The Garden Pavilions of the Duke of Weiguo', with a poem on 'Feasting in Master Zhu Baoying's Rishe Garden' the following year.[31] These are the only garden poems of the 1520s, the decade Wen spent partly (1523–6) in Peking, where the sequence on the imperial park discussed in the previous chapter was produced.

Poems on the theme of gardens resume in 1530, with 'On a Picture of the Eryi Garden'; a prose colophon reveals that Eryi Garden was the property of the high official Yu Tai (*jinshi* of 1502; MRZJ 370) at Wuxi. But after that, easily identifiable garden verse becomes rather rare in Wen's work. There is a long gap until 1549, the year of 'Congratulating Master Qian of Dongshe on the Construction of a Detached Villa'.[32] In 1551, by which time he was in his eighties, Wen wrote 'The Pond Pavilions of the Western Garden', 'A Small Party at Zhifu's Eastern Garden on People Day', and another poem on going in the second month to see the flowering plums in the same garden of Wang Zhifu, alias Wang Ting (1488–1571; MRZJ 46), a successful official of Suzhou origin.[33] A new generation of social contacts is reflected in a poem of the same year, 'He Yuanlang's Ao Garden', where the dedicatee is He Liangjun (1506–73; DMB 515–8), whose garden was at Huating to the east of Suzhou.[34] In 1552 Wen wrote 'On People Day Wang Zhifu Made an Appointment for Me to View the Flowering Plums in his Eastern Garden but it was Cancelled because of Rain'.[35] This doubtless incomplete list of properties cited in Wen's collected works closes in 1554 with 'The Garden Pavilion of the Yuan Clan, on the day *shang ji*', and 'A Small Party in the Wang Clan Eastern Garden on People Day', the latter demonstrating ties into extreme old age with the family of an early patron, Wang Ao. Among the last poems he wrote, in 1557, was 'A Cypress Planted by the Hand of Fan Wenzheng', memorializing the Song statesman Fan Chengda, who remained in the Ming one of the fixed standards of gentlemanly behaviour, a paragon of integrity much as Wen himself came to be viewed.

There is nothing particularly idiosyncratic about this list, which could be duplicated from the collected works of other members of the Suzhou elite without difficulty. A bald tally such as this gives no sense of the poems as works of art, or of their reception among those whose property they celebrate, but it does yield some suggestive lines of further enquiry. The thirty-two citations, covering some twenty-four different sites, the vast majority of which are in Suzhou, gives us some insight into linguistic usage, and in particular into the very wide variation in the names used for what I am lumping together as 'gardens'. Wen's most common usage is 'pond pavilion' (*chi ting*), which occurs four times, but he also has 'garden pond' (*yuan chi*), 'garden pavilion' (*yuan ting*), 'thatched hall' (*cao tang*), 'hermitage' (*an*), 'estate' (*zhuang*) and 'detached villa' (*bie shu*) as well as even, on just one occasion, simply 'garden' (*yuan*). Almost always is an owner specified, though that owner is often a 'clan' (*shi*) rather than an individual. The garden here emerges as often a family, not a particular, property.

Perhaps more surprising is the distribution of garden poetry throughout Wen's lifetime. The early examples are mostly written for relatives, like the physician Qian Tongai. Then come patrons and teachers of an older generation, like Wang Ao, Wu Kuan, Bai Ang and Xu Jin. What is striking is the extent to which poems explicitly about gardens become very rare in Wen Zhengming's work after his return from Peking in 1526, with only five sites not celebrated before that date being the subject of poems. This is surely paradoxical. If Wen was notably 'living in reclusion' after his withdrawal from politics, and if gardens were key signifiers of a reclusive lifestyle, would we not be entitled to expect the opposite? May we not begin to suspect that far from signifying above all reclusion and withdrawal, garden properties were read by Wen and his contemporaries in a more complex way that also admitted of their ambivalent status as luxury property? A young man, seeking ties of patronage with powerful figures in the higher reaches of the bureaucracy, might be expected to produce verse celebratory of the gardens of potential patrons, but once past middle age, and having self-consciously assumed the role of the refuser of social ties, Wen Zhengming no longer could afford to be associated with the intensely social space of Suzhou's gardens, the scene above all of parties small and large, of interactions both competitive and harmonious. A garden was a dangerous place for a Ming recluse, it implied too many ties.

This view may perhaps be reinforced by considering Wen's prose work on gardens. Only two descriptive prose 'Records' by Wen exist on the subject of property belonging to others. The earlier of the two is the 'Record of the Garden of the Unsuccessful Politician' of 1533, executed for a man with whom he had relations dating back to his youth, and who must have been very elderly by this time (Wen himself was in his sixties). The second is his 'Record of Dwelling in the Mountains at Jade Maiden Pool', an account of the estate, twenty miles south of the city of Yixing, of Shi Ji (1495–1571; MRZJ 105), a man whose great wealth (much of it dispensed in acts of charity) was not matched by a particularly spectacular official career. Following the death of his mother in 1534, and the necessary retiral, he, like Wang Xianchen, took the opportunity to lay out an extensive property. This was particularly rich in explicit associations with Daoist spirituality, and may have invoked some personal response in Wen Zhengming. We simply do not know how the networks of patronage, of favour and counter-favour operated in this respect. But there is a sense in both cases of what might be called the evening-out of cultural and economic capital. There can be no doubt that both Wang Xianchen and Shi Ji were, with their official status and their very considerable wealth, better provided with the latter than was Wen Zhengming. Yet he was a figure renowned on an empire-wide basis, while they (most particularly Wang) remain rather shadowy figures. Again we see the role of the garden in equalizing different forms of status, allowing a rich man to attract the notice of particularly prestigious literary and cultural figures. It is noteworthy that the anonymous editor, when selecting Wen Zhengming's work for publication, omitted the 'Garden of the Unsuccessful Politician' piece altogether, suggesting that it may have been executed in the course of rendering the type of social obligation which his status as a 'lofty recluse' is particularly supposed to have precluded. Along with a large quantity of verse written similarly as occasional work, it was perhaps not the kind of writing a man sought to be remembered by.

All the preceding has been predicated on the legitimacy of the individual subject as the unit of analysis. But there must hang a question-mark over the degree to which the single adult male is individually comprehensible, and whether we should not begin to take the contemporary sources seriously by applying our attention equally to the larger family unit.

What of the property Wen Zhengming and his family owned themselves? Later biographical sources certainly exaggerate his supposed poverty as a means of reinforcing the image of 'purity': there is no need to take this presentation with absolute literalness. There is evidence that the Wen family, if not in the front ranks of the Suzhou plutocracy, were nevertheless possessors of quite reasonable amounts of wealth. (Bear in mind that one of the 'impure' tasks delegated to Madame Wu was 'the purchase of real estate'.) The evidence for this can be inferred from a much later source, but one whose compiler plausibly had access to records dating back centuries. This is the *Wen shi zu pu* ('Genealogy of the Wen Clan'), compiled c. 1730 in a single *juan* by Wen Han, a descendant in the eighth generation. Its 'Monograph on Residences and Memorial Arches of Successive Generations' (*Li shi di zhai fang biao zhi*) is our main source for understanding property (including gardens) and the transmission of property within the males of the Wen family.[36] Although the existence of a genealogy is one of the key features taken to mark the constituting of a kinship group into the formal type of organization called a 'lineage', and which often involved the communal holding of property, there is no suggestion that the Wen were technically a 'lineage' in the Ming period. Such formal organization was rather rare in Ming Suzhou, though it had been common in the Song period and was to become so again in the Qing.[37] Wen Zhengming praised the institution in a preface he provided for the genealogy of the Chen lineage,[38] but he seems not to have created an organization by himself (and in any case as a younger brother was not formally in a position to). The transmission of property within the Wen patriline was governed by customary law, in which each male received an equal share of his father's property at that father's decease. A closer look at the Wen genealogy allows us to see certain pieces of that property moving through the generations. However, by no means every male member of the family has his dwelling recorded in this way, and it is clear that some members of the family are more famous than others in a ranking that does not necessarily accord with simple seniority, or with status through degree-holding or official rank.

32 Wen Zhengming, *Farewell at Tingyun*, 1531, hanging scroll, ink and colour on paper. Museum für Ostasiatische Kunst, Berlin.

The earliest residence mentioned in the genealogy is that of Wen Zhengming's father, Wen Lin. We are told that it was

north-west of Deqing Bridge. Within it was the Halting Clouds Lodging (*Ting yun guan*) [illus. 32]. His son the Expectant Official Zhengming also lived in it, and the name Halting Clouds was still used.

This residence is also mentioned in the lists of dwellings in the Wu county gazetteer of 1642, which includes poems alluding to the 'lake rocks' that decorated it.[39] Wen Lin's younger brother, Wen Sen, lived close by. The property is described in slightly more detail in the entry on Wen Zhengming himself:

Before the Expectant Official's three-span Halting Clouds Lodging was a jade mountain and one great wutong tree, while behind were over a hundred stems of bamboo. The Living-Room of Direct Speech (*Wu yan shi*) was east of the Lodging. In the centre were the Magnolia Hall (*Yulan tang*), the Jade Chime Mountain Studio (*Yu qing shan fang*) and the Singing So Tower (*Ge si lou*).

There is no mention here of a garden, and indeed the description seems to suggest a relatively small area of ground in which architectural structures predominated: one hundred stems of bamboo does not sound like an awful lot (illus. 21). The property remained the home in the next generation of the second son Wen Jia, who added the Shading the Sun Hall (*Yin ri tang*) to it. His cousin Wen Boren (1502–75), the oldest son of Wen Zhengming's elder brother, Wen Gui, is described in bald terms as initially living 'at Han Village in Dongting'. In later years he moved to the western foot of Tiger Hill. Such a move from a rural, if not exactly remote, area by the lake to the most fashionable suburb just outside the city walls to the north-west was one made by increasing numbers of the elite in the middle years of the sixteenth century.

In the next generation we have the first explicit record of a large-scale garden belonging to a member of the family, with the property of Wen Zhaozhi, elder son of Wen Peng, whose residence is not mentioned in the genealogy even though he was Wen Zhengming's elder son, and hence would have received an equal distribution of the estate with Wen Jia. Wen Zhaozhi is someone whose involvement with garden and landscape was on a wholly different plane from that of his forebears. Though without a degree, he passed from being a student of the imperial academy to the post of Office Manager (*lu shi*) in the Directorate of the Imperial Forest Park, and was afterwards known to the family records, as was standard, by his official title –

'Master Imperial Forest'.[40] Although a relatively lowly rank, it gave him direct responsibility for (and presumably access to) the gardens of the imperial palace complex. The fact that he was the first member of the family to build a noteworthy garden in Suzhou on his return there in 1586 is again suggestive of the role of Peking as model and inspiration for developments in garden culture in the southern city. It was clearly on a larger scale than anything the family had possessed before:

Master Imperial Forest's Pagoda Reflection Garden (*Ta ying yuan*) was at the foot of Tiger Hill. With prasine wutong trees and tall bamboos, clear pool and white rocks, it was a totally outstanding garden grove (*yuan lin*). The living rooms were lofty and bright, and in the centre was a pavilion. The pagoda was reflected in the pool, hence the name.

The genealogy then quotes a 'Record of the Pagoda Reflection Garden' by a later owner of the property and a distant relative, Gu Ling:[41]

My lord cleared the grasses and built a hut on the southern slope of Tiger Hill, naming it the Ocean Surge Mountain Estate (*Hai yong shan zhuang*). He excavated the ground, and a spring and pond were formed, wherein the reflection of the pagoda was seen. He thereupon changed the name to Pagoda Reflection Garden.

It is a curious fact that there is a real degree of discrepancy between the family genealogy and other sources as to which were the noteworthy gardens of Suzhou and its environs. For example, the impressive surrounding garden receives no notice in the Wu county gazetteer of 1642. It was, however, celebrated by its owner, in whose collected poetry the poems on gardens play a much greater role than in any of his forebears save Wen Zhengming. Many of these are non-specific, with titles like 'Autumn Night in a Garden Grove' or 'A Garden Pavilion'.[42] There are poems on the gardens of others, such as 'Borrowing a Bed in Yao Yuanbai's Reclusion in the City Garden', 'The Garden Pavilions of the Xu Dukes of Weiguo' (both of these sites were in Nanjing), 'The Garden of the Chuan Family at Kunshan' (described as 'a chance visit') and 'A Party in the Garden Pavilions of Gu, Sir Wenkang'.[43] There are a few poems inspired by his tenure of office in the Imperial Forest Park, such as 'The Imperial Park' and 'Fasting Overnight in the Imperial Forest'.[44] But there are also a considerable number of poems on his own garden, and on the delights of building and owning such a property: 'With Assistant Instructor Huangfu in the Pagoda Reflection Garden', 'Building a Garden at

South Village on Tiger Hill, and My Delight at Suddenly Trapping the Reflection of the Pagoda in a Pond', 'Restoring a Garden', and the charmingly simple quatrain 'Returning':

> Returning home in old age I rebuilt the Pagoda Reflection Garden,
> Where the flowers smile and the birds speak.
> All I ask is quiet for the body and repose for the mind;
> I do not long for the clamour of carriages and horses at my gate.[45]

The sentiments may be conventional (and they are repeated in numerous other poems on the theme of 'Return', all of which draw on Tao Yuanming's famous sequence of the same title), but there is no need to argue that they are not sincere. However, as we shall see, Wen Zhaozhi was in his retirement far from inactive in the wider social world.

Wen Zhaozhi had a younger brother, Wen Yuanfa (1529–1602), who enjoyed a bureaucratic career as magistrate of Pujiang county and Vice-prefect of Weihu prefecture, with the honorific ranks of Grand Master for Forthright Service, Advisor in the Left Secretariat of the Heir Apparent, and Expositor-in-waiting in the Hanlin Academy.[46] His dwelling, with its Hengshan Thatched Hall, Orchid Snow Chapel, Cloud-driving Belvedere, and Wutong Flower Courtyard, is also listed in the genealogy, but not in the more public textual record of the gazetteer. Wen Yuanfa was the author of an important piece of autobiographical writing, which gives additional detail about the family genealogy, but confusingly lists different names for the features of his dwelling. He also wrote a work entitled 'Random Notes on the Study of Horticulture' (Xue pu sui bi).[47]

It was in the next generation, the generation of those men born in the third quarter of the sixteenth century who reached maturity only in the seventeenth, that several members of the Wen family simultaneously became the possessors of notable gardens, which are described in the genealogy in some detail. One of those belonged to a man who was far and away the most significant political figure produced by the family – Wen Yuanfa's eldest son, Wen Zhenmeng (1574–1636; DMB 1467-71). He was the family's first gainer of the jinshi degree (in 1622) since the double success of his great-great-grandfather and great-great-grand-uncle in 1472 and 1487. Furthermore, he was in that year zhuangyuan, the holder of the highest place in the examination rankings, the only member of the family to achieve this distinction, which more or less guaranteed empire-wide fame and a glittering political career. His advance in the bureaucracy was, however, tortuous and blighted by factionalism, in which he was identified with the 'Restoration Society' and the Donglin party at court.[48] He did in the end reach the supreme bureaucratic post of Grand Secretary (in 1635), but died shortly after. This did nothing to dim the lustre of his renown as far as the family was concerned. He was the only member of the family to have a formal posthumous title confirmed by the emperor (*Wensu*, 'Cultured and Reverential'), and in the genealogy he is the only person whose death is described by the honorific word *hong*, only to be used in reporting the death of those who had reached the highest offices.[49]

Wen Zhenmeng's residence was written up in the Wu county gazetteer of 1642, and the passage was subsequently copied into the genealogy:

The Residence of the Eastern Belvedere Scholar, Zhenmeng, was north-east of the Baolin temple. In the centre was the Relationship-of-Generations Hall, in front was the Herb Patch, with piled up mountains and excavated pond, where he constructed the Stone Classics Hall and the Verditer Gem Islet. Groves and trees shone off each other, and it was the most splendid site in the west of the city.[50]

The genealogy includes further information on this splendid magnatial garden:

In the middle of the Herb Patch were the Birth-of-Clouds Villa and the Relationship-of-Generations Hall. In front of the Hall was a broad courtyard, with in front of the courtyard a great pond of five or so *mu*. South of the pond were piled up stones which form the Five Old Peaks, twenty feet high. In the middle of the pond is a hexagonal pavilion called Washed Prase. To the right of the Hall is the Verditer Gem Islet. The courtyard is planted with five willows, several spans in girth. In addition there is the Chapel of Sudden Enlightenment, the Hall of Stone Classics, the Chapel of Concentration-on-Distance, and the Crag Screen.

In addition to this urban garden, the genealogy describes what seems to be a separate suburban villa:

The Bamboo Bank is set in seclusion with its back to the hills, the dwelling's door facing onto a deep torrent, with a small living-room of several spans and single long covered walkway. The Bamboo Bank Mountain Hall is in front of the Stone Living-room, and is the place in which Wen Zhenmeng studied. Later were rebuilt the Bamboo Bank Thatched Hut, the Xiang Clouds Lodging, the Southern Clouds Hermitage, and the Floating Autumn Shallows.

The original site of Wen Zhenmeng's Herb Patch garden still survives in north-west Suzhou, though known by the name *Yi pu*, 'Art Patch', a name given to it by a subsequent owner in the early Qing. The layout, and even the scale, bear no relation to the gazetteer and genealogy descriptions, and, as with the Garden of the Unsuccessful Politician, certain names must be judged to be the only things that survive from the Ming period.[51] A few of these raise the possibility of a programme, with political overtones, in the choices made for the names of features in the garden of this somewhat austere and self-consciously 'pure' figure, who was involved in the publication of popular morality books.[52] For 'pure' by 1620 was a term with resonances in the factional politics of the age, being the self-appellation of those who placed opposition to the influence of prominent court eunuchs like Wei Zhongxian (1568–1627; ECCP 846–7) at the centre of their agenda. The term 'Relationship-of-Generations' (Shi lun), the name of the garden's principal hall, has Confucian overtones. It recalls the Ming lun tang ('Hall of Making Relationships Clear'), the central structure in the Confucian temples that were a visible focus of elite status in every county of the empire.[53] There is another explicit allusion in the case of the 'Chapel of Sudden Enlightenment' (Meng sheng zhai), where meng sheng is a phrase first used in this sense by Zhu Xi, one of the patriarchs of what was by the Ming period orthodox Confucianism. Even more obviously Confucian in reference is the 'Hall of Stone Classics' (Shi jing tang).

Wen Zhenmeng was involved with at least two other prominent Suzhou gardens besides those of his immediate family, in the role of giver of names to garden structures and features. These names would then be inscribed, in the calligraphy of the namer, over the door of the relevant building. As with the writing of garden poetry and prose accounts, the execution of these name-boards played a major part in the establishment of ties of patronage, clientelage and alliance among members of the elite, and again the sources convey the sense that having someone important, like Wen Zhenmeng, inscribe these boards brought honour to the garden's proprietor. Wen was responsible for some of the name-boards for the 'Truly-Thus Small Building' (Zhen ru xiao zhu) built at Guangfu shan outside Suzhou by Wang Qifeng.[54] He was more involved in the Returning to the Fields Garden (Gui tian yuan) of Wang Xinyi, built on the site of the Garden of the Unsuccessful Politician celebrated by his great-grandfather. He suggested the name and provided the name-board for the whole garden and was active together with other Suzhou worthies in providing names for the structures. The main hall, the 'Orchid Snow Hall' (Lan xue tang), was named by him.

Wen Zhenmeng's younger brother was Wen Zhenheng, author of

the 'Treatise on Superfluous Things', owner in his own right of a luxurious garden also situated in the north-west corner of urban Suzhou, and celebrated both in the gazetteer of 1642 (written when the owner was still alive) and in the family genealogy:

The residence of the Palace Penman, Zhenheng, was in Gaoshi Lane, west of Shima Ditch, and was the ruined patch of the Feng family. Built therein were the Four Charms Hall, the Embroidered Sword Hall, the Caged Goose Belvedere, the Slanting Moon Walkway, Many Fragrance Tower, Whistling Terrace, Roaming the Moon Tower, and Jade Bureau Chapel. Tall stems and curious rocks, square pools and sinuous torrents, crane towers and deer enclosures, fishskin couches and swallow curtains, even delicate shoots and tender grasses, peaks in bowls and sprays in dishes – nothing was lacking to makes its splendour and its fame an outstanding piece of extravagance.[55]

The genealogy adds the names of seven further structures, augmenting the sense of a garden steeped in the luxurious excess that moralists of the period were increasingly driven to protest, and which Wen Zhenheng's own 'Treatise' (written when he was a much younger man) also often attacks as 'vulgarity'. (His writing on gardens in the 'Treatise' is examined in the following chapter.)

A third member of this generation is credited with a garden in the family genealogy, though on a far more modest scale. He is Wen Congjian (1574–1648), a cousin of Wen Zhenheng and Wen Zhenmeng, being the son of their father's first cousin Wen Yuanshan (1554–89). The site of this was at Peach Blossom Bank (*Tao hua wu*),

where he built a living-room of three spans, and took over a hall of his forebears, naming it the Magnolia Courtyard. It was over a *mu* in area. In front of it he planted several 'wooden slaves' [orange trees], and behind it a hundred stems of bamboo, of a striking intensity of pure shade. By the side were planted three *mu* of bamboos, named the Half-starved Garden, with the Misty Moon Terrace, the Service of Tea Chapel, the Paired Tree Mound, the Inkstone Washing Pond, the Phoenix Tail Ridge, the Verditer Moss Road, the Cassia Lane, Flowering Plum [? – character unreadable] and the One Rainhat Hermitage.

Wen Zhenmeng died nine years before the trauma of the Manchu conquest of Suzhou in 1645, but his younger brother was one of its victims, starving himself to death rather than submit to the new dynasty. Wen Congjian went into hiding, only to die a few years later, and his Magnolia Hall was destroyed in the upheaval. No further gardens, or indeed residences, of any significance are assigned in the genealogy to members of the Wen family, the final entry in the

33 Stone memorial arch to Grand Secretary Xu Guo (1527–96), erected
1585. Zheng village, Huizhou district, Anhui province.

34 The pagoda, Tiger Hill, Suzhou, erected AD 961.

35 The 'Cloud-capped Peak', now in the Lingering Garden (*Liu yuan*), Suzhou. This great Lake Tai rock was already famous in the Ming period, when it stood in the now-vanished garden of Xu Shaopu.

36 View of an 'artificial mountain' (*jia shan*) in the Garden of the Master of the Fishing Nets (*Wang shi yuan*), Suzhou, probably 19th or early 20th century.

37 General view of the Astor court looking south from the Moon-
viewing Terrace, Metropolitan Museum of Art, New York. Built by
craftsmen from Suzhou, this is closely based on a courtyard in that

city's Garden of the Master of the Fishing Nets (*Wang shi yuan*) as it
appears today.

38 A double-tree peony blossom, growing in a Suzhou garden today. These rare species were the increasing focus of attention in gardens of the later 16th century.

39 An ornamental species of *Prunus*, growing in the Lingering Garden (*Liu yuan*), Suzhou, today. This is a purely ornamental species, raised for its blossom.

40 Market gardening in the immediate environs of Suzhou in the late
1980s. The regularity of the strips is a major difference between this
scene and the situation in Ming times, but note the cultivation right up
to the edge of the canal.

'Residences' monograph being for Wen Nan (1597–1668), grandfather of the text's compiler, Wen Han. He, we are told,

lived by the side of the Expectant Official's [i.e. Wen Zhengming's] old lodging, his residence was named Small Halting Clouds. Several spans of the old living room were thick with dust and never entered. An ancient pine grew in the courtyard, secluded orchids crowded beneath it. The window lattices were ornamented and bright, the tables and couches of an antique elegance, with pictures, calligraphy and bronzes arrayed to left and right. He was naturally fond of inkstones, and collected twelve of them, hence he named his chapel the Chapel of Twelve Inkstones.

A sequence can perhaps be discerned in the Wen family property, which matches the broad outlines of garden development in the Ming proposed in the preceding chapters. Despite the family's modest level of prominence from the beginning of the dynasty onwards, it is only in the latter part of the fifteenth century, with Wen Lin, that residences become aesthetic sites. However, they remain quite modest, in terms of individually named features, all the way through the first half of the sixteenth (Wen Zhengming's dwelling has only four). From the 1580s, when Wen Zhaozhi returns from his official career as a functionary of the imperial garden department, the pace and scale of involvement intensifies. Wen Zhaozhi is the first member of the family to have a garden clearly identified as such, with the crucial feature of a large pond, as opposed to a courtyard containing plants. The next generation, the final one whose members were to live under the Ming ruling house, dramatically improve on this, with the gardens of the brothers Wen Zhenmeng ('the most splendid site in the west of the city') and Wen Zhenheng ('an outstanding piece of extravagance'). Their residences have, respectively, ten and fifteen named features, while that of their cousin Wen Congjian has eleven. This growth in the garden as a site of aesthetic interest and elaboration could perhaps be paralleled by a close study of other elite Ming genealogies, and is supported by numerous commentators of the day.

How was the luxury landscape of the garden, and the dwelling it accompanied, paid for? Unfortunately we know very little about the costs of creating a garden, but they could be proverbially large. Sources speak of 'thousands' of ounces of silver spent in the arrangement of ponds and artificial mountains. When the property of the disgraced Grand Secretary Yan Song was confiscated by the state in 1562, his principal residence in the city of Nanchang was valued at 7,850 ounces of silver, of which 1,000 ounces was specifically given as the value of the 'flower garden' (hua yuan).[56] A site known as the 'Duke's Flower Garden' at Jiangning was deemed in the 1650s to be worth 100,000 ounces of silver, having been brought by a group of local officials, each contributing the still considerable sum of 300 ounces.[57] It is not beyond the bounds of credibility that at least the most successful members of the Wen family, like Wen Zhenmeng, spent comparable sums.

The source of the Wen family's wealth was property in land. Quite how much was owned is impossible to say for certain, since elite writing is reticent on the distasteful details of income, but it is possible to make some crude calculations that might give us some idea of the order of property involved. The 'Monograph on the Tumuli and Graves of Successive Generations' in the genealogy gives, in addition to the location and size of the tomb of each male Wen, a note of the quantity of 'tomb-fields' (mu tian), land specifically set aside for the upkeep of the grave.[58] This land was worked by 'grave-hands' (fen ding), whose names are also given. The 'Family Rituals' of the twelfth-century philosopher Zhu Xi, a text that enjoyed prescriptive and unchallenged status as a guide to proper action among families like the Suzhou Wen in the Ming, gives a simple formula for deciding how much 'tomb-fields' a given grave should have:

On first erecting a sacrificial hall, calculate the size of the current fields, and for each altar set aside one part in twenty as sacrificial fields. When 'kinship is exhausted' for any ancestor [i.e. after the fourth generation] convert the specified land into grave fields.[59]

We might thus hypothesize that the 4.8 mu of tomb-fields surrounding the grave of Wen Hui (1399–1468) represent a twentieth part of the landed property left at his death, used for the support of his cult in the ancestral hall until the 1570s or 1580s, and then diverted to the support of his tomb. The amount of land left by him at his decease would thus have been 96 mu, a perfectly respectable holding when, as we have seen, 10 mu was reckoned to be enough for subsistence. Not every male in the family had a discrete grave site, since a considerable number were buried by the side of ancestors, and shared in the income from their tomb-fields. The grave of Wen Lin had approximately 8 mu of tomb-fields, implying a landholding of 160 mu, while his brother Wen Sen had 5 mu, implying 100 mu in his lifetime. Wen Zhengming himself had 9.3 mu in death, 186 in life. His brother would have had the same. Wen Yuanfa had the largest allocation of tomb-fields for the family in the Ming dynasty, at 12 mu, giving 240 in life. In fact, we have a way of cross-checking this figure, since Wen Yuanfa describes himself in his 'Autobiography' as possessing '300 *mu* bequeathed by my forebears. . .sufficient for my daily needs'.[60] The calculations based on tomb-field ratios may thus if anything be an *under*estimate. Three-hundred *mu* of land held by an individual was a reasonable estate in late sixteenth-century Jiangnan, certainly far exceeding that needed for self-sufficiency, and putting the Wen on a par with similar families like that of Gao Panlong (1562–1626; DMB 701–10), leader of the Donglin party of scholars and officials.[61] All protestations of poverty and hardship by the Ming elite must be taken as relative. It was wrong to flaunt wealth, but it was also wrong to overdo the 'poor scholar' act, as can be seen from Wen Yuanfa's defence of his older brother, Wen Zhaozhi, who must, given the equal division of property, have owned land on something like the same scale:

Although he was poor in his youth, it is not in his nature to put on an air of forced frugality. . .he has never in his life talked about poverty, and his clothes remain decent, so that even his intimates do not know him for a poor scholar.[62]

He Liangjun, whose garden was celebrated by Wen Zhengming, was scornful of those who refused to live up to the lifestyle their wealth would support, by (for example) using porcelain tableware when they could afford gold and silver.[63] This was the kind of solecism a member of the Wen family would have been careful to avoid.

The Wen family, then, was quite rich, and its riches came from the standard source of the peer group, property in land. No discourse of land or landscape in the period could escape this fact – or if it appeared to, it did so in a deliberate inversion of what actually supported the lifestyles of the practitioners of those discourses.

THE PUBLIC LANDSCAPE

In addition to the ownership of large quantities of private productive land, and of the deliberately unproductive landscape of gardens that, though ostensibly private, were (as we have seen) often accessible, the members of the Wen family impinged on what might be called the 'public landscape' of Ming Suzhou. They did this in a number of ways. For a start, their graves were to a considerable extent public sites, in the sense that their locations were known to other members of the elite, and recorded in texts such as gazetteers. The early nineteenth-century Suzhou writer Qian Yong, in a passage on the wealthy of the region in the Ming period, links together 'dwellings and graves' (*zhai mu*) as the two visible components of a family's prosperity, and gives the sense that the number of maintained graves was an important index of a surname's prominence.[64] The corollary of this concentration on 'dwellings and graves' is that productive property is invisible. We are told where a family lived in great detail, and considerable precision is expended on locations of the physical reminders of past notables, including their gardens; we may be told in general terms that such-and-such a family owned 300,000 *mu* of land, but its location is not a matter of public record.

The Wen family's prominence was physically present in the landscape of Suzhou in other way than simply dwellings and tombs. One of these ways was through the presence of shrines, *ci*. Such shrines to local officials and departed worthies were omnipresent in the Ming, but could only be established with official approval. They could similarly only be maintained as long as the prestige of the person enshrined therein lasted, and cults were continuously being obliterated.[65]

Several shrines honouring members of the Wen family, usually in connection with other worthies, existed in Suzhou. The most important of these was the shrine of the hero-official of the Song dynasty with whom they claimed kinship, Wen Tianxiang. He had no personal connection with Suzhou, and the presence of a shrine to him may perhaps be seen as a reflection of the family's prestige, and influential connections, in the Ming. (Wen Tianxiang also received honours in a temple in Peking, and was effectively part of the Ming 'state cult'.) The shrine was first set up in 1511 in Wu county, on the petition of the Regional Inspector of Southern Zhili, Xie Shen (*jinshi* 1499; MRZJ 886).[66] Public funds were assigned to the building, and to the supply of pork, lamb and other sacrificial necessities, which the Prefect of Suzhou offered in person twice a year. The main inscription for the shrine was provided by Wang Ao, doyen of the Suzhou elite and patron of Wen Zhengming, who at this time was in his early forties.

This original shrine, which also housed an academy called the Wenshan Academy, was deemed to be too cramped, and so a new one was built in 1541, in the eastern half of the Suzhou urban area. By this time Wen Zhengming's prestige was scarcely rivalled (he was in his seventies), and it was he who provided the calligraphy for the text of Wen Tianxiang's famous 'Song of Righteous Anger' that accompanied the stone statue of the martyr in the main hall. That the Wen family should have one of their ancestors publicly commemorated in this very visible way must have been a reflection of their standing among their peers, as well as the kind of connections in the bureaucracy that they could mobilize to sustain recognition by the state.[67]

Other shrines commemorated additional members of the family: Wen Zhengming was reverenced at the Shrine of the Five Worthies in the Zhiping Temple, Wu county (along with his friends Wang Shou, Tang Zhen, Wang Chong and Tang Yin), and together with his teacher Wu Kuan at the Shrine of the Luminous Worthies at Yaofengshan. He shared a shrine, established in 1686 on official instigation, with his great-grandson Wen Zhenmeng. The latter was also honoured in a Shrine of the Three Worthies at Tiger Hill. In addition to these, most of the male members of the family in the principal line were remembered publicly in the Shrines of Local Worthies attached to the Suzhou Prefectural School, and the schools of Wu and Changzhou counties.

Even more prominent in the landscape than shrines were commemorative arches (illus. 33). They were one of the most impressive features of the urban scene, in the eyes of the Portuguese visitor to Ming China, Gaspar da Cruz:

In all the streets of the principal cities, which are royal or main highways, there are very many and very sumptuous triumphal arches, whereas Cantao has but few and not sumptuous. These arches in the principal cities, besides being very fair, sumptuous and very well wrought. . .are erected upon eight columns, very large and very thick; and they are placed in such sort that they form three arches crossing the street, that in the middle being larger than the two at the sides, the eight columns being arranged in pairs. They are topped by a very fair and curious edifice of wood. It is roofed with very fair porcelain tile, which gives it much grace and beauty, and those arches are made of such width and in such wise that many people can stand underneath protected from the rain and the sun; whereupon underneath them are sold many fruits and toys and a great variety of wares.[68]

These arches, again requiring official sanction for their erection, fulfilled to some degree the same role as the *loggie* to be found in contemporary Italian cities; they proclaimed the importance of certain families, by providing public space. The Wen family were honoured by several of these arches in the Ming period, all of them clustered in the streets around the family's principal urban dwellings in the fashionable north-west of the city. In Zhongjie Street, the Arch for the Father and Sons of Equal Excellence commemorated Wen Hong (1426–79), Wen Lin (1445-99) and Wen Sen (1464–1525), all three holders of the *juren* degree.[69] The same street was spanned by the Arch for the Elder and Younger Brother of Equal Renown, celebrating Wen Lin and Wen Sen as both being *jinshi* successes. Wen Sen on his own was granted the Embroidered Garments Arch, alluding to his censorial office. The Hanlin Arch commemorated Wen Zhengming's brief tenure in that illustrious institution, while the Signal Chastity Arch, set up in the 1620s, celebrated a daughter of Wen Yuanfa, the wife of one Tao Ruzhe. The fact that it was set up in Zhongjie Street, in the family's north-western 'power base', shows that the lustre was shed on her natal family. (Another virtuous Wen wife was given an arch in the Kangxi reign: 1662–1722, but after that the family lacked the clout to arrange such visible markers of status.)

Lastly, the family could make its mark on the landscape through the building of bridges. These acts of public charity both connected space (the state built the city walls, the main type of visible spatial division) and symbolized elite control over it. Gates and bridges (there were roughly 400 of the latter) are the main way texts have of orienting themselves, of giving directions in Ming Suzhou. Wen Zhengming built the Halting Clouds Bridge close by his own urban dwelling, and named after it, while Wen Zhenmeng publicly displayed his examination triumph with the Zhuangyuan Bridge, adjacent to the family graves in Wu county.[70]

In a classic article entitled 'A Millenium of Chinese Urban History: Form, Time and Space Concepts in Soochow', Frederick Mote has argued for the domination of rural concepts of space governing its use within urban areas, of the importance of market gardening within the city area, and the consequent lack of distinctively urban open space. Similarly he writes that

The ostentatious use of great wealth in traditional China could never have produced the great town houses and formal gardens of Europe. . . . Nor did traditional Chinese cities have their fashionable quarters, or slum quarters, such as those that have existed in the West. All residential streets looked the same, more or less, masking the life of individual homes behind uniform walls. The result is that Chinese cities were full of great surprises and intriguing deceptions, even mysteries.[71]

The stark contrast implied here between China in the Ming period and Europe, expressed through radically different deployments of space, may in fact be overdrawn. Anyone passing through north-west Suzhou in the late sixteenth century or early seventeenth would have received clear and repeated messages that this was the area of residence of a prominent, wealthy, officially successful kin-group. The illiterate fruitsellers passing daily under the arches commemorating moral worth (and its result, high office), and the visiting member of the elite perhaps allowed access to family properties in the form of elaborate gardens, was receiving a message not so very different from that being given to their contemporaries in Italy by the piazzas, fountains, palace facades and belvederes of the great cities.

If ostensibly private space was perhaps more 'public' in the Ming period than has hitherto been recognized, the theoretically accessible space of places of public resort was capable of parallel claims to appropriation by powerful individuals and families. This is perhaps noticeable in the case of Tiger Hill. This site, to the north-west of the Suzhou urban area, was dominated by a Buddhist monastery with the distinctive landmark of its pagoda (illus. 28, 34). Though tradition- ally attributed to the Sui dynasty (581–618), modern archaeological investigation has shown that this was built originally between AD 959 and 961.[72] The temple is known to have been substantially renovated in the Yuan reign period of Zhizheng (1341–68), with further work in the Yongle (1403–24),[73] Xuande (1426–35) and Chongzhen (1628–44) reigns. The proximity of the site (which in addition to the monastery possessed legendary connections with the earliest rulers of the region) to the city walls made it a major place of public resort for all levels of Suzhou society, the subject of innumerable poems as well as a large quantity of pictorial represen- tation. Yuan Hongdao, who was magistrate of Wu county at one point in his career, summed up its popularity in this way:

Tiger Hill is perhaps seven or eight *li* outside the city walls [of Suzhou]. The hill itself is lacking in precipitous cliffs or deep ravines, but simply because of its proximity to the city, not a day goes by without flutes, drums and fancy boats clustering there. On any moonlit night, flowery morning, or snowy evening, visitors come and go like the threads of some great tapestry, and the day of the Mid-autumn festival is the most popular time of all.[74]

We have seen that several members of the Wen family had residences at or near Tiger Hill. One of these was Wen Zhaozhi, the author, in 1578, of a 'Gazetteer of Tiger Hill' *(Huqiu shan zhi)* which, according to his own preface, was written at the instigation of the Buddhist monks. This gazetteer is in four chapters plus one preliminary chapter (in fact only one double-page) comprising illustrations.[75] Chapters Three to Five are taken up with samples of prose and verse about Tiger Hill and its environs, but chapter One is divided into a number of categories, such as the basic history of the site, its streams and rocks, temples, flora, canals, secular personalities associated with it, graves, famous monks, and notable occurrences. The section on 'Personalities' (ren wu) is relatively lengthy, and is subdivided into figures before and after the Xuande reign, the point in the early fifteenth century when the monastery was substantially rebuilt.[76] What is striking is the percentage of the thirty-four figures named who are either members of the Wen family, or who are demonstrably linked to them by well-established ties of patronage, intermarriage, or the teacher–pupil relationship. Wen Hong, Wen Lin, Wen Zhengming, Wen Peng, Wen Jia and Wen Boren are all given notices. So are Wen Zhengming's literature teacher Wu Kuan (of the Eastern Estate), calligraphy teacher Li Yingzhen (1431–93; DMB 1471) and patron Wang Ao. There are both the paternal and maternal grandfathers of Zhu Yunming (1461–1527; DMB 392–7), Wen Zhengming's lifelong friend and fellow student of Li Yingzhen. There is Tang Zhen, another close friend, and his brother-in-law, Zhu Xizhou (1463–1546; MRZJ 129). There are numerous other friends of Wen's, such as Yang Xunji (1458–1546; DMB 1513–16), Tang Yin, Peng Nian (1505–66; DMB 1117–18), the brothers Yuan Zhi and Yuan Bao (1502–47 and 1499–1576; DMB 1626–7), Huang Luzeng and Huang Xingzeng (1487–1561 and 1490–1540; DMB 661–5). Lu Shidao (jinshi 1538; DMB 1473) was one of Wen Zhengming's students. Huangfu Fang was a personal friend of the gazetteer's author, Wen Zhaozhi. This is a real portrait of a coterie, of a relatively small circle. Given the crowds that are known to have enjoyed the amenities of Tiger Hill, and given Suzhou's total population at this period (approximately 500,000), what Wen Zhaozhi is putting forward is not a cross-section of the elite (never mind the broader population), but a programmatic claim that Tiger Hill is really 'ours', that the only famous people who have spent time there are 'our' people. He is throwing across the landscape a network of connections, symbolically taking possession of it for the Wen family interest. His text is not a neutral reflection of the landscape but a prescription as to how the landscape ought to be; it creates as much as it describes.

4 The Represented Garden

If the terms 'garden'/*yuan* come to seem less like the name of a thing than a way of categorizing certain types of land use, and if those manners of categorizing are dependent on the deployment of representations in word and image, how are those words and images distinguished in the Ming period? If gardens are not a thing transcendentally existing before they become the objects of representation, but instead are crucially created through those representations, then it becomes important to understand those representations not as 'evidence', but instead to 'substitute for the enigmatic treasure of "things" anterior to discourse the regular formation of objects which emerge only in discourse'.[1] What is 'writing about gardens', and what are 'pictures of gardens'?

'Garden' appears nowhere in the lists of subject-matter for painting found in the earliest texts on the subject.[2] As I have argued, 'the garden' is spread thinly through a range of Ming discourses: the agronomic text, the household manual, the topographical gazetteer, the family genealogy. In the early Ming period there simply is no 'writing about gardens', in the sense of a coherent, cross-referencing text. In Foucault's sense of discourse as 'practices that systematically create the objects of which they speak',[3] gardens are not in the early Ming a discursive object. By about 1620 or 1630 at the latest, this was no longer the case, and 'writing about gardens' had become a possibility, a possibility that is essentially being exploited in the same terms today, the present text not excluded.

Once 'gardens' have been constituted as a discursive formation, it is literally unthinkable that they were ever *not*. Thus it is that a modern work, such as Jin Xuezhi's *Aesthetics of Chinese Gardens*, sets out to constitute a lineage, or an archaeology, of itself, with a systematic listing of garden writing set out in a chapter entitled 'The Flowers of Theory Fill the Garden with the Colours of Spring'.[4] This situates the first embodiment of theory about gardens in architectural writing, while pointing out that the earliest 'architectural treatises' in fact contain no mention of gardens at all. The author then goes on to discuss the genre of *yuan ji*, or 'garden records', giving as the earliest proto-examples the essays 'Record of my Thatched Hall' and 'Preface to "Essay on Dwelling by a Pond"' by the Tang poet Bo Juyi (772–846), as well as the 'Record of the Flowers and Trees

[seen] while Living in the Mountains at Pingquan' by his contemporary Li Deyu (787–850). The status of these texts as, in modern eyes, the foundations of subsequent writing on gardens is confirmed by their inclusion as the first three items in the collection of 'garden records' published in 1983 under the editorship of Chen Zhi and Zhang Gongshi. This consensus is further extended in a listing of important 'garden records' of the Song dynasty, particularly the eleventh century; Jin Xuezhi describes this as a period that saw a great expansion in the production of this kind of text, and lists twelve pieces, ten of which are also reprinted by Chen and Zhang.

Instead of going on to list extensively Ming and Qing period garden records, Jin Xuezhi turns his attention to 'theorists' of the garden. He cites from the Song writer Shen Gua (1031–95), who gives a short list of early figures associated with gardens: Tao Yuanming, Bai Juyi, and another Tang writer, Li Yue. These are all poets who have written of the delights of reclusion and self-sufficiency. Jin Xuezhi adduces as the only Song theoretical work on gardens Du Wan's 'Stone Catalogue of Cloudy Forest' (Yun lin shi pu). This work, with a preface dated to 1133, although not apparently printed until the late Ming period, lists different types of stone and discusses their suitability for different uses. But many of the one hundred and ten minerals it contains are described as being 'suitable to be made into utensils'. In fact, references to the display of rockwork in a garden context are no more numerous, and it is arguably as much a book written from within the pharmacopoeic tradition as it is from any tradition of writing on garden matters.[5]

With the late Ming, Jin Xuezhi can adduce some work that does appear to be 'about gardens' in a recognizable way. There is Wang Shizhen's 'Compilation of Famous Gardens and Estates Ancient and Modern' (Gu jin ming yuan shu bian), a compilation of earlier authors' 'garden records' no longer extant, though the author's preface does survive.[6] There is the 'Treatise on Superfluous Things' by Wen Zhenheng, described here as 'a thinker on garden aesthetics'. Above all there is the Yuan ye ('The Craft of Gardens') by Ji Cheng, described as the 'most important and the richest' piece of theoretical writing on gardens in the Ming period. Its value lies above all in the fact that it is 'systematic', xitong de, something on which great stress is laid. The importance of 'system' is echoed by a writer of the Republican period, Tong Jun, whose Study of Jiangnan Gardens was completed in 1937, though not published until 1963. Here xitong is such a pervasive word that it is tempting to translate it as 'discourse', since it is the possession or absence of this quality that allows statements to be made and to have meaning. most particularly as applied to a discussion of gardens. What Jin Xuezhi is doing in the *Aesthetics of Chinese Gardens* is building just such a system, where 'surviving classic gardens' (such as the Garden of the Unsuccessful Politician) validate the textual record of the past, and where that textual record supports current practice as the embodiment of a long, coherent and unbroken tradition.

TOURING AND MAPPING THE GARDEN

In what follows I will look at the rhetoric of some of these Ming texts, in particular at two 'records' dealing with landscape from the mid-Ming period, and at the rather different set of strategies deployed in texts of the late Ming, particularly those by Wen Zhenheng and Ji Cheng.

The former are both by Wen Zhengming, being his 'Record of the Garden of the Unsuccessful Politician' of 1533, and his 'Record of Dwelling in the Mountains at Jade Maiden Pool', which is not dated precisely but was probably written later in the same decade, i.e. when the author was in his sixties.[7] What links them is not the type of site they describe – one an urban setting bounded by walls and dominated by architectural structures and fruit trees, and the other a considerably larger area away from any city, where the principal features are strange geological formations and natural (or semi-natural torrents). Although both of these writings by Wen are included as 'garden records' in the modern compilation by Chen Zhi and Zhang Gongshi, it is doubtful if either of the sites they treat are assimilated to the same category of 'gardens' by Wen himself, or by their owners. However, the two *texts* are certainly part of the same genre of writing, one which had an established place in Ming bibliographical practice. 'Records' formed a standard category in authors' collected works. From the Tang period (618–906), the word *ji* began to be used in the titles of short pieces forming part of the 'new and thriving genre' of travel literature, where to 'form the title of a travel piece the word *chi* is usually suffixed to a placename, sometimes with the additional world *yu* (travelling) between or as the first character of the title'.[8] In the sixteenth century this travel-literature format of the *ji* began to be used for more personal, even autobiographical purposes (the idea of life as a journey), as a way of escaping the conventions of historiography, where self-revelation was more difficult. The whole point of the 'record' was that it was a 'flexible and amorphous format', equally suitable for intensely personal spiritual examination and the more casual (if no less fraught) discharge of social obligations through the celebration of the property of a patron, or friend, or other connection.

The origins of the genre in travel literature are clearly visible in both of Wen Zhengming's texts. They open by situating the site to be described within space, relating it to some landmark with which the audience is presumed to be familiar ('between the Lou and Qi Gates' or 'south-west of Lord Zhang's Cavern, no more than three *li* away'). Then the figure of the owner is brought forward, as the person responsible for 'dredging and channelling', who 'cleared the soil and put on rocks, stopped channels and guided the flows'. Thus right at the beginning a close personal relationship is established between a single named owner and the site, which exists only through his heroic efforts, and his alone, unsupported by kin or by connections. (This is in contrast to the number of gardens listed in gazetteers as the 'X Family Garden', and to the involvement of such sites in networks of patronage, for which I have argued in chapter One.) Following this, the narration begins to move through space, creating the space as it describes it before the reader's eyes.

I use here the words 'place' and 'space' in the sense in which they are defined by Michel de Certeau in *The Practice of Everyday Life*. Place, for de Certeau, implies an indication of stability, where two things cannot be in the same place, and the term governs the distribution of coexistent elements. Space, by contrast, exists 'when one takes into consideration vectors of direction, velocities and time variables'. De Certeau continues:

Thus the street geometrically defined by urban planning is transformed into space by walkers. In the same way, an act of reading is the space produced by the practice of a particular place: a written text, i.e. a place constituted by a system of signs.[9]

Spaces imply operations, which in turn require subjects to carry them out. Hence the Garden of the Unsuccessful Politician cannot be recorded unless it is in some sense visitable, a rhetoric of accessibility that I would see as paralleling the actual accessibility of Ming gardens for which I have argued in previous chapters. It is narration, stories, which 'carry out a labour that constantly transforms the places into spaces or spaces into places'. Here, the narrative of the visit, formally derived from the record of journeys through the landscape, and by the Ming associated with accounts of journeys through life, 'life-stories', performs the task of turning a list of pavilions and rocks – a list of places – into the space of the garden.

There is a further helpful distinction to be made here between two ways of describing space and movement through this space. These de Certeau characterizes as 'maps' and 'tours'.[10] The 'map' type of description says 'William's bedroom is next to our bedroom'. The 'tour' type of description says 'You go up the stairs and turn right and you come into William's bedroom.'

In other words, description oscillates between the terms of an alternative: either *seeing* (the knowledge of an order of places) or *going* (spatializing actions). Either it presents a *tableau* ('there are. . .'), or it organizes *movements* ('you enter, you go across, you turn. . .').

De Certeau further argues for 'seeing' and 'acting' as 'two symbolic and anthropological languages of space', the former acting out chiefly in scientific discourse, with its neutral observer and totalizing vision, while the latter is more characteristic of 'ordinary' culture, the 'everyday life' he is attempting to theorize.

What relevance does this have to Ming garden descriptions? Is Wen Zhengming's 'Record of the Garden of the Unsuccessful Politician' a 'map' or a 'tour', and does it yield any insights into 'everyday life' and its practices? One modern historian has written of the very great difficulty of 'thinking space' for early modern China, hampered as one is on the macro-level by an organicist tradition in the written record, emphasizing the standardizing, normative practices of the unitary state.[11] In this written record, all space is reduced to the same type of place. Might an attention to the spatializing practices in the large corpus of site descriptions surviving from the Ming period not perhaps provide a strategy for reading past this?

The space of Wang Xianchen's garden is in the first place created by himself: 'He built a hall on the south side. . . . In front of the hall he built the many fragrances bank' (always remembering, of course, that the pronouns necessary to make sense in English are not present in the Chinese text). Verbs of action and of motion are pervasive in the following account: 'Crossing Little Flying Rainbow and going north, then following the water and going west, the bank has many lotuses. . .'; 'Following the pier and going north the area is more remote. . .'; 'Again going east you emerge at the rear of the dreaming in Seclusion Tower. . .'; 'Following the Water and carrying on to the east fruit orchards fill the view. . .'. 'Map'-like sitings of individual features, which serve to direct the gaze of a viewer rather than the feet of a walker, are also present in some numbers: 'Further to the west and in the middle of the stream is a gazebo. . .'; 'On the east bank earth has been piled up to form a terrace. . .'; 'To the east of Bamboo Torrent are a hundred flowering plum trees. . .'; 'In the middle of the patch is a pavilion. . .'. Thus, rhetorically neither the 'tour' nor the 'map' predominates, but instead there is the effect of constantly swooping in from a vantage-point to move through the space, then rising again to enjoy a gaze that sees all simultaneously. The final sentence of the description of the garden, before it moves on to discuss the owner and his justification for building it, has just this sense of pulling suddenly back from ground level to a height where a complete panorama is visible, in the form of an inventory of garden structures:

In all there is one hall, one tower, six pavilions and twenty-three studios, balustrades, ponds, terraces, banks and torrents, making a total of thirty-one [the whole], by name the Garden of the Unsuccessful Politician.

The alternation of seeing and moving imparts a sort of instability to the text that makes the space very hard to grasp. If there is a gaze, if we imagine the garden spread out before an observer who views it from a vantage-point, where is that observer positioned, and how is the garden oriented? Does it face south, so that the owner in it may occupy the correct position of a host towards that direction? Or are we looking at a map, where cartographic convention generally decreed that 'south' should be at the top of the sheet?[12] This instability is only exacerbated by the several mechanisms of locating place or direction employed within the text. There are the directional markers, of north, south, east and west, along with combinations such as north-east. There is the use of 'ahead' or 'in front' (qian), and 'behind' (hou), together with 'left' and 'right'. Occasionally Wen Zhengming employs yang and yin, literally 'sunny' and 'shady', terms that can refer to the north side of a river but to the south side of a hill; given the presence of flowing water on the site it is not always clear which of the pair is referred to. The surface impression is of topographical precision, but in fact this is not the case, and it is, on the contrary, difficult to reconstruct a ground-plan of the Garden of the Unsuccessful Politician on the basis of Wen's 'Record' alone. Partly this is to do with the studied lack of definition of boundaries. There is a distinct sense that the narrator is on the inside (socially as well as physically), but no sense of where inside and outside are differentiated.

This runs directly in the face of what constitutes a garden, a yuan in etymological terms, where the idea of enclosure and boundary is very important. In the householder's manual, the Bian min tu zuan, published in Suzhou almost contemporaneously with Wen Zheng-ming's 'Record', the only point at which the concept of yuan/garden appears is in a discussion of thorn hedges, as if the boundary was the major element constitutive of the space within.[13] The lack of a sense of boundary serves to distinguish the space described in the 'Record' from wealth-producing space, from actual fields of rice and other crops, where the configuration of the interior space is of no account (being absolutely homogeneous), but the dimensions and positioning of external boundaries are crucial. However, there is another way in which a boundary is presented to us, through the very medium of telling the garden in words:

. . .the story plays a decisive role. It 'describes', to be sure. But 'every description is more than a fixation', it is 'a culturally creative act'. It even has distributive power and performative force (it does what it says) when an ensemble of circumstances is brought together. Then it founds spaces.[14]

Even a fragmented narrative, with no single standpoint, is continually concerned with marking out boundaries, between what is to be told and what is not to be told, between what is there and what is not. But in Wen's record the space is both experienced and seen in a privileged way, where the interior is given priority over the exterior, and even that interior is to an extent fluid in the inter-relations of its various constituent parts.

A first hypothesis to account for this might draw attention to the distaste felt by advanced aesthetic theory, most pronouncedly in the realm of painting, for formal likeness, and might argue that the fuzziness of Wen's verbal strategies is only a parallel to the equally non-precise visual representations they were designed to accompany. This appeal to the history of painting in the Ming may in the end turn out to be a legitimate one, but I should like to resist it for just a little bit longer.

The orientation of the moving or seeing subject in the 'Record of the Garden of the Unsuccessful Politician' is in no sense an eccentric one, but is repeated in the other Wen text, 'A Record of Dwelling in the Mountains at Jade Maiden Pool'. Though the differences between the two sites are very great, the similarities between the two texts are nevertheless striking, with the resulting effect of assimilating both a flat urban space and a hillside riddled with caverns to the 'same' kind of space. Again the property is located, and the association with the named owner brought to the foreground:

Shi Gongfu of Liyang buried his mother on the mountain, and some of the local people sold him the land, which Gongfu acquired with joy. He subsequently cleared the soil and put out rocks, stopped channels and

guided the flows, split and opened, cut and mowed, fully bringing forth
the splendour of the whole mountain. The secluded cliffs and inaccessible ravines, numinous pools and remote valleys are all prime examples,
yet this pool in truth stands at the head of them.

We then proceed to the same intermingling of 'map' and 'tour'
descriptions, of seeing while stationary and experiencing through
movement, which distinguishes the other text. If anything the 'map'
type is more to the fore, in that the sense of motion through the site
is often conveyed by the movement of water rather than of the
narrator: 'The current flows downhill to the west, takes a turn to the
south and comes into a bay where craggy rocks pile up, like dragons
and horses bending to drink, like smooth columns straight and
lofty. . .'. The language of the 'Jade Maiden Pool' piece is however
considerably more euphuistic, and is dominated by words for water
and the movement of water – leaping, spraying and splashing in a
constant flux of motion. There is the same desire to inventory the
property in terms of nameable sites, as if only that which can be
named can be visited, and only these places can give space meaning:

. . . there are thirty-one terraces, gazebos, towers, belvederes, shrines,
lodges and bridges. The groves, ravines, cliffs and watercourses which
can be named number twenty-three, with other odds and ends which I
have not bothered to record, and which do not appear here.

NAMING IN THE GARDEN

The importance attached to the naming of features in gardens
throughout their existence as aesthetic sites in China has often
been noted. The completion of the garden of the Jia family, in the
eighteenth-century novel 'Story of the Stone' (also known as 'The
Dream of the Red Chamber'), is only achieved when the structures
within it are named and embellished with inscriptions in the form of
appropriate poetic couplets. As one of the family says,

All these prospects and flowers – even the rocks and trees and flowers
will seem somehow incomplete without that touch of poetry which only
the written word can lend a scene.[15]

This is not a uniquely Chinese phenomenon. Garden inscriptions
(often drawn from Roman agronomic writers like Columella or
Varro) were an important part of Italian Renaissance landscape
practice, and in eighteenth-century England a property like The
Leasowes, garden of the poet William Shenstone (1714–63), had an
elaborate structure of thirty-five quotations from classical literature
built into it to create a 'moral or emblematic landscape'.[16]

Naming has a history. The names of features on the Wangchuan Estate of the poet Wang Wei (699–759), whose representations of his property were to become among the most imitated images in Chinese painting, are by and large plain and descriptive: 'Lake Pavilion', 'South Residence', 'White Stone Rapids', 'Bamboo Rest House', 'Pepper Orchard'.[17] Robert Harrist has shown that it was not until the Northern Song dynasty (960–1127), and the expansion of garden culture in and around its capital of Kaifeng, that the names of features within the garden became the subject of conscious exegesis, and he writes of 'a burst of writing addressed to the origins and meanings of names for studios, pavilions, ponds, and other sites associated with gardens'.[18] These names were present within the sites in the form of name-boards. But there is no clear evidence that more lengthily poetical inscriptions, such as became standard later, were incorporated physically into the gardens of Suzhou at the time of the late fifteenth-century garden revival, and the names of individual features in these early gardens tend towards the prosaic, often with a rural flavour: the Eastern Estate of Wu Kuan has its Wheat Mound, Vegetable Patch and Mulberry Orchard. Some of the individual features within the Garden of the Unsuccessful Politician are similarly simple generic descriptions: Lotus Bend, Apple Orchard, Angling Crag, and as we have seen the same names reappear in other gardens. These are simply names like 'the gazebo' or 'the conservatory', rather than specific toponyms. We have more evidence for the factors contributing to names of features in Wang Xianchen's garden, in the form of the short prose postfaces to Wen Zhengming's thirty-one poems on the garden.[19] In twelve cases the poet makes it clear that a literary allusion (usually one to Tang dynasty poetry) lies behind the choice of name. In thirteen cases the name simply seems to be a description, though almost no description is without some distant tinge of allusion to an educated person. One name, Jade Spring, is that of a famous spring in Peking where the garden owner passed part of his career, and the import of three of the names is unclear to me, though they too may well contain allusions present sensibilities are too dull to grasp.

In the case of the Garden of the Unsuccessful Politician it is the poems, as much as the prose text, that carry the main message of the garden's programme (if programme is not too strong a word). The first of them, on the Hall like a Villa, alludes to the belief that the garden was built on the site of the dwelling of Lu Guimeng (died c. 881), the Tang poet who together with his friend Pi Rixiu (c. 834–c. 883) created much of the imagery that was to be deployed by writers on the beauties of Suzhou in later times. Wen cites a saying by Pi to the effect that 'Luwang's [Lu Guimeng's] dwelling is not outside the walls and ramparts, yet is spacious like a villa in the suburbs', and goes on his own words:

What need is there to be outside the city to really understand?
From a patch close at hand one can clearly have distant thoughts . . .

This is the concept of *shi yin*, 'reclusion in the city'. The theme is strengthened by poem number Two, the preface to which tells us that the owner, Wang Xianchen, was recuperating from illness at Jiuli Lake, near his official post in Fujian province, when he repeatedly dreamed of the word 'reclusion'. Poem number Seven praises Wang further by linking him with two further culture heroes of the past, the posts Du Fu (712–70) and Su Shunqin (1008–48), the latter the builder of the original Surging Waves Pavilion (*Canglang ting*). The fact that Su returned to his native Suzhou from the capital at Kaifeng, while Wang had come back from Peking, justifies the continuation of Su Shunqin's name in the form of a pavilion entitled Little Surging Waves (*Xiao Canglang*).[20] As well as making allusion to famous poets and recluses, with whom the patron is compared (poem Fifteen explicitly compares him to the great alchemist Tao Hongjing: 456–536), several poems make reference to fruit, and in particular to its suitability for gifts. There are appropriate allusions also to the world of office-holding as a snare and a delusion, with those on the Sophora Tent and the Sophora Rain Pavilion both alluding to a well-known Tang prose tale, 'The Governor of the Southern Tributary State', in which the hero falls asleep, dreams of a great and noble career, and wakes to discover the splendid realm he has visited is no more than an ant-hill. Although the poem is under composition in the eighth month, when the examinations are due to take place, the author is now aged, and will indulge in such dreams no more. One of the longest poems is Twenty-nine, on the Jasper Patch, which contains the most explicit connections between the garden and the idea of the land of the immortals, but it is also explicit about the owner's return from the capital, and the fact that he has retained his integrity in the face of political adversity.

There is in the naming of the structures, torrents and rocks of Jade Maiden Pool none of the imagery of natural fruitfulness and increase, nor of political hopes surrendered but with integrity preserved, which surrounds the Garden of the Unsuccessful Politician. Instead, if not exactly a coherent programme, then a very clear and explicit different body of references can be read here, allusions to immortals and the semi-divine beings of Daoism. The Pool is in proximity to

Lord Zhang's cavern, associated with the Daoist patriarch Zhang Daoling, and a plot recorded by Wen Zhengming's own painting teacher, Shen Zhou.[21] It is a site where 'Tradition has it that a Jade Maiden used to cultivate purification'. The names of individual features on the estate are steeped in Daoist sensibilities, and in allusions to the holy and numinous character of the property – 'Belvedere of the Radiance of Jade', 'Jade Yang Mountain Dwelling', 'Jade Void Hall', 'Immortals' Perch', 'Alchemy Room', even a set of eight small buildings named after and arranged in the configurations of the hexagrams of the 'Book of Changes'. Several of the buildings are explicitly designed for religious worship. The interest of Shi Ji (1495–1571; MRZJ 105), the owner of Jade Maiden Pool, in Daoism is well attested, but it was an interest that did not impede the assembling of considerable wealth and a wide circle of social contacts. A student of the official and philosopher Wang Shouren (1472–1529; DMB 1408–16), he passed the *jinshi* examination in 1532, and reached the post of Vice-Minister of the Court of the Imperial Stud. Clearly a man of very great wealth, he was a notable founder of charitable estates and charitable schools to support the education of poor scholars, a provider of relief grain during famines in 1543 and 1544,[22] and an organizer of local militia forces against the 'Japanese' pirates who infested the lower Yangtze region in the mid-sixteenth century. His seventieth birthday was celebrated by a number of luminaries.[23] Though living amidst the full panoply of Daoist reclusion, Shi Ji was clearly a man who could marshal some of the most politically and culturally prestigious figures of his day to celebrate both his property and the longevity that attested to his moral worth and success in the Daoist arts.

Wen Zhengming's 'Record of Dwelling in the Mountains at Jade Maiden Pool' very much *is* a celebration of the property's owner. This marvellous site

has never been casually discussed, and though on investigation one finds that the worthies of the Tang have repeatedly sung of the 'Jade Pool', nothing apart from this had ever been heard of. Over the more than eight hundred years from the Tang to now, Gongfu is the first person to promote it. Is it that this marvellous country, Heaven's secret, must await the worthiness of this man before yielding up its splendours? Gongfu has a disposition to pure beauty, and all necessary talents; he does not immerse himself in the world, but puts forth his emotions in hills and ravines. He seeks out the rare and plucks out the marvellous, brings forth the obscure and penetrates the occluded, that the arcane causes of things are made manifest . . .

Shi Ji will be remembered, it is asserted, for the marvels of 'Jade Maiden Pool', which he has restored and brought to public notice; 'at another time gentlemen who are fond of the marvellous may roam here, and it may be that some of them will know of Gongfu.' This advertisement of reclusion, this publicizing of eremitism in the figure of a man famous for being withdrawn and inaccessible will not seem incomprehensible to anyone who has considered the lifestyles of the rich and famous in the late twentieth century. In the two Wen Zhengming prose pieces there are, however, two different models of reclusion being advertised. That ascribed to Wang Xianchen in the Garden of the Unsuccessful Politician is one based on the ideas of self-sufficiency in material things, and the morally ennobling nature of certain types of work on the land. The great model to which this type of allusion looks back is Tao Yuanming (365–427), with his back turned on government office and his rows of chrysanthemums by the East Fence. The much more mystically informed type of reclusion practised by Shi Ji, with his worship of Jade Maidens and his references to the alchemical production of wondrous elixirs, has its roots in the practices of other contemporaries of Tao Yuanming, such as Tao Hongjing or Ge Hong. These two reclusive traditions, which perhaps once represented different emphases if not quite personal social strategies, are still distinct in writings of the early sixteenth century, but they show a tendency to coalesce as the Ming dynasty wears on into a less specific form, one that could be adopted without necessarily implying great personal commitment to the ideals that animated the two traditions' great early practioners. A *shan fang*, or 'mountain studio', was now a state of mind rather than a physical location remote from the city.

PICTURING THE GARDEN

As far as is known, Wen Zhengming provided no pictorial record of Jade Maiden Pool to accompany his prose 'Record'. However, in the case of the Garden of the Unsuccessful Politician, the 'Record' and the thirty-one poems were created as part of an integral album, with thirty-one pictures, executed in ink, showing places within the garden. These too have their rhetoric. In particular, the album format as applied to the garden is dominated by the rhetorical figure of asyndeton, sudden 'cutting' from one scene to another without transitions. While the prose narrative by and large walks us from one pavilion or rock to another, taking account of the space in between, the pictures do the opposite, presenting instead a series of totally discrete views, with no sense of how they are to be joined one to

41 Xu Ben (died 1393), *The Stone-Lion Garden* (*Shizi lin tu*), album leaf,
ink on paper. National Palace Museum, Taipei, Taiwan.

another. The album is different from the handscroll or hanging scroll formats of picture, where scenes not visible within the field of vision of a single observer are present within the same pictorial frame. The scroll formats are more like narrative (in Greek *diegesis*, 'passing through'), while the album sets boundaries and is, in de Certeau's terms, more a collection of 'places' rather than one being concerned with 'space'. If the writing is a problematic source for the reconstruction of a ground-plan, the pictures are simply an impossible one. That is not what they set out to do.

The album format, breaking a single site down into a smaller visual units, had been used several times in Suzhou to depict property before Wen Zhengming applied it to the Garden of the Unsuccessful Politician. An album attributed to Xu Ben (died 1393) shows the Lion Grove (*Shizi lin*; illus. 41), while Du Qiong created one in 1443 containing ten views of the Nancun Villa of Tao Zongyi (1316–1403).[24] Wen's teacher, Shen Zhou, had used it for an album of views of Wu Kuan's Eastern Estate, which passed to Wen, and by descent to his son Wen Jia, from whom it was subsequently stolen. This album no longer survives.[25] Shen also painted in the 1490s an album of twelve views of Tiger Hill (illus. 28), which defined the iconography of the site for subsequent Suzhou painters.[26] All these albums, and the manner of representation they embodied, as transmitted through Shen Zhou to Wen Zhengming, who in turn employed it in the two separate albums he made of the Garden of the Unsuccessful Politician, are distinguished among other features by a high point of view, looking down from an eminence on the sites which are pictured, in a way which the actual topography of urban Suzhou makes impossible.

The implications of such a viewpoint have recently come to be of some importance to theories about the meaning of landscape representation in early modern Europe. John Barrell has demonstrated that, in eighteenth-century England, very explicit connections were made between the physical eminence that afforded a broad panoramic view and the social eminence that went with ownership of property in land. It was the ability to see further in the metaphorical sense, to grasp general principles, and the interrelationship between seemingly unconnected phenomena that justified the hegemony of the gentry. They were men of vision, possessed of a broad sweep of understanding denied to those (women, mechanics) whose horizons were more narrowly defined. A correct taste in landscape – on the part of those landowners whose own interests were altruistically deemed to be those of the total body politic – was crucial, and that correct taste was one for the panorama, the lofty viewpoint. Those who are actually down on the ground cannot grasp the larger scheme of things.[27]

Is this of any help at all in considering Chinese representations of land, gardens not excluded, in the Ming period? It is worth remembering first of all that the production of these representations was in the hands of landowners. In Europe at this time the landowner may have been patron to the painter, but was very unlikely to produce images of his own or another's land in his own hand, whereas Shen Zhou, Wen Zhengming and other Suzhou artists of the late fifteenth century and early sixteenth were all established landowners in their own right. The people who were involved with a revival of garden culture in Suzhou, and with the creation of certain new or revived forms of representing landed property, such as the discontinuous album, were involved with land on a daily basis as the chief support of their social eminence.

The metaphor of height could be deployed in this situation in much the same way as it was in England two hundred years later. Height equalled enlightenment, in the famous couplet by a Tang poet on the ascent of a pagoda:

If you wish to exhaust the panorama of one thousand *li*,
Climb one more storey of the tower.[28]

'Climb one more storey of the tower', *geng shang yi ceng lou*, came to mean 'a step to enlightenment' in the Buddhist sense. The notion of an encompassing panorama as a good thing in its own right appears in Wen Zhaozhi's account of Tiger Hill, when he says that it is better than 'deep mountains and great waters', whose splendours cannot be taken in at a single glance.[29] The idea of *yi lan jin zai mu*, 'everything taken in by the eye at one glance', not only relates to the aesthetic of miniaturization and pictorialization discussed above, but it contradicts a widespread modern understanding that one of the key principles of Chinese landscape design is an opposition to seeing everything at once, and a fondness for breaking a site like a garden into a number of discrete views. This is clearly contradicted by Wen's words. Such a total view implies height.

We have already encountered the term *qing gao*, very widespread in Ming usage and meaning literally 'pure and lofty, or high'. A *gao shi*, 'lofty gentleman', was a person of superior moral and intellectual qualities, qualities that, though they might be temporarily manifested in a man living in reclusion, were precisely those that separated that man from the vulgar throng below, and placed him squarely among the governors, not the governed. Height was a moral quality, in a context where political theory admitted of no distinction between moral worth and the right to rule. Wen Zhengming makes this explicit in his inscription on a painting entitled 'Living in a Tower', *Lou ju tu*, done for the retired official Liu Lin (1474–1561; MRZJ 860) in 1543, where he exploits the ambiguity in the term *gao*, meaning, both literal and figurative 'loftiness' (illus. 22).[30] In her study of an important imaginary set of views of a real garden, the 'Garden of Solitary Delight' built in 1073 by the Northern Song statesman Sima Guang, and painted some time in the early sixteenth century by the professional painter Qui Ying, Ellen Johnston Laing draws attention to the frequent appearance of towers and other storied structures in literary and pictorial descriptions of gardens.[31] She shows how Qiu Ying, in depicting the climactic final site of the handscroll, the 'Tower for Viewing the Mountains', suddenly introduces a much more distant (though equally high) point of view, rendering this tower on a smaller scale from all the rest of the garden (illus. 27). Sima Guang's prose preface to his garden (written by Wen Zhengming on the scroll in question) makes explicit that this high point is to enable him to see the mountains beyond the city of Luoyang, just as that paragon of eremitism, Tao Yuanming, lived in reclusion with a view from his door of the Southern Mountain. This congruence of sensibility with the great figures of the past was easily evoked by a distant prospect. Laing argues also a Daoist motive in a view of hills, a view that takes the gazer outside the world of men. As a third connotation of height she adduces that

A favourite theme in Chinese poetry is the survey of the past, a review of history conveyed by titles or lines referring to ascending a height, by images evoked by looking into the distance, by poetic comments contrasting the permanence of mountains and rivers with the brevity of human life by recalling historical personalities. This ascending 'to have a look'. . . means rising above the here and now and looking into the past.[32]

It is possible to argue that this survey of the past, as the surest guide to practical political action in the Ming here-and-now, is also a trait associated purely with the owners of the land and rulers of the polity. Only they are 'high' enough to draw the lessons from history that will enable them today to order the body politic correctly. The vulgar mass is 'down there', and the gentleman is physically elevated. As Xiang Yukui, grandson of the great collector Xiang Yuanbian and the man who united the Qiu Ying painting with the independently existing Wen Zhengming essay, wrote in a colophon of his own dated 1644, the painting 'lifts one above the sordid bustle of life'.[33] Actual towers were important too. Gui Youguang wrote a 'Record of the Tower for Seeing the Village(s)', pictorializing the productive landscape into fields 'like a painting, that the owner can see but where he does not live'. The tower in Wang Xinyi's Returning to the Fields Garden in Suzhou in the 1630s gave a view, not of hills concealing the haunts of immortals, but of the family's fields of glutinous rice.[34]

Another sort of innovative pictorial format, showing named property owners in conjunction with land, often land in the form of gardens, came into being at about this time, and again it is associated with the small group of Suzhou artists who would much later be grouped as the 'Wu School'. They share with the albums and the Qiu Ying scroll mentioned earlier a high point of view, from which the viewer gazes downwards towards a specific piece of property. These are the handscrolls, usually short in length, that portray an owner in a named piece of property, a property that often supplied one of the owner's by-names, or *bie hao*. From this is derived *bie hao tu*, or 'by-name pictures'.

This name for the specific genre was already in use in the later sixteenth century, when it was identified as being both an innovation and a distinctive genre of Ming painters by the connoisseur and artistic theorist Zhang Chou (1577–?1643; DMB 51–3). He explains the phenomenon thus: 'Subjects for painting in ancient and modern times have become fully developed from their origins down to our Ming dynasty. . . . In the Ming there are the *bie hao* [pictures], like Tang Yin's "Keeping to the Plough", Wen Zhengming's "Chrysanthemum Patch" and Qiu Ying's "Eastern Grove" and "Jade Peak".'[35]

We have already noted the close identification, in terms of names, between a garden owner and his property. Many great Ming gardens were known simply by the name of the owner – 'The Garden of Xu Wenbi, Duke of Dingguo'; 'The Garden of Administrative Commissioner Xu'. Even when a garden had another name it was not necessarily used; Ming sources are just as likely to call the 'Dipper Garden' of Mi Wanzhong in Peking simply the 'Mi Garden'. Conversely, features on the property often provided the owner with a by-name, the only name an adult Ming male chose for himself. This *hao* was therefore intended to be something intensely personal, evocative of its bearer's aspirations and points of moral or intellectual reference.[36]

James Cahill has noted that 'Chinese scholars regularly used their studio names to designate themselves and are called by these names',

42 Huang Gongwang, *Dwelling in the Fuchun Mountains* (*Fuchun shan ju tu*), 1347–50, section of a hand scroll, ink and colour on paper. National Palace Museum, Taipei, Taiwan.

and points out that the picture of a scholar in his studio is therefore a kind of portraiture, regardless of the lack of individualized resemblance in the delineation of facial features.[37] It is unclear whether a name like 'Sophora Rain' (*Huaiyu*), the *hao* of Wang Xianchen, was applied first to himself or to the Sophora Rain Pavilion in the Garden of the Unsuccessful Politician, or whether the two namings were simultaneous, but the effect is a blurring of the distinction between owner and property that is played on in a number of ways in the 'by-name pictures'.

As Zhang Chou recognized, the phenomenon of painting pictures of an individual's property is one that can be traced back to the Yuan period. Richard Vinograd has recently demonstrated that Wang Meng's 'Dwelling in Retreat in the Blue Bian Mountains' scroll of 1366 records the topography of land important to his patron, Zhao Lin. He further argues for the fourteenth century as a period when Chinese painting began to concern itself with specific locales in a way it had not done hitherto, particularly with settings

closely tied to the artist or recipient both by bonds of ownership, personal association or family history. The landscape of the scholar–amateur painter in the Yuan period was to a considerable extent what might be termed the landscape of property.[38]

This Yuan type of depiction of property, which perhaps has it roots in the much-copied subject of Wang Wei's Wangchuan Villa, is exemplified by works like Zhu Derun's 'Beautiful Wilds Studio' (*Xie ye xuan tu*) and Huang Gongwang's 'Dwelling in the Fuchun Mountains' (*Fuchun shan ju tu*), as well a Wang Meng's 'Blue Bian Mountains' discussed by Vinograd (illus. 42). In all of these the focus of attention is in the natural scenery outside the dwelling or retreat that is the ostensible subject of the painting. The human element is continuous with the greater setting, and often the owner of the dwelling is not represented at all. It is the existing scenery that is the basis for garden and landscape painting in the Tang–Yuan period. This undergoes a major change in the Ming.[39]

The topographical representation of landscape, including owned landscape, does not disappear totally from Ming art, even if it is downgraded in aesthetic theory. John Dardess has shown how the elite of Taihe county patronized a local school of landscape painters, whose work is now lost, for whom topographical accuracy of the actual landscape of the region was a major factor in the desirability of the work. The patrons of these artists made no great claims for these works as art, viewing them instead as 'a technique whereby an immovable, inaccessible scene was approximately represented on paper, and made portable, so as to provide those far from the native soil with something to stimulate sentimental attachments and nostalgic reverie'.[40]

This kind of topographical representation was practised by artists closer to the cultural centre. Anne de Coursey Clapp's study of Tang Yin, bosom companion of Wen Zhengming has shown how important such work was in the relationship between Tang and his 'great patron' Wang Ao, editor of the Suzhou gazetteer of 1506. He produced for Wang Ao a number of topographic works, some of them described in their titles as 'true views' (shi jing). These may indeed manifest Wang's 'local pride, and deep devotion to the land of his birth', but they do so through the medium of representations of land that he at least partly owned, particularly the Dongting peninsulas.[41]

The typical format of the by-name picture is fairly standardized, consisting of a large inscription giving the name of the site and the person (they are one and the same) to be commemorated, followed by the painting itself, followed by a prose 'record' and a greater or less number of poems. These elements are typically by different hands. The pictorial part is often quite short as handscrolls go, so that it can be taken in at a single view (like an album leaf) without the need for unrolling. This meant that 'a limit was put to the length of the picture so that the viewer's attention would be fixed squarely on the patron'.[42] The central figure is typically very much larger than in the studio paintings of the Yuan, and is very frequently seen in social intercourse with a guest, often with servants present. As well as antecedents purely from within the realm of painting, these representations of the reciprocities of elite hospitality can perhaps be loosely related to a type of object that predates the earliest surviving Ming bie hao tu by some fifty years. These are a type of carved lacquer-box or dish, dating from the early years of the fifteenth century, and surviving in some numbers, which portray gentlemen in what might loosely be called garden settings. In the example illustrated here (illus. 43), two men are seated as host and guest on a terrace in front of a pavilion, from which are about to emerge two servants bearing dishes and trays of refreshments. The man on the right, undoubtedly the guest, has his back slightly turned towards the viewer and carries at his side a qin zither, companion of the gentleman's leisure hours. The tray was made in a workshop in the new northern imperial capital of Peking. A comparison of the imagery of such a picture with any one of the surviving Suzhou 'by-name pictures' reveals a similarity of iconography, which is probably explicable on the level of the function of both types of object within the nexus of reciprocal gift-giving on the part of the elite.

Although the exact function of the lacquer-boxes and dishes is not entirely clear, it seems likely that they were used for presentations of items such as fruit or sweetmeats, which formed an important part of relationships between the elite. The box or dish was not retained by the recipient of the gift, but returned with a small reciprocal gift, often destined as a reward for the servants who carried out the errand. While it would not be true to say that imagery such as the scene on the dish illustrated here is universal (some show scenes of departure, and others clearly encode allusions to lines of poetry), it is worth pointing out that a very large number of them do have these 'host and guest' scenes (illus. 25). The point of such a scene is surely that it refers to a situation of elite solidarity within an over-arching framework of unequal power. The host's position is always ritually superior to that of the guest, something that is manifested in seating and standing positions, as well as in the order of taking tea or wine, and of exchanging presents. The host, the superior party, is by definition always 'at home', on his own property, the words used for 'host' and 'owner' being exactly the same – zhu. It is arguably significant that 'home', or 'property', is always represented not by an interior scene (something to which there would have been no technical impediment), but by one outside. One explanation for this would be an appeal to a supposed Chinese characteristic of the 'love of nature', but this begs the question of whether the love of nature was equally distributed among all social actors within the polity, between genders, age groups, tenants and landowners. It is not 'the Chinese' who are represented as 'loving nature' in the gift-exchanges of lacquer-boxes or in the by-name pictures, but those Chinese who owned property on which nature in the concrete could be enjoyed.

What is immediately noticeable about the Suzhou bie hao tu in its earliest manifestations is the very close overlap of the people involved with the practice, both as patrons and artists, with the group of leaders of the revival of actual garden culture in the late fifteenth century and early sixteenth. The earliest Ming by-name picture identified is the Shen cui xuan tu ('Deep Purple Studio'), a work no longer extant by the sixteenth century, when Wen Zhengming added a picture to the surviving genuine colophons.[43] The earliest surviving by-name picture is a short handscroll, now in the Palace Museum, Peking, entitled Yousong tu, 'Befriending the Pines' (illus. 23). It carries the seals, though not the signature, of Du

43 Dish, early 15th century, carved red lacquer on a wooden core.
Victoria and Albert Museum, London.

Qiong (1396–1474), one of the earliest painters of the 'Wu School', and the man whose conscious revival of the Pleasure Patch, one of the great but decayed Song gardens of the city, could be seen as participating in the garden-culture revival in Ming Suzhou.[44] The identity of the inhabitant of the pavilion, who sits in the attitude of a host, dressed in his red official robes and hat, would be completely lost to us were it not for the record of the painting in the connoisseurly notes of Zhang Chou, the preface to which is dated 1616. Zhang reveals that Yousong is the name of the pavilion, and the by-name of the painter's brother-in-law Wei Yousong (his actual name was by then no longer known), and he laments the fact that a colophon by Wen Zhengming's nephew Wen Boren (1502–75) deals only with the stylistic affiliations of the picture, saying nothing about the circumstances of presentation or the meaning of the name 'Befriending the Pines'.

Thus by 1616 the emphasis in a work like this had shifted from the identity of the sitter, whose position had called the picture into being, to the eminence of the artist. Since it was customary for the artist only to sign a picture of this type in a very brief manner, without inscribing the actual image further, once the supporting apparatus of colophons and poems is lost (whether deliberately or not), the identity of the sitter cannot be recovered, though the format of the picture will usually be enough to suggest, tantalizingly, that an actual person is represented. Du Qiong's picture of his brother-in-law is not a portrait, and nor should the rendering of his property be considered as a topographical painting. The subject-matter of the representation is the hao, 'Befriending the Pines'. The effort has gone not into the explicit rendering of the structure but of the inner meaning of the name. There remains nevertheless an element of literalness in this: pines shade the building, while dwarf pines in pots stand on the square stone table. The whole question of the validation or otherwise of the 'accurate' representation of physical phenomena in Ming painting is a complex one, and there is certainly not a single 'Chinese' view, even if there are recurring themes in the writings of a relatively homogeneous body of elite artistic theorists.

From the late fifteenth century, the production of bie hao tu by the elite Suzhou artists becomes a very common phenomenon. The listing of thirty such pictures in a recent article by Liu Jiuan is surely only a very preliminary assessment, given that Clapp is able to cite twelve such works by Tang Yin alone, out of a recorded output of some fifty-seven works, 'whose subject matter and inscriptions state or plainly imply that they were made to honour individuals under special circumstances'.[45] Tang Yin may be a special case, in that he derived the major part of his income from such work, but they were equally prominent in the oeuvre of men for whom they were more a part of a network of reciprocal obligations than a source of immediate financial gain. Shen Zhou's *Suian tu*, 'Profound Hermitage' is dated 1500 and has colophons by Wu Kuan and Li Dongyang. It commemorates the dwelling of one Yang Yiqing, who passed the examinations in the same year as Wu, and who is a neighbour of his (presumably in the south-east of Suzhou city, close to the Eastern Estate). Liu Jiuan lists eight identifiable *bie hao tu* by Wen Zhengming (not all of which survive, and surely only a fragment of his output), which demonstrate the wide nature of his connections. One of them, the *Dongyuan tu*, 'Eastern Garden', was painted in 1530 for Xu Zhenzhi of Nanjing, the aristocratic descendant in the fifth generation of Xu Da, first Duke of Dingguo. Despite the protestations in the biographical literature created immediately after his death, contact with the aristocracy could not always be avoided even by those who sought to keep themselves 'pure and lofty'.

One feature shared by all these works is their concentration on the owner in a structure, the studio or hermitage of the painting's title, with the world outside the property rendered more or less as a void. This can be seen in scrolls like Du Qiong's 'Befriending the Pines' and Wen Zhengming's 'Studio of True Connoisseurship' (*Zhen shang zhai tu*). The latter was executed for the collector Hua Xia (active 1514–59) in two separate versions dated 1547 and 1559, the year of Wen's death.[46] Like the two albums of views of the Garden of the Unsuccessful Politician, the existence of authentic multiple versions of the identical subject may be more to do with meeting continuing obligations than with any purely artistic necessity of grappling again with the same problem.

In treating the relationship between inner and outer, between the garden and the natural landscape, the artists of early sixteenth-century Suzhou typically give the prime role to the former, in a reversal of the practice of the Song and Yuan predecessors, where the natural landscape of rivers and mountains is pre-eminent. Of course the *bie hao tu* do not represent the entire output of Suzhou artists, but their innovatory features do hint at new attitudes to the relationship between owner and property at the period. This relationship, exemplified by the shared name, is very much closer than it had perhaps been previously. This may well have had something to do with the fact that in the sixteenth century the nature of the self became one of the topics that increasingly attracted the attention of elite thinkers. The great outpouring of autobiographical writing that begins in the mid-Ming is a written counterpart to these essentializing portraits in an ideal and self-created landscape, whose very physical features are conjured into being at the will of the autonomous upper-class male.

What is rather striking at least about surviving by-name pictures is that in the majority of cases they are paintings by relatively famous artists of relatively obscure subjects. In a number of cases the identity of the sitter is no longer recoverable, or if a name is known it is of someone who left no literary works himself, nor any trace on the voluminous contemporary biographical literature, such as makes up the bulk of Ming gazetteers. This almost certainly reverses the relative levels of prominence at the time of the pictures' creation, when it was the subject of the scroll who outweighed the painter in social terms, even though the painter might be a quite prominent member of the elite in good standing. It is at least arguable that the shift in emphasis from 'property', broadly conceived, to aesthetics, a shift that took place in the actual practices of garden and landscape design in the course of the sixteenth century, is paralleled in the case of the paintings by a loss of interest in the subjects as owners of property, and an almost total concentration on the identity of the artist. No one wanted to own the 'Studio of True Connoisseurship' scroll because it was *of* Hua Xia, but because it was *by* Wen Zhengming. This process, or shift, had taken place by the end of the sixteenth century, if the evidence of writers like Zhang Chou is to be relied upon. Art's power to act as a site where the social world is denied thus came to act on landed property and the representations of that property, as the rate of exchange between economic capital and cultural capital perhaps underwent adjustments.

Some of these paintings were clearly commissioned from artists whose economic position gave them no option but to produce work to order. They might even be individuals of such low status that their names were never recorded as part of the process. However, many pictures, and the texts that accompanied them, and which were of equal or greater importance, were the products of members of the elite for whom distance from market relations was an important part of their personal prestige. This does not mean that power relations between all members of the elite were egalitarian. On the contrary, when two men met, considerations of relative hierarchy based on age, bureaucratic rank (if any) and family prominence were to the fore. This gives us a way of thinking about these by-name pictures of garden scenes, which, like the fruit grown in those gardens, existed

162

to make manifest existing inequalities.

Explanations of the gift relationship, by and large deriving from the work of the French anthropologist Marcel Mauss, have stressed that gifts create relationships, that a gift is given to evoke a reciprocal gift and thus to make connections where no connection had existed before. Some more recent work takes a slightly modified view, and one that perhaps fits more closely with the Chinese case:

Presentations of this type are not the origin points of debt, as models derived from Mauss might indicate, but are rather the points at which debts of relatedness are expressed, or at which debts arising from particular services are extinguished.[47]

Thus paintings of property, privileged access to property, and gifts of certain types of 'pure' produce from property as well as other forms of exchange (most notably of women) serve to sketch out for us, in a fragmentary form, a few of the lineaments of the obligations that bound the Suzhou elite together, not in some harmonious whole, but in a constantly shifting web of clientelage, patronage, debts incurred and debts wiped clean. Wen Zhengming did not paint the studio of Hua Xia in order to generate a relationship where none previously existed, but to objectify a relationship already pre-existent, the precise meaning and power structure of which is now irrevocably lost to us. But (and here perhaps the initial insight of Mauss retains its vitality) the status of a gift in late imperial property law was an imprecise one, in which the giver's attachment to the thing given was never entirely severed.[48] Consequently, the gift of a painting, plus colophons of an individual's name and property, continued to act as a gauge of connections between the recipient and donor(s). In the words of a sentence I have previously used as a justification for attention to the close particulars of material culture, 'even though from a theoretical point of view human actors encode things with significance, from a *methodological* point of view it is the things in motion that illuminate their social and human context'.[49]

As we have seen, these pictures very quickly came adrift from the reciprocal social obligations that had created them, as they entered the sphere of the market simply as 'works of art', and became subject to the categorization of being 'a real Wen Zhengming'. Their capture by the realm of aesthetics is paralleled by changes in the actual topography of gardens, but more especially in the way they are written about and represented pictorially. At a very crude level there is an observable change in the long term in the manner in which garden sites are represented by the conventions of cartography. Song period maps show gardens by means of a pond (often rectangular) and a grove of trees. Qing maps of the city of Suzhou represent the garden sites by conventional representations of the piled-up rocks of the 'artificial mountains' and by architectural structures. A *yuan* is no longer a place of trees but a place of rockery and pavilions. It was in the sixteenth century, above all, that this transition took place.

By the end of the century, many of the conventions of garden representation invented or revitalized a hundred years previously retained their vitality, though applied to properties that might be very different from those in, for example, the Eastern Estate. For these were now largely conceived within an aesthetic framework derived from pictorial conventions, at a time when those pictorial conventions that were becoming dominant stressed the undesirability of topographical accuracy in the rendering of place. Although these views have become standard in the literature of art history, we are on less secure ground on attributing them as universally held views of all actual or potential patrons. We must also take on board the perception of some representations as being read topographically, in situations where without some explicit statement we might be unlikely to accept them as in fact falling into this category. For example, one Qing colophon on the now-lost first Wen Zhengming album of the Garden of the Unsuccessful Politician laments that the passage of time has wrought innumerable changes on the actual garden, but that the album preserves for us the layout (*wei zhi*) of the original site as it was in 1533. This is despite the fact, as noted above, that Wen goes to some lengths in the album *not* to connect the various discrete scenes in such a way as to make a reconstruction of the whole possible.

We must also resist the temptation to subsume all representations of gardens and property to those that have come down to us from a small number of elite artists like Wen Zhengming, while ignoring the much larger body of landscape representation in the Ming period found in maps, illustrations to gazetteers and other less prestigious sources. We need a grasp, for which the materials are not yet at hand, of the total 'visual economy' of the Ming period, to understand how typical or atypical the work actually is that has been the almost exclusive focus of attention. Here the boundaries between what we call a 'painting' and what we call a 'map' are of some interest. In Chinese both words can be rendered by the term *tu*, something that can also mean an arrangement of text (like a genealogical chart) without overt pictorial content at all. In the seventeenth century Gong Xian was to draw a clear distinction between *tu*, which are merely pictures, and which can include maps and diagrams, and *hua*, which is painting within a self-consciously historical tradition, and where subject-matter takes second place to style as the subject of aesthetic contemplation.[50] James Cahill has translated *tu* as 'functional pictures', and this may be the area into which most of the mid-Ming pictures of property, from Tang Yin's 'true views' done for Wang Ao, to Wen Zhengming's work for Wang Xianchen, can be placed. A later member of the Wen family, Wen Boren, is recorded as having painted in 1561 a pictorial scroll showing coastal defences against the 'Japanese pirates', and in the same year as having executed a set of 'Fifteen Views of the Fan Garden' for Gu Congyi.[51] The former work would, if it had survived, be considered under the discipline of cartography, and the latter as a work of art, but we ought to be less confident in asserting a clear categorical division of the two works in the mind of their creator or the patrons for whom they were made.

What is not in doubt is that by the late Ming the disposition of features within a garden was seen as an essentially artistic activity. The great arbiter of taste, Chen Jiru, asserts in one couplet on a particular property that

> The owner has no vulgar attitude,
> In building a plot we see his cultured heart (*wen xin*).[52]

This was the attitude that was to be dominant on into the Qing period and down to the present day. In early eighteenth-century Suzhou, the writer Li Guo (1679–1751) could encapsulate the theory of the 'cultured heart' as the key to a fine garden, while at the same time describing the 'Ink Estate' (*Mo zhuang*) of one contemporary 'as if melded into a scroll':

Previous generations would say that there is no man of culture (*wen ren*) who does not love mountains and waters (*shan shui*), since mountains and waters are a thing which pushes away vulgarity. . .when vulgarity is pushed away then one can study and investigate principle (*li*), one can see the Way.[53]

The assimilation of property to nature, in the form of 'mountains and water', is here complete, and it is this category, rather than the portraits in a pavilion of an earlier age, that Li has in mind when he considers a given garden as being 'like a painting'. So too, when Wang Xinyi describes his Returning to the Fields Garden in terms of the styles of painters, it is to the great masters of the fourteenth century that he turns for terminology. Qi Biaojia describes his own garden in compositional terms, comparing 'the skills used in constructing the garden to those of fine craftsmen such as a physician, a general, a painter or an essayist'.[54] Dong Qichang completes the process, with his claim that, as the possessor of two of the most important early pictorial renderings of estates, those of the Tang luminaries Du Fu and Wang Wei, 'some of the gentlemen's gardens can be painted, but my paintings can be gardened' (ke yuan).[55] By the early nineteenth century, not only were Wen Zhengming's paintings accepted as the best guide to the original appearance of the Garden of the Unsuccessful Politician, but it was perfectly possibly to look at the crowd visiting an actual garden landscape in spring and be reminded above all of a famous painting.[56]

TEXTS OF THE GARDEN

The period from c. 1620 that saw the assimilation in one sense of the garden to 'mountains and water', and of both to ideas about the desirability of stylistic over representational criteria in judging painting, also saw the emergence of other ways of talking about 'gardens', in the genre of writing about luxury consumption that flourished particularly after 1590. Although there is relevant material in some of the earliest examples of this genre, such as Gao Lian's 'Eight Discourses on the Art of Living' of 1591, and Tu Long's related 'Desultory Remarks on Furnishing the Abode of the Retired Scholar' of 1606, none of it is as extensive as the great quantity of 'garden-related' material in Wen Zhengheng's 'Treatise on Super-fluous Things', probably completed between 1615 and 1620.[57] What is immediately apparent is that the word 'garden' (yuan, or its cognates, such as pu) appears hardly at all anywhere in the book. Instead, the garden is presented not as a single coherent site, with boundaries and consistent internal features, but as a bundle of scattered characteristics, each one of which is subject to the types of discrimination on the grounds of taste that are the main purpose of the 'Treatise'. The key distinction invoked is the one between 'elegant' and 'vulgar'. The work's tone of languid and world-weary explanation of what (to people like us) should be self-evident, is captured typically in the opening section of its first chapter, 'Dwell-ings and Cottages', which has already been quoted in chapter Two. What the rest of the section on dwellings does is to disintegrate the idyll of reclusion invoked in the opening passage into a multitude of distinctions and discriminations. These are, for example, applied to gates, which must have two or four leaves, never six, and which should be fitted with genuine archaic bronze ring-handles (alternatively with 'purple bronze' or steel, but never yellow or white brass). They must be lacquered vermilion, purple or black.[58] The author proceeds through steps, windows, balustrades and screen walls, before embarking on the main categories of structure: halls, 'mountain chapels', 'small dwellings', Buddha halls, bridges, tea-houses, chambers for playing the qin-zither, washing-chambers, alleyways and courtyards, towers and belvederes (above three storeys is 'very vulgar'), and finally terraces.

Every taboo creates the possibility of a transgression, and in the case of the 'Treatise on Superfluous Things' it seems more likely that it is what Wen Zhenheng reprehends that gives us a clearer picture of how gardens were laid out in early seventeenth-century Suzhou. The things he fulminates against are unlikely to be entirely imaginary, and some of them have become commonplaces of garden design in the present century. Bridges made out of foraminate Great Lake rocks are vulgar, but not so vulgar as is placing a pavilion in the middle of a bridge, a feature that became so common in the Qing period that it was transmitted to Europe as one of the great clichés of Chinoiserie, an infallible signifier of 'Chineseness'. Stone bridges should never have three arches, and plank bridges must never have two angles in their plan, all of these being distinctions the point of which it is hard to grasp nowadays, except that it is the sheer *fact* of distinctions existing at all that legitimizes the text.

This 'disintegration' of the garden as a coherent property in favour of commentary on its individually considered constituent parts is carried over into chapter Two of the 'Treatise', on 'Flowers and Trees'. In the initial comments it is made clear that though some degree of practical edible or pharmacopoeic value still clings to certain plants, that is no longer their main purpose. They are for looking at, thus:

Grasses and trees must not be confusedly jumbled up, but must be planted appropriately so that the whole year round they form an unbroken pictorial composition (ru tu hua). For example, peaches and plums must not be planted in a courtyard, since they are for looking at from a distance, while red flowering plums and brown peaches provide a few accents in a grove, but should not be planted in numbers. . . . As for arbours of beans or vegetable patches, or the specialities of the mountains, they are of course not odious, but they should form a separate area of several qing of open space; it is not an elegant thing to have them planted in a courtyard. . . . As for the cultivation of orchids and chrysanthemums, there are ancient prescriptions for these; transmitting them to the gardeners and managing these matters are suitable concerns of a recluse.[59]

The mention of gardeners (*yuan ding*) provides the first use of the word *yuan* in the text. Individual flowers and shrubs are then listed, with notes as to their suitability. They include tree peony and peony, magnolia, crab apple, camellia, peach, plum, apricot, flowering plum, daphne, roses and Banks' roses, rosa rugosa, kerria, Lagerstroemia, pomegranate, hibiscus mutabilis, Michelia, jasmine, rhododendron, pine, hibiscus syriacus, cassia, willow, boxwood, sophora, wutong, toon tree, gingko, tallow tree, bamboo, chrysanthemum, orchid, mallow, poppy, tawny daylily, Hosta, Pentapetes phoenicia, lotus, narcissus, Impatiens and plantain. All of these plants, which outnumber greatly the handful of generic types found in the description of the Garden of the Unsuccessful Politician by the author's great-grandfather, are subject to discrimination as to variety, colour, suitability for various positions and suitability on the grounds of gender. For example, two varieties of peony should not be planted together, while it is vulgar to combine camellia and magnolia, something 'people often do, since they flower at the same time, the red and white being dazzling'.[60] Similarly, peach and willow are a vulgar combination. The flowering plum, described as 'the floral companion of the recluse. . . most antique [of flowers]', should be planted in great quantities: 'You should plant several *mu* of them, and sit or lie among them when they blossom, to purify both the spirit and the bones.'[61] The plum, by contrast, must always be planted singly, never in clumps. Roses are altogether a suspect item:

I once saw in someone's garden a screen made from bamboo, with five-coloured climbing roses across it. The Banks' roses were trained on a wooden frame, called a 'rose arbour'. When they flowered he would sit beneath it – what difference is there between this and dining in the market-place? However, neither of them can be planted without a framework, so perhaps they should be planted round the women's quarters for the servant girls to pluck – this is just about acceptable.[62]

This discrimination on the grounds of gender is one made elsewhere in the 'Treatise' with respect to manufactured goods, and it is applied equally to wooden balustrading and to the kinds of birds that may be kept as pets.[63] The 'West Lake Willow' (*Tamarix chinensis*) is condemned for having 'an effeminate air'.[64]

The introduction of the 'market-place', a space which is the very antithesis of everything the gentlemen's garden stands for, as a space of promiscuous social mingling and unregulated consumption, is taken up elsewhere in the text, suggesting a regularly understood opposition between the two. Of orchids it is said 'You must plant only one pot in each location, otherwise is looks like the Tiger Hill flower-market', while the discussion of 'Vegetables and Fruit' maintains that 'all matters relating to food and drink must be antique, elegant, refined and pure, without the slightest hint of the market-place butcher or vintner'. The section on the vegetable rape charts the distance between Wen Zhenheng and his forebear Wen Zhengming, who was happy to sing the praises of a man whose avowed aim was to 'peddle vegetables'. By 1620 even playing at a vegetable peddler was unacceptable:

It is suitable to order the gardeners to plant a lot of them to provide side dishes, but this must be done without thoughts of profit in the market-place, which makes you no more than a vegetable peddler.[65]

The garden is now not merely a site of 'reclusion in the city', but a site utterly *unlike* the urban scene, defined by the transgressive commercialized promiscuity of the market-place. As market relations penetrated all parts of exchange within the world of the Jiangnan elite, so that everything from artworks to garden rocks became subject to its corroding touch, the garden as inversion of the commercial world came to seem more and more necessary. The more the garden was actually penetrated by buying and selling, the shriller grew the claims that it was a place absolutely apart, absolutely unlike, and the tighter grew the discriminations that preserved its otherness.

Again and again Wen cannot avoid drawing attention to the fact that most of the elements of the elegant garden can be bought and sold. Suzhou was a centre of a major commercial flower-growing industry. Of rugosa roses, 'in Suzhou there are acres of them, and a huge profit is made when they flower'. Of jasmine: 'When it flowers a hundred boats converge on Tiger Hill. Thus the flower-market is at its most flourishing in early summer.'[66] Not even the chrysanthe-mum (illus. 44), the flower *par excellence* of Tao Yuanming, the greatest of all recluses, can escape:

When the chrysanthemums flower in Suzhou the aficionados (*hao shi zhe*[67]) invariably obtain several hundred stems, of multicoloured hue, arranged in rows as an object of amusement; this is to vaunt an appearance of wealth and nobility. Those who truly appreciate flowers will obtain rare varieties, arranging one or two stems in an ancient vase, the petals erect and beauteous, the leaves dense and luscious, and they will place them by their table or couch, toying with them as they sit or recline, until the flowers fade; this is to obtain the nature and essence of flowers.

44 *Chrysanthemum, bamboo and garden rock,* woodblock print, from *Gao Song's Chrysanthemum Album (Gao Song ju pu),* 1550.

Wen goes on to discuss varieties of chrysanthemums, including edible ones, and lists the 'six necessities and two prohibitions' of growing them, technical horticultural knowledge of a type hardly seen elsewhere in the 'Treatise'. The inappropriateness of this specialized body of skill is brought sharply into focus when he seems to recall himself and asserts that 'These are all things which the gardeners must know, they are not the affair of our sort'.[68]

One of the longest sections in the chapter is that on 'Amusement with Pots' (*Pan wan*).[69] Wen Zhenheng opposes at least one of the choices of plants made by his slightly older contemporary Gu Qiyuan, calling dwarfed plantains 'ridiculous', and seems in general to favour larger versions of *panjing*.[70] He reverses what he says is the fashionable view that those for the table are superior to those used in courtyards and walkways, and gives pride of place to the Tianmu pine (*Pinus taiwanensis*), specimens of which should ideally be between one and two feet high. As is now standard, he makes the link with named famous painters: an ideal tree should fit one description of Ma Yuan, another of Guo Xi, another of Liu Songnian (c. 1150–after 1225), and a fourth of Sheng Mou (active c. 1310–60). He decries a fashionable trick of having flowers sprout from a chunk of incense wood, and lists other acceptable trees, which include the familiar flowering plum, as well as *Lycium chinensis* and *Ligustrum quihoi*. The Damnacanthus, which he associates with Hangzhou, is 'in between elegance and vulgarity'. The rest of the entry discusses acceptable types of dish, acceptable forms (round, never square, with long narrow ones being 'particularly tabooed'), rocks, and placings, with a limitation of two being placed on the number to be set in any one spot.

Wen's material in this chapter is exclusively on the *consumption* of flowers, with very little information as to how they are to be grown. As we have seen, knowledge of this type was for him beneath the dignity of 'our sort' of people. He thus has nothing to say, for example, about the techniques used for the forcing of flowers in the late Ming, and their production out of season. There has been a total rift between the discourses of 'horticulture' and of 'gardens', the latter now characterized purely as objects of luxury consumption. The same is true of his discussion in chapter Three of his 'Treatise' on 'Water and Rocks'. His introduction to the subject takes in some of the large cosmological themes that are associated with these natural phenomena, as well, incidentally, as providing the first example of his usage of any of the terms for 'garden', in what is the nearest he gets to an overall programmatic statement:

Rocks lead one to antiquity, water leads one to remoteness. In a garden grove (*yuan lin*) water and rocks are the most indispensable things. They absolutely must return and encircle, thrusting vigorously, and must be grounded in a suitable manner. One peak is the eight thousand feet of Mounts Tai and Hua, and one dipperful of water is ten thousand *li* of rivers and lakes. There must also be tall bamboos, old trees, strange creepers, ugly trees, bent twisted and thrusting out; dark cliffs and prasine torrents, bubbling springs with a surging flow, as if one were entering among deep precipices and inaccessible ravines; these make the splendid landscape of a famous region.[71]

However, the discussion of individual features under this rubric has none of the atmosphere of broad cosmological vistas that much secondary literature invariably brings into play in the discussion of rocks or water in the 'Chinese garden'. Wen's note on pools clearly envisages construction on a lavish scale, anything up to ten *mu* in area, 'the broader the more splendid'. Any islands must be clearly differentiated from those in fish-rearing, and only willows may be planted at the edge, never peaches or apricots. 'At the broadest point place a water belvedere, one like those in a painting being fine.'[72] His account of stones is concerned not with any supposed coherence of 'stones' as a particular kind of cosmological manifestation, a symbol of eternal verities, or a congealment of the life-force of the universe, but with differentiating between types. He makes this very clear in his first entry, on 'Ranking stones' (*Pin shin*):

Of stones, Lingbi are best and Ying stones come next. But these two types are very expensive and hard to buy, large ones being particularly difficult to obtain, so that anything over several feet is in the class of marvels. Small ones can be placed on the table, those with a colour like lacquer and a sound like jade being the best.[73]

He then ranks according to shape, and dismisses some other currently available stones, including cinnabar, while the flashing gemstones *shiqing* and *shilü* are 'vulgar'. His subsequent account of ten individual named kinds of stone concentrates on their sources, and the forms in which they are found, with additional notes such as the fact (of Taihu stones) that 'the artificial mountains which are valued at Suzhou are all made of these stones'.[74] Novelty was no necessary bar to acceptability in the elegant garden: the 'newly appeared' stones from Mount Yaofeng, near Suzhou, are 'antique, simple and delightful' once they have a bit of moss on them.[75] Kunshan stones are, however, 'valued by the vulgar, and are not elegant objects'. Little pieces of 'coarse agate' from Shandong are very expensive and hard to obtain, and are acceptable in moderation, though Wen notes that when 'recently I saw someone who was surrounded with several dishes of them, it ended up looking like a shop'.[76]

Chapter Four, on 'Birds and Fish', contains an entry that almost poignantly encapsulates the dilemma faced by Wen Zhenheng, the forlorn promoter of elegance in a market culture. For centuries, the white crane had carried a heavy freight of associations with those who, through moral worth and religious exercise, had sloughed off the mundane and vulgar world and achieved the status of untrammelled immortal. Wen writes of them:

Among empty woods and wild gullies, green pines and white stones, only this gentleman is suitable. The rest of the feathered tribe is not worth considering.

However, even these 'gentlemen', these symbols of immortality, of Daoist eremitism and quietistic withdrawal were market commodities. Breeding them commercially, as Wen himself cannot forbear to reveal, was the chief industry of a village called 'Crane Nest Village', situated in Huating to the east of Suzhou, and which supplied the whole of Jiangnan.[77] The full kit necessary for a hermit's life was available for cash.

Perhaps what sums up the changes in garden discourse between the early sixteenth century and the early seventeenth is the existence of Wen's chapter Twelve on 'Vegetables and Fruit'. For these have now become completely separated from the plants which bear them, situated back in chapter Two on 'Flowers and Trees'. The same species can appear in both places, for example the flowering plum, which in the latter is the inseparable companion of recluses, and in the former is 'although an ordinary fruit, they encourage sleep and slake the thirst, and have their own qualities'.[78] As with purely ornamental species, there is a great expansion in the number of fruits and vegetables available to the rich consumer in Suzhou's markets, not just cherries, peaches, plums, flowering plums, apricots, several varieties of oranges, loquats, bayberrys, jujubes, pears, chestnuts, gingko nuts, persimmons and water chestnuts (which were all grown locally), but imported grapes, lichees, pears from Shandong and apples from the north-west. Vegetables to tempt the palate included *Wu jia pi* (*Acanthopanax spinosum*), whose 'prolonged consumption will lighten the body and brighten the eye', various beans, mushrooms, gourds, aubergines, taro, wild rice stem (*Zizania caduciflora*), yam and rape. Note that, just as the staple crops that had filled the Eastern Estate have vanished, and just as fields of rice or other grains are noteworthy by their absence from painting, the only foodstuffs that can be assimilated to the discourse of elegant living are fruits and vegetables. Grains, meat and fish have no place in the world of 'Superfluous Things'.

'The garden' as a coherent site is only fleetingly present in the 'Treatise on Superfluous Things', being broken down into literally hundreds of objects with an autonomy of their own, both in terms of the discrimination of taste and in terms of the market in which they circulated. Yet it does cover almost all the 'ingredients' from which a late Ming aesthetic garden could be assembled. It differs in this respect from what is the only explicit 'garden-making' treatise, the slightly later *Yuan ye*, by Ji Cheng.

The existence of a complete English translation of this work, under the title 'The Craft of Gardens', and its use by Osvald Sirén in *The Gardens of China* (1949) makes a full discussion of its content unnecessary.[79] It represents an entirely independent textual tradition from the 'Treatise on Superfluous Things', and appears to borrow no material from the earlier work, but its method of operation is similar, as in disaggregation of 'the garden' into a large number of discrete features.

The author, Ji Cheng, clearly belonged to a less privileged social stratum than did Wen Zhenheng, although he was probably an educated man of modest means, who enjoyed the patronage of Ruan Dacheng (c. 1587–1646), a major political figure who later historiography was to saddle with much of the opprobrium for the fall of the Ming dynasty. The existence of a preface, dated 1634, by Ruan Dacheng is the traditional explanation for the almost total obscurity into which 'The Craft of Gardens' fell between its publication and its 'rediscovery' by Chinese architectural historians in the inter-war period, though this must now be modified by the discovery that it was still being exported to Japan in the early eighteenth century.[80]

While the exact purpose of 'The Craft of Gardens' remains open to debate, a number of commentators accept it as an artefact in which gardens and skills relevant to the creation of gardens are themselves commodities, and the text is therefore assimilable to what I have elsewhere argued as 'the commodification of knowledge' in the late Ming. The presumed audience for this lay text is among those for whom increased prosperity made it possible to consider the emulation of consumption patterns that had previously been restricted to a few. The text stresses again and again, to those who might be thinking of doing so, that, for those who lack the correct degree of taste, it is highly dangerous to lay out a garden according to one's own inclinations. The litany of egregious errors into which it is possible to fall is backed up by the claim that it will be much safer to employ a 'master' of the craft, who will undertake the direction of workmen in the practical tasks. This role is clearly intended for none other than Ji Cheng himself, a man whose self-characterization in his authorial preface begins with the only credentials that by this point really matter:

As a young man I was known as a painter. I was by nature interested in seeking out the unusual; since I derived most pleasure from the brushes of Guan Tong and Jing Hao, I paid homage to their style in all my work.[81]

The 'master' is to be a master above all of pictorial composition, using the physical elements of buildings and rocks (he has correspondingly less to say about plants) in the way a painter would use brushstrokes. As I have argued, this was by the late Ming an absolutely standard way of considering gardens, now formed into a discursive object about which it was possible to make statements of the normative kind found in the writing of both Wen Zhenheng and Ji Cheng. It is possible to see a text like 'The Craft of Gardens' as being not necessarily the culmination of a long, if inchoate and unrecorded, tradition of essential wisdom about landscape, but as being a response to a historically specific politics of taste and consumption. For as we have seen the word *yuan* by no means signifies at this point the aesthetic landscape only, and instead remains a site of contest in a situation where it can equally be made to refer to a productive space. By 1630 it is possible to assert, by means of completely ignoring any other possibility, that a 'garden' is purely a place of rocks and pavilions. This is what Ji Cheng does. By associating gardens above all with painting, from which the mimesis of productive land is excluded, this assertion is reinforced. But it is an assertion that is in an insoluble tension with the market forces that actually govern the ownership and transfer of *all* property, gardens included, despite appeals to 'nature' as the ultimate validating principle for the kind of cultural product Ji Cheng was manufacturing.

The subsequent oblivion (or at least obscurity) of Ji Cheng's text can on one level be explained by his association with the odious Ruan Dacheng, in that it may have been a contributing factor to the book's omission from the great eighteenth-century imperially sponsored bibliographical compilation, the *Si ku quan shu*. This would clearly have damaged the book's prospects of a wide circulation. Perhaps a broader answer can be sought in the fate it shared with a number of late Ming works, including the 'Treatise on Superfluous Things', which have at their heart the project of enshrining 'consumption' as a discursive object, of setting 'things' and the social order in a stable and correct relationship. The degree of development of the market, and the concomitant growth in a mechanism of fashion applied to a wide variety of commodities and knowledges, could not but doom this project to failure, while the traumatic political changes of the Manchu conquest made it look in retrospect like a frivolous dilettantism. The formulation in the later seventeenth century and eighteenth of an 'orthodox', again imperially sponsored, position, on the question of representationalism versus the exultation of stylistic affiliations in painting closed down one type of treatment of land in its aesthetic dimensions. The intellectual currents that marginalized the Ming way of talking about the world of material culture closed down another, even if the absolute aestheticization of the garden in practice triumphed, and continues to set the framework for all discussion of the subject down to the present.

5 The Landscape of Number

By the late Ming, any given piece of landed property, and in particular any piece of land capable of categorization as a 'garden' (and so listed in sources such as gazetteers), was subject to the pull of a number of discursive fields, some of which have already been discussed. The field of agronomy, backed by the sanctions of classical political economy, was particularly powerful, but was increasingly challenged by that of aesthetics, embodied in the discourse of painting. Issues of public access and private reclusion also subjected a site to contradictory, sometimes unresolvable, tensions, while other areas of concern, among them the discourse of plants, acted to complicate the picture yet further. This chapter will continue this process of complication, by holding the artefact of the garden up to scrutiny in the light of a number of other Ming practices, such as geomancy (the art of selecting auspicious locations for dwellings and tombs), mensuration and surveying, all linked by what contemporary sources would have described as *shu xue*, the 'study of number'. The term *shu xue* is used in modern Chinese to designate the scientific discourse of mathematics, but to translate it that way in a Ming text is both misleading and anachronistic. As Ho Peng Yoke has pointed out,[1] a more satisfactory, though still limited, translation would be 'numerology', incorporating 'the art of predicting the future, both in the natural and human world'. While explicit linkage between this area of concern – highly important both theoretically and on a practical level – and the world of garden culture may be hard to find in the Ming sources, there remains enough evidence to argue that for the garden viewed *as property* it was of overwhelming importance. It pervaded understanding of land to such a degree that explicit reference to it was generally deemed to be superfluous, and we must make do with hints and allusions in passing, but its very ubiquity makes it an area that must be addressed. It was underpinned by the prestige of the most enigmatic and endlessly fascinating of the canonical books, the 'Book of Changes' (*Yi jing* or *Zhou yi*: 'Changes of the Zhou Dynasty'), whose eight trigrams and sixty-four hexagrams not only provided the basic building blocks of numerology, but which supplied metaphors and images penetrating aesthetic discourse as well. Richard Smith has noted how it was the name of a hexagram that provided the eighteenth-century poet Yuan Mei (1716–98) with the imagery justifying his creation of a famous garden, and it was the trigram *gen*, in one of its correlative meanings of 'north-east', which provided the name of the 'magic marchmount' built in the imperial capital in the early twelfth century.[2]

GEOMANCY AND LAND

The modern literature on geomancy is now quite extensive, though still small in proportion to the importance of the subject in Ming life.[3] It appears in Ming sources under a number of names, with the classically more prestigious terms of *di li*, 'principle of the earth', and *kan yu*, 'cover and support', being seen more frequently than the modern colloquial terms of *feng shui*, 'wind and water'.[4] In at least one Ming source, a discussion of the geomancy of the secondary (though original) imperial capital at Nanjing is simply headed *shan shui*, 'mountains and water', a term more usually translated as 'landscape', especially when viewed as the subject of painting.[5] The two sets of ideas were clearly understood as being at some level intertwined. Whichever name was deployed, the same one could be used to cover two rather different schools of geomancy. The first was the possibly more learned but less widely used cosmological method, dependent on the geomancer's compass and on elaborate calculations (illus. 45). This was associated in tradition with the province of Fujian. The second school was supposed to have its origins in Jiangxi, and to be concerned more with skilled 'reading' of the existing forms of the landscape, and the selection of the 'lairs' (*xue*) where auspicious influences might be expected to congregate.[6] The difficulties of the textual evidence, and in particular the often deliberately obfuscatory account they give of when and by whom they were written, make it especially hard to construct any *historical* account of geomancy, taking full account of diachronic changes in its technical procedures and its reception in the wider society of its practitioners and the consumers of their skills. Nevertheless, it is clear that the views on geomancy held by those Song dynasty giants of the 'school of principle', whose philosophical positions were largely normative among the Ming elite, were fairly relaxed. Geomancy was not heterodox. Patricia Ebrey has shown that Zhu Xi, whose 'Family Rituals' provided norms of social behaviour for families like the Suzhou Wen, and whose commentaries on the Classics provided access to bureaucratic advance through the examinations, was generally accepting of the metaphysical assumptions underlying geomancy, assumptions that accorded well with his own cosmological views.[7] This is not to say that there were not numerous Ming dynasty critiques of the *practice* of geomancy, and elite

45 Geomancer's compass, first half of 17th century, varnished wood.
National Museum of Denmark, Lyngby.

scepticism of the efficacy of its prescriptions. Such critiques are actually quite common. But they are not the same thing as rejection of the cosmological principles that were supposed to supply its explanatory force, which were widely accepted by educated people, who may in any case have accepted at least grave geomancy as being (as Harriet Zurndorfer appropriately points out) a 'necessary evil'.[8] While dismissing it as superstition, Matteo Ricci was forced to accept that geomancy was a study in which were occupied '*molte persone gravi*'.[9]

In his extensive observations on and collection of anecdotes about geomancy in the late Ming, contained in the *biji* text *Wu za zu*, the Fujianese writer Xie Zhaozhe shows himself to be typical in his scepticism, a scepticism that is justified on pragmatic rather than theoretical grounds.[10] Despite his critiques (all to an extent *topoi*, which can be found in a variety of writers), Xie Zhaozhe demonstrates in immediately contiguous passages that he was fully conversant with the technical language of geomancy, with its search for the 'true dragon' (*zhen long*). He knows that 'If the dragon is true then the "lair" (*xue*) is true'. The extent to which geomantic terminology was a widely disseminated type of language, available to the educated many, and not just the arcane specialist interest of a few remains debatable, but the evidence here and elsewhere suggests that it may have been broadly familiar to a relatively wide segment of the elite. Xie's most trenchant criticism in fact ends up by subverting itself:

Of those who are gulled by the 'principles of the earth' my fellow Fujianese are the worst. There are those who employ a hundred stratagems yet do not succeed in an entire lifetime. There are those who are deluded by the geomancers[11] and who are ruined by burials in the end. There are those rich and noble families who obtain a piece of land which is basically excellent, but because they fear it has defects and is not beautiful to look at, they construct mountains of earth, convert fields into slopes, surrounding them with walls and leading in water, building bridges and constructing terraces. The expense stretches to 10,000 strings of cash, the labour to ten years. It is as if one corrected the defects in one's ears or nose by carving or plastering – it disorders the truth, and to what purpose? And furthermore to exhaust the labour of man in stopping up the veins of the earth not only cannot bring good fortune, but will hasten disaster.[12]

He concludes the section with a story of a relative of his who was himself a skilled geomancer (itself an interesting fact, in that it tells us that members of the elite possessed and practised this skill without recourse to professionals) and who was widely praised, until he retired from office, whereupon he

built a dwelling on the West Lake [at Hangzhou], facing the city, with its back towards the water, and with great watercourses on all four sides. Everyone said it was a doomed location, but he did not heed them. He left it to his descendants, who declined rapidly into poverty. Several hapless individuals were executed. They could not keep the property, and sold it to be a clan shrine.[13]

Geomancy might be a difficult, even an impossible, skill to practise effectively, but the veins of the earth were not to be tampered with lightly, while the siting of both graves (yin zhai, 'dwellings of yin/darkness) and of living accommodation (yang zhai, 'dwellings of yang/light') could have immediate and lasting consequences for an individual and for his kin. These were not eccentric views. It was the fear of damage to 'the veins of the earth' that led the elite of Taihe county to oppose large-scale gypsum mining there in the fourteenth century, and their action finds many echoes in later Ming literature.[14] Writing specifically of the gardens of Nanjing, Gu Qiyuan at the very beginning of the seventeenth century ascribes their rarity in the early Ming to government prohibitions on digging ponds, 'lest they damage the vital breath (qi) of the earth in the imperial capital'.[15] It was perfectly possible for a sixteenth-century author like Lang Ying (1487–1566; DMB 791–3), in the course of the same passage, to recount the origins of the science of the 'principles of the earth' with respect while inveighing against the 'lascivious warlocks and blind dotards who cover the empire'.[16] When we read in a Ming source that a certain person was violently opposed to geomancy, it is quite likely that the opposition was to charlatan practitioners (and by the more fastidious of elite definitions, all *professional* practioners were likely to be charlatans) rather than to the perfectly orthodox cosmology that underlay it.[17]

Wen Zhengming's own work shows a certain acceptance of at least the more classically grounded parts of geomancy, and a willingness to use some of its terminology, even if only in a rather casual manner. In his description of the imperial gardens, Wen Zhengming calls *Wan sui shan*, 'Longevity Hill', the *zhen shan*, the 'protecting hill of the Great Within', using a term that is principally meaningful in the context of geomancy, and the theory of defence against evil influences permeating from the north. The hill is described as being 'to the north-east of the imperial city, beyond the Xuanwu Gate. . . .On it groves of tree extend their shade. It is particularly rich in rare fruits, another name of it being the Garden (or Orchard) of a Hundred Fruits (*Bai guo yuan*)'.[18] The creation of a geomantically positioned artificial hill in the north-east of the imperial city would be likely to evoke in Wen's readership the memory of the 'North-eastern Peak', the *Gen yue*, built in the Northern Song capital of Kaifeng under the emperor Huizong in a (successful) attempt to cure his lack of an heir.[19] The term *gen* is the name of one of the eight trigrams, the patterns of three broken or unbroken lines that, found in the *Yi jing*, or 'Book of Changes', were the basic building blocks of all numerology and prognosticatory sciences in the Ming period. It is also a term Wen Zhengming uses in his descriptive tour of the Garden of the Unsuccessful Politician, where as we have seen he bafflingly mixes several types of orientating terminology, using 'left and right', and 'north and south' as well as the trigram names, with their more arcane flavour.

A yet more explicitly 'geomantic' landscape, described by Wen with every sign of approval, is that of Jade Maiden Pool, and in particular the section around Jade Void Hall, where

surrounding the hall are eight rooms of three spans, taking their aspects from the trigrams of the 'Changes', and their names from the directions; they are called 'Pure Yang', 'Central Yang', 'Beginning Yang', 'Following Yang', 'Bright Yang', 'Penetrating Yang', 'Arriving Yang', and 'Ascendant Yang'.[20]

The text continues: 'Emerging from "Ascendant Yang" to the north. . .', which implies that 'Pure Yang', where the sequence begins, is at the opposite point of the compass, i.e. the south. There are two possible sequences for the trigrams, one beginning in the south being the 'Former Heaven' (*xian tian*) sequence, where the trigram *gen* in fact takes the position north-*west*. Only in the 'Latter Heaven' (*hou tian*) sequence, which has its starting point in the east, does the character *gen* line up to the north-east.[21] This 'Latter Heaven' order is the one employed on a rare surviving pair of Ming period geomancer's compasses, or *luo pan*, which can be identified as having been in a European collection as early as 1653 (illus. 45).[22] Although it is possible that Wen failed to notice the inconsistency between the two systems (the one he himself used in specifying directions in the Garden of the Unsuccessful Politician, and the one used in laying out the circle of pavilions at Jade Maiden Pool), it is more likely that such cosmological sophistications were much more widely available to educated discourse than they are to modern scholarship, which is only beginning to cast off missionary impatience with Chinese 'superstition', and take seriously the abiding elite fascination with the *Book of Changes*.

Perhaps even more telling is another passage in Wen's description of Jade Maiden Pool:

To the south of Ripple Cliff is Lord Yang Grotto. There are three lairs in this grotto, the last lair being rather deep, and called White Dragon Depository.[23]

The word here translated as 'lair' is *xue*, the technical term in geomancy for a favourable site, being the lair of the invisible dragons whose bodies comprise the topographic movement of the landscape. It is for the *xue* that the geomancer searches, and at the *xue* that graves and dwellings must equally be sited, if disaster is to be avoided. Such a word could scarcely be used in a Ming text without evoking resonances of geomancy, whatever Wen Zhengming's personal views.

If the 'pure and lofty' Wen Zhengming, often held up as the very model of 'Confucian' rectitude, was so deeply involved, even if only at the unconscious and allusive level, with ideas and individuals connected to divination and geomancy, is this not likely to have been even more true of the general run of the Ming upper classes? I would argue that it was, and that a geomantic perception of landscape was very widely shared by the elite, to such an extent that it rarely shows up in biographical notices, being something largely taken for granted as part of an educated person's mental furniture. What effect then, if any, did the pervasive nature of geomantic ideas have on the actual disposition of the landscape, when it came to the laying out of any given piece of property as an aesthetically conceived garden?

A certain amount of valuable work has been done already on the connections between geomantic ideas and aesthetic notions, though the majority of this has concerned itself with landscape *painting* rather than with the actual manipulations of the terrain involved in garden construction.[24] Roger Goepper has demonstrated some of the links between geomantic terminology and that used in treatises on landscape art as far back as the Song, and has pointed out that Wang Wei, revered in the Ming as the founder of the prestigious 'Southern School' of painting, was believed (possibly erroneously) at the same period to be the author of an influential work on geomancy.[25] John Hay, in his study of Huang Gongwang's 'Dwelling in the Fuchun Mountains' handscroll (illus. 42), has attempted to correlate geomantic notions of landform with a single surviving work.[26] Susan Bush has shown that technical terms from geomancy formed part of the critical vocabulary of at least one major seventeenth-century theorist of painting, and John B. Henderson has argued that, from the early seventeenth century, a burgeoning critique of the correlative cosmology that underlay geomancy can be used to explain both a growing scepticism of geomancy itself, and a congruent growing attention to irregularity and distortion in the art of the age.[27] The temptation is very strong to conflate landscape painting with the actual practice of garden culture, especially since we have seen that from the later sixteenth century it was standard practice to perceive gardens as possessing stylistic features derived from individual, named artists, but before accepting the temptation it would be as well to assemble some of the very scattered evidence of a relationship between gardening and geomancy, which is nothing like as plentiful or as explicit as might casually be supposed.

Occasionally, however, a very clear statement can be found in the sources. In the Wu county gazetteer of 1642, there is an account of the Sprouting Garden (*Mi yuan*), an urban property of some 20 *mu* built inside the Xu Gate on the site of the earlier Green Waters Garden (*Lü shui yuan*) by a certain Zhang Shiwei at some unspecified period in the Ming dynasty. The account of it says quite clearly, 'Every building is placed according to the prescriptions of the geomancers', using the term *xing jia*, 'experts on forms'.[28] This tantalizing reference is in fact the *only* mention of geomancy with regard to a garden in any of the three Ming gazetteers of Suzhou, and serves only to raise further questions. We might dearly wish to know something of the owner, Zhang Shiwei, of his connections and of the circles in which he moved. Are we to assume that in all the other gardens of Suzhou and its environs the buildings were placed *without* reference to the views of geomancers, and that Zhang Shiwei is to be viewed as uniquely credulous or superstitious? Is the point of the notice that, unusually, the *buildings* were placed according to geomantic prescription, whereas it might be quite standard practice to take note of their calculations when involved in large-scale earth-moving, for example in the dredging of ponds or creating artificial mountains? Certainly it is very hard to read the Ming treatise on building and carpentry, the 'Classic of Lu Ban', without coming to the view that it would be very difficult to move the quantities of soil necessary for a major Ming garden, to dig ponds, dam streams or cause them to flow, and to build structures (including structures of several stories and structures over water) without taking geomancy into account. This text overwhelmingly provides evidence for the view that, if geomancy was as widely believed in as the evidence would suggest, then the construction of a garden in the sixteenth century can scarcely have been a neutral or unproblematic activity, without any cosmological or spiritual/religious dimension. However, as the modern translator of the 'Classic of Lu Ban' perceptively points out, 'it is clear that what is called "geomancy" for a large part consists of ritual calculations, the outcome of which hardly shows in the finished building'. He continues:

Geomancy as a whole, including the 'siting branch', is a ritual in the first place. Its prescriptions and regulations force the geomancer, the carpenter and the owner to make complicated calculations, but it can always be manipulated in such a way that in the end it is possible to build the house which conforms best to the personal needs of the owner and the requirements of the building site. In other words, precisely the same house would have been built if geomancy would [sic] not exist.[29]

This seems entirely sensible, and applicable all the more strongly to gardens. Certainly, in the Ming novel *Jin ping mei*, a geomancer is called in to determine the auspicious time to begin construction of the garden, but he has no input into what we could call its design.[30] The renderings of individual gardens found in Ming painting do not provide us with the opportunity to read individual features or juxtapositions of features as being informed by geomancy.[31] It would, however, be rash to assume that such a relationship had not been taken into consideration at the time of construction.

Some idea of the kinds of consideration that may have been in play during the building of a late Ming garden can be dimly discerned from *juan* Three of the 'Classic of Lu Ban', a collection of seventy-one quatrains describing the benefits and perils of different sites and layouts of land. Some of these have immediate relevance to gardens. For example:

If there is a rock resembling a wine jar,
The house changes into a 'site of fullness'.
The family will be rich, and as soon as a wish is pronounced,
Gold and silver are poured out by the peck.

Or again:

There may be a triple rock at the back of the house,
But the granaries will be full of grain.
Rocks behind the house mean average luck,
But if there is a pond as well, one will be completely at leisure.[32]

The accompanying images (illus. 46) show the kind of elaborately contorted rock that could be found in gardens, and it is certainly

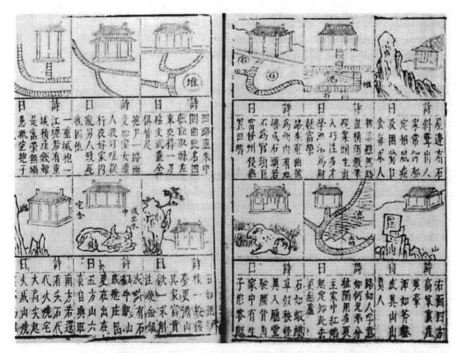

46 Auspicious and inauspicious configurations of landscape, woodblock print, from the *Classic of Lu Ban* (*Lu Ban jing*), contained in the *Complete Book of the Geomancy of Dwellings and the Creation of Happiness* (*Xiang zhai zao fu quan shu*).

plausible that individual stones and *jia shan*, or 'artificial mountains', were placed in a way that was deemed to have a beneficial influence on the household. At the very least, extremely pointed forms, associated with the element 'Fire', were to be avoided, given the risk of an incendiary outbreak they might bring upon the property.

The links between geomancy and aesthetics were flexible ones, both being modulated by the criteria of 'suitability', which is frequently invoked in discussions on how to make a fine garden, or a fine dwelling. An early seventeenth-century geomantic text, the 'Complete Book of Creating Good Luck in Houses of All Directions' (*Ba zhai zao fu zhou shu*), puts it in this way:

The shape of a house is of the highest importance. If the shape (*xing xiang*) is unfavourable, the house will be hard to live in definitively. Whether a house is favourable or unfavourable, unlucky or lucky, can be told by the eye. As a rule, a house is favourable if it is square and straight, plain and neat, and pleasing to the eye. If it is too high and large, or too small and tumbledown, so as to be unpleasing to the eye, then it is unfavourable.[33]

Though framed in relatively simple language, this is essentially the same argument as that put forward at almost exactly the same period in Wen Zhenheng's 'Treatise on Superfluous Things':

In general, the form should follow the function, since everything has that which is suitable to it; it is better to be antique and eschew the fashionable, to be simple and eschew the skilful, to be plain and eschew vulgarity; for a graceful sparseness, an elegant purity, arises from the basic nature. It is not something which can be lightly discussed by those who have to strive to explain things.[34]

We have already seen how Xie Zhaozhe, in his discussion of geomancy with regard to graves in his native Fujian, complains that all the rich are essentially allowing aesthetic criteria to override those of geomancy when, having obtained land which is 'basically excellent', they go on to modify it by large-scale construction work, out of fear that it is 'not beautiful to look at'.[35] His description of the steps then taken to remedy these aesthetic defects, with the owners choosing to 'construct mountains of earth, convert fields into slopes, surrounding them with walls and leading in water, building bridges and constructing terraces', might equally be one of the many formulaic complaints made about the excesses of the wealthy in garden construction, where exactly the same language is used. Perhaps this interpenetration of geomancy and aesthetics is more easily grasped if we consider that they are applied equally to sites, graves and gardens, as walled and tree-filled spaces which exist to display the prestige, the social prominence, the wealth and the taste of the families that constructed them. It would be hardly surprising, therefore, if graves and gardens were treated in some ways alike.

Such late Ming writing as is explicitly concerned with garden construction displays relatively little overt concern with geomancy. Nevertheless it is noticeable how in the chapter on 'Dwelling and Cottages' in his 'Treatise on Superfluous Things' Wen Zhenheng makes rather frequent use of the term *ji*, 'taboo', when describing unacceptable details of the structure of buildings, or the layout of structures. For example, a propos of paths, he says, 'At every entrance to a gate [the path] must curve slightly; too straight is tabooed'. He certainly uses it of buildings many more times than he does of writing utensils or other moveable luxuries.[36] This is very much a word from the geomantic treatises, and from the 'Classic of Lu Ban',[37] a word that has its origins in the archaic language of the 'Book of Changes'. Wen also uses the quintessentially geomantic term *xue*, in the statement that the recluse's dwelling is a 'lair'.[38] In his discussion of rocks, pride of place is given to the famous sonorous stones from Lingbi county in Anhui province, the most attractive of which are said to be in the form of 'a reclining ox' (*wo niu*).[39] This very shape of stone is the subject of one of the admonitory quatrains in the 'Classic of Lu Ban':

> If there is a rock resembling a reclining ox,
> The site becomes a 'bringer of farms and fields'.
> And if there are hills all round the place,
> Domestic animals will thrive well.[40]

The congruence here seems too close to be merely a coincidence, and we therefore have geomancy used to smuggle into the aestheticized garden an unspoken concern with the prosperity of the productive estates of the family.

Geomantic attitudes, or geomantic awareness, may pervade a text like the 'Treatise on Superfluous Things', though few very explicit connections are made. Perhaps they were so obvious the author simply had no need to. The same thing is not quite true of Ji Cheng's 'Craft of Gardens', written in the following decade. Here the very few references to geomancy are concerned with advising the prospective garden builder not to pay too much attention to its strictures. There is certainly an assumption that a geomancer will be involved in the choice of the site for a garden (although, as we have seen, the skill may actually lie in choosing the moment to begin work on a site already selected for other reasons). The first section of the treatise is concerned with the selection of a site, and is entitled *Xiang di*, using a word that in the context of studying the human face rather than the surface of the earth means 'physiognomy', in the sense of fortune-telling from the lineaments of the countenance.[41] One sentence in this passage reads:

When you are taking geomantic readings to locate the garden, it is advantageous to have an area of water, and when starting to work on the main plan, you should go straight to the water source.

In the section on the layout of buildings within the garden, which is described as the single most important element in its success, the author firmly states that 'In choosing the direction the buildings face in, do not be bound by what the geomancer tells you'.[42] Again there is no sense that one should dispense with the services of a geomancer, whose skills might be all the more necessary to negate any bad influences resulting from an overridingly aesthetic choice of disposition of the garden's structure. However, on the whole there is less of a geomantic 'feel' about 'The Craft of Gardens' than there is in the 'Treatise on Superfluous Things' (there are, for example, no 'reclining ox'-shaped rocks), something that is not entirely surprising given the emphasis in the former text on placing one's trust entirely in a wholly different kind of specialist, the aesthetically informed master of the craft of landscape design, none other than Ji Cheng himself.

I have argued that geomancy was a widely disseminated element in the mentality of the Ming elite, which pervaded almost at an unconscious level their thinking about landscape. It was a part, but only a part, of the body of knowledge subsumed under the title of 'numerology', or *shu xue*. It is now time to examine the impact of another part of that body on the Ming reading of land and landscape, in a way that will take us away from gardens and towards the larger landscape of fields within which they were set. This is the subject of mensuration, and in particular of the planar geometry that was of such intimate concern to the Ming state and to those members of the elite (potentially every single one of them) who acted as the agents of its governance. Number, and the measurement that it made possible, had a practical as well as a spiritual significance.

MEASUREMENT AND MAPPING

The Ming polity rested on the ownership and taxation of productive land, and on control over the labour to work it. Although by the Ming period a private market in land was universal across the empire, all educated people would have been aware of statements in classical texts of political economy, asserting the state's ultimate ownership (embodied in the person of the emperor), and its right periodically to redistribute land.[43] The utopian 'well field system', in which equally sized rectangular parcels of land were allotted to taxpayers, may have been accepted as a device of the ancient sage–kings that could not effectively be revitalized in a decadent age, but there is evidence that, at least on the north China plain, such state-ordained, rectilinear topographies dating back at least one thousand years did exist and do still exist on the ground.[44] A study based on aerial photographs suggests powerfully the ability of the medieval Chinese state in its dry agriculture heartland to impose patterns of land management, if not of landholding, which speak eloquently of its normative power. Such physical regularity had probably never been a feature of the lower Yangtze area, and it certainly was not so in the sixteenth century.[45] That is not to say that there was not a network, at least on the conceptual level, of state topography cast over the landscape of the Suzhou region. The county (xian) might have been the basic building block of administration, but recent studies have shown that the sub-county units of cantons, townships and wards had a greater impact on the organization of social life than was hitherto accepted.[46] This was due to an acceptance by the state of the 'natural' geography of the region, rather than an attempt to impose an unfeasibly regular system, which would have involved major redistribution of land. Not that major changes of ownership arrangement did not also take place at the command of the state. As the power-base of a rival claimant for the imperial throne, Suzhou was ever under the particular disfavour of Zhu Yuanzhang, the Ming founder. Most of the land in Suzhou prefecture was technically confiscated from its owners in the early Ming (making the survival of the Wu family's Eastern Estate all the more miraculous), though in fact no state agency ever administered it, and the rent on the land was simply merged with the land tax. At the beginning of the Ming period, private property was, in the words of the leading scholar of the subject 'insignificant' in the Yangtze delta. Beginning in 1547, the government simply wrote off its property in land, returning it formally to private ownership, in 'one of the milestones of Ming financial history'. The back rents were shared out among all landowners, significantly raising the burden per acre on everyone, and generating major dissatisfaction among the elite.[47] When in mid-century this was compounded by the pressure of a new and more accurate land survey, these grievances became ever more acute.

Taxation of the land depended above all on number, on the accurate surveying of land areas, and the registering of those areas in two complementary forms of document, both of which included graphic representations of the terrain involved. These in theory were the 'yellow registers' (huang ce), which showed each individual piece of land with details of its owner and its tax liability, and the 'fish-scale map registers' (yu lin tu ce), which revealed the interrelation of all the plots in a given area, locked together like the scales of a fish. Accurate and prompt collection of the land tax depended on these cadastral surveys, which were therefore of the utmost importance. As with many early modern states, in Ming China the link between the possession of maps and the possession of power over the land represented in them was quite explicit. Security at the main depository of the cadastral maps in the secondary capital of Nanjing, on an island in the middle of a lake which was itself walled all around, was extremely tight.[48] Geographical information in general was treated as a state secret, and even local officials were only allowed to see the central copies of the maps (as opposed to the copies held locally) on a strict 'need-to-know' basis. In 1522 a Korean interpreter bought in a Peking bookshop a copy of the comprehensive geography of the empire, the Da Ming yi tong zhi ('Comprehensive Gazetteer of the Great Ming'). An official complained that 'No foreigner should be allowed to purchase books of this kind', and the work was confiscated, the unfortunate Koreans being confined to their compound, their shopping privileges not restored until 1534.[49] Although we have very little evidence for the place of these real maps in everyday life, we can guess that they played a major part in forming the mental picture of the landscape held by every landowner, or at least by his agents responsible for management of an estate. It would be extremely valuable to know whether maps of any kind, either individual productions or copies of the 'yellow registers', were kept by families, and to know something of how they were used. They seem, for example, not to have been used in arguing land cases before a magistrate, but were they ever produced for the kind of private elite dispute mediator represented by Wen Zhengming in his retirement? The collected works of certain Ming individuals do contain representations of their landed property, and they appear also in certain Ming family genealogies.[50] Maps may have been all the more necessary in that a given family's property was likely to consist not of a compact and homogeneous latifundium, but of a scattering of fields across quite a wide area.[51] It has been demonstrated that any plot larger than two mu (roughly the size of four tennis-courts) had to be discounted on selling, because only a small percentage of buyers could afford a piece of that size. A free market in land therefore had the effect of accelerating the breaking up of the land into ever smaller units.[52] The situation was further complicated by the fact that the land the state and the elite sought to exploit in the Suzhou region was literally shifting under their feet. Water-management practices that were profitable in the short term increased the severity and frequency of floods, which had the effect of totally altering the topography. The landscape was actually, as well as figuratively 'restless'. This rendered the fish-scale map registers particularly pointless, as they were not updated to reflect the constant flux of appearing and disappearing land.[53] The frequent changes in the ownership of gardens, even their physical disappearance and reappearance, which are referred to in the sources, make them more, not less, like other types of landholding. This was exacerbated from about the beginning of the fifteenth century, with the withdrawal to the cities of most of the landowning class, and their consequent loss of interest in maintaining drainage and irrigation facilities for the public good.[54] According to regulations promulgated in the late fifteenth century, responsibility for the upkeep of the dikes facing on to a watercourse rested with the individual proprietors, in proportion to keep the amount of land they possessed that fronted directly onto the water. This land was the most desirable, favoured by better irrigation, access to the fertile mud necessary for manuring the fields, and ease of transport of the harvested crops. The creeks bordering these fields were themselves pieces of private property, which might be owned by absentee landlords interested only in the fishing rights and profits from the sale of the valuable mud.

Faced with this problem, the state attempted to alter the basis on which the obligation to maintain dikes and waterways was calculated, from one based on the length of property fronting onto the water to one based on the total area of land owned. This change in the relationship between inner and outer, periphery and centre, began to be discussed c. 1500, and was complete by the end of the century.[55] It clearly made *area*, rather than linear measurement, the key issue between the individual owner and the state, and it did so at exactly the point that the question of land area, and the measurement of land, was pushed even more forcefully to the forefront of the elite's consciousness by the first serious attempt since the founding of the dynasty to resurvey landholding and record it in accordance with actual conditions on the ground. The fact that this survey was carried out using an entirely new method of calculating land area meant that questions of surveying, of geometry and of number may well have been closer to the surface of consciousness of many members of the elite than traditional accounts of the classical humanistic education would normally credit.

How much mathematics, and what sort of mathematics did the educated elite of Jiangnan know? Teleologically oriented accounts of the development of Chinese mathematics view the sixteenth century as pretty much a dark age, devoid of important advances in technique, a stagnant period between the achievements of the Yuan dynasty and the introduction of Euclidean geometry and other European mathematical practices at the very beginning of the seventeenth century. However, this fails to take account of changes in the social role of mathematics, and of important changes too in the application of already existing techniques, particularly in the field of geometry and surveying.[56] These were the cornerstones of Ming mathematics, the areas to which manuals and textbooks devote the greatest amount of space. This had always been the case.[57] As Kang Chao points out, however, these formulae, which remained in use down to the Ming dynasty contain no example of the measurement of an irregular quadrilateral, in actual practice one of the most common forms in which a field could be found, particularly in south China. The method empirically used between the Han and the Ming for determining the surface area of this shape involved a crude multiplication of half of the products of the addition of opposite pairs of sides. This method of treating a quadrilateral as if it were a rectangle always resulted in an overestimate.[58] In 1578, under the direction of Grand Secretary Zhang Juzheng, orders were given to every magistrate to survey the land in his jurisdiction using a new method, called the *kai fang fa*, 'creating a square method'. In this method, any quadrilateral to be measured is first surrounded notionally by a rectangle, which can easily be measured accurately. From this total are then subtracted the areas of the right-angled triangles bounded by the notional exterior and the actual field boundary. These are also easy to get right, and so an accurate area for the field can be arrived at. This relatively simple method, which needed no more tools than the chain or the surveyor's measuring-rod, was still to prove too cumbersome in practice, and it was never used again after this survey, which lasted from 1578 to 1582.[59]

It is reasonable to assume that the magistrates who were ordered to undertake this land survey using the new technique had some understanding of what they were being ordered to do. As we have seen, no very high level of numeracy was involved. For example, although he is hardly of significance to the history of mathematics, the amount of attention given to questions of land surveying by the famous official Hai Rui (1513–87; DMB 474–9), especially during his tenure of office as magistrate of Chun'an and as governor of Nan Zhili province, based in Suzhou (1569–70), speaks eloquently of the importance he attached to it, including the technical aspects that are often deemed to be of less importance by humanistically trained modern sinologists.[60] His essay 'On the Principles of the Measurements of Fields' (*Liang tian ze li*) takes the putative reader, presumably a local official like himself, step by step through all the procedures involved, beginning with the marking of a blank sheet of paper with the points of the compass. There are also helpful diagrams of the types of document that should result from the exercise (illus. 47, 48).[61] Hai Rui's relative success in resurveying Suzhou, achieved in the teeth of considerable opposition from landholding families, both with and without official status, was instrumental in convincing Zhang Juzheng that a new cadastral survey of the entire empire would be feasible. He was not the only official to carry out a mapping project of his area on his own initiative.[62]

A conscientious official was certainly more likely to encounter opposition than support from the locally powerful, given that the main aim of the survey was less to increase state revenues from the land tax than it was to curb simple tax evasion and equalize the tax burden. The point was to ensure social harmony by preventing the rich from offloading the entire tax burden for a district onto the poor. When Tu Long (1542–1605; DMB 1324–7) attempted to carry out the survey as magistrate of Qingbu, east of Suzhou, between 1578 and 1582, he was thwarted by the influence of the retired grand secretary, Xu Jie (1503–83; DMB 570–6), whose family had huge quantities of land in the area, which they were unwilling to have recorded. Several members of Wen Zhengming's family occupied the kind of posts in which issues of land and the measurement of land were prime concerns: his father, Wen Lin, was both a magistrate and a prefect, his son, Wen Peng, was magistrate of Pujiang in Zhejiang province, and his grandson, Wen Yuanfa, was (most unusually) magistrate of the same county, during the decades when the great cadastral survey was carried out. Wen Yuanfa alludes in broad terms in his autobiography to the difficulties of collecting taxes in Pujiang, where 'the land is barren and the people are devious and addicted to

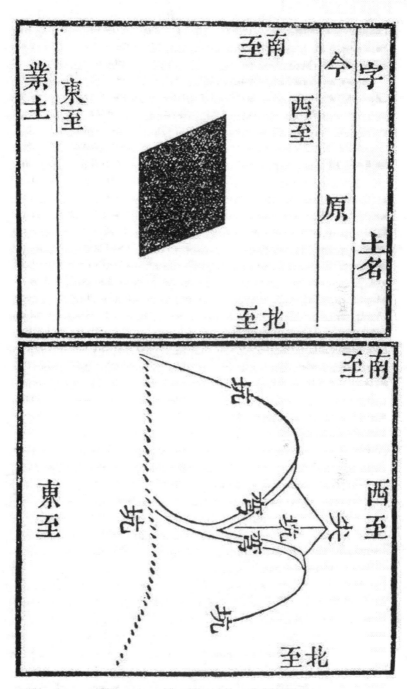

47 How to record the ownership of irregular plots of land.
48 How to record the position of plots of land.
Two woodblock print diagrams from Hai Rui, *Works of Hai Rui* (*Hai Rui ji*), after *Hai Zhingjie wen ji* (1594).

trickery'. The local powerful families attempted to bribe him, then to threaten him, finally to impeach him, if he did not relax his rigour, although, in the end, he survived the ordeal.[63]

For a man like Wen Yuanfa, and equally for his opponents among the wealthy of Pujiang, knowing how to calculate the area of a piece of land was hardly an arcane, if still not an everyday skill. It was necessary to the magistrate, for the purpose of registration and taxation, but it was necessary too for the private landholder (often one and the same person at a different stage in his career), since land had to be bought and sold and divided equally among a number of heirs. There are some intriguing implications of this for an understanding of the visual culture of the Ming period. Michael Baxandall has argued that volume and the representation of volume was an issue among the producers and consumers of painting in fourteenth-century Italy, men whose education was dominated by mathematical exercises in which gauging – the accurate measurement of volume – played a central role.[64] While it can in no sense be argued that any mathematical skill played an equally prominent part in a Ming landowner's education, the fact remains that if a Ming gentleman knew any mathematics at all it was likely to be a simple planar geometry. How such a way of looking at area, and in particular at a number of interlocking irregular planar fields, might play out in a manner of regarding space and pictorial space is a tantalizing subject, but one that would take us even further from the central issue of land and landscape (illus. 40).

The wide dissemination of geometrical consciousness, to put it no more strongly than that, in the sixteenth century was not matched by any very great measure of prestige. Quite the reverse. Ming calculations were by and large put to practical ends, chiefly land measurement, as we have seen, but including other types of sum necessary to a commercial society. Commercial growth meant that more calculations were now being done more often by more people, and were often now beginning to involve the relatively new device of the abacus. The abacus is attested by pictorial evidence from 1436, and is mentioned in an essay of 1513 by Li Dongyang, celebrator of Wu Kuan's Eastern Estate.[65] The associations of the subject with mercantile operations made it all the more imperative for those who wished to be 'pure and lofty' to distance themselves from the very concept of number, as 'practical studies' came to be seen as irremediably tainted. This rejection of mathematical knowledge thus becomes a historically specific, quite recent event rather than a timeless characteristic of 'the Chinese scholar'. Even in the mid-

Ming the wider elite may not have been so absolute. The skilled Ming eye, looking down on a garden perhaps from an eminence, may well have been able to add an appraisal of area, of the differing proportions of irregularly shaped water and disparate parcels of land (which, after all, only mirrored the wider landscape beyond the walls), to other types of appreciation.

THE AESTHETICS OF OWNERSHIP

If the garden/*yuan* stood in formal opposition to the field/*tian* in the Ming system of categorizing landscape, it did so also by virtue of its coherence. It was a single place, where a family's fields could be very widely scattered. In this respect a garden is an 'anti-field', but an opposite that serves to sharpen the definition of what it opposes. One could go further and argue that the garden of the late fifteenth century, such as the Eastern Estate, with its very clear connections to an idea of fruitfulness and production, was a sort of symbolic core of a family or individual's dispersed landholdings, much as the villa of the contemporary Venetian *terraferma* acted as a symbolic centre for a number of parcels of land.[66] The Eastern Estate may be categorized as a 'garden' in the gazetteer, but both its name (*zhuang* is very close in usage to the Italian 'villa') and its gathering into a small compass of several types of land use (rice, wheat, mulberries, fruit, vegetables) mark it as an ideal estate in little, where the whole can be taken in visually and without the necessity of fatiguing excursions to different localities beyond the comfort of the city walls. Both 'estate' and 'garden' are property, subsumable under the same heading and subject to the same legal and social constraints as to their disposition, at least formally. These constraints are historically specific, and 'property' is thus every bit as much a culturally constructed category as 'garden' itself, subject similarly to historical mutation and to conflicting interpretations.

Much secondary literature on Chinese society at this period alludes to what are considered to be the 'weak' property concepts with which it operated. An oft-cited article by H. F. Schurman proposes the lack of an idea of freely disposable private property as one of the crucial reasons for the different patterns of development in early modern China and Europe (and, by extension, for the underdevelopment of the former).[67] This to a large extent disregards the actual historical circumstances of the emergence of the idea of 'private property' in European countries, where, for example in England, it can be shown not to have emerged until 1656, at a point when the previously dominant rights of the Crown were in abeyance.[68] The idea of private property in land as the *ne plus ultra* of modernity and as being a wholly desirable attribute unique to Western civilization over a very long historical span, has a considerable genealogy in orientalist writing as well as in more recent scholarship.[69] It is invoked by Frederic Mote in a passage that makes an explicit contrast between a 'private' involuted China and an externally oriented, more dynamic Italy, and which is worth repeating here. For Mote, the 'often noted' fact of weak property concepts

may explain the lack of heavy investments in ostentatious family buildings; traditional China's elite seem never to have equated elite status with the use of magnificent buildings, no matter how splendid their lifestyles otherwise were. The *palazzi* of Renaissance Italian cities did more than protect their noble inhabitants; they outfaced each other in an enduring confrontation of status and property, one in which princes had to out-rival counts and dukes, and kings were pressed to grander demonstrations. Chinese society displays different mechanisms.[70]

Coupled with this has been an assertion that the Chinese rich did not spend on external display (e.g. on the facades of their houses) or on what was effectively public space: there were to be no *piazze* in China.[71] This of course begs the question of just how 'public' the *piazze* of early modern Italy actually were (in Verona, at least in the sixteenth century, the main square was becoming 'an increasingly exclusive precinct whose dignity and *gravitas* had to be upheld', and where first stalls and benches, and subsequently wheeled vehicles of any kind, were banned).[72] That aside, it might be wondered just how much difference there in fact is between the facade of an (inaccessible) Roman palace and the grandiose gate of the (relatively accessible) Garden of the Grand Preceptor, in telling the passer-by that the owner of this property is an important person. To sixteenth-century European visitors to China, the splendid facades of the houses of the rich and powerful were a very visible part of the contemporary street-scene. Above all, it could be argued that these status displays share the fact that they are taking place in a context of *competition*, in a fluid and unstable social climate where it is a matter of some debate as to who are the powerful and the important. In an 'enduring confrontation' between clearly differentiated hierarchically ordered persons (counts, dukes), there were certain mechanisms, like the all-important matter of precedence in procession, which could not be challenged, or could only be so at points of crisis. In the much more fluid, competitive (one might say 'modern') society of Ming

China, competition through cultural display played an even greater part than it did in contemporary Europe. The display of culturally prestigious property, like fabulously expensive paintings and antiques, or urban real estate configured as a great garden, was one of the surest ways of establishing its possessors in a prominent role. An example of this kind of brutally obvious competitive behaviour, which incidentally involved the owners of the sites of two of the most famous of mid-Ming Suzhou gardens, is recounted by the early nineteenth-century chronicler of anecdotes about Suzhou, Qian Yong. In an entry headed 'A Wealth Competition', he tells the story of a certain Mr Zhu, who in the Kangxi reign (1662–1722) was 'the richest person in the Suzhou region', and who lived on the site of the old Eastern Estate of Wu Kuan. He became involved in a bout of competitive consumption with a neighbour, a certain Zhao, who was an officer in the forces of the local satrap Wu Sangui (1612–78).[73] The feud between Zhao and Zhu began when the former staged a feast at which silver drinking-cups were given to all the guests as keepsakes. Zhu retaliated by hanging up lanterns made from strings of real pearls at the New Year festivities, whereupon Zhao sent his servants round to smash them (the anecdote would be meaningless if the decorations on Zhu's property were not generally accessible as part of the festival). Zhu then invited Wang Yongning – Wu's son-in-law – round to dinner, 'and when the feast broke up they wandered in the garden, where the shattered lanterns were placed to one side'. Wang asked his host how this had happened, and Zhu blamed Zhao, but tactfully pointed out that he had done nothing about it, since Zhao was under the patronage of the great Wu Sangui. In deference to his host, Wang Yongning then had Zhao transferred to another post, leaving Zhu the winner of this costly potlatch. That it should have taken place in a garden is perhaps fitting, if they were indeed – as I have argued – now seen principally as sites of conspicuous consumption, as property to be flaunted.

But who were the possessors of property? Who owned things? At a theoretical level the imperial state had many pre-eminent rights, though in a fact a private market in land had long been accepted. At a ritual level, and particularly in association with the acquisition of land for graves, divine powers might need to be consulted. Each county, sub-prefecture and prefecture had its *cheng huang*, usually translated as 'city god', though their powers extended over the entire landscape of the administrative unit, not just the urban administrative centre. Worshipped by officials like Wen Lin and Wen Yuanfa, they were enthroned in halls decorated with murals of 'mountains and rivers' (*shan shui*), presumably (though this is not explicit in the source) the actual landscape over which they presided. Unfortunately, we have no idea what these murals looked like, though they once must have been familiar components of the Ming elite's visual culture, and which combined the concerns of an official state topography with geomantic considerations.[74] The individual as well as the state might have to deal with the claims of higher powers on the land. The practice of drawing up *mai di juan*, 'land purchase certificates', in which the burial tract was 'bought' from the deity of the soil, was not a strictly canonical one, but it was certainly indulged in by the Ming elite.[75]

It may well be correct to say that collectivities such as families 'owned' much of the property in China, and other members of the family might in some cases have pre-emptive rights of purchase. The Song Confucian theorist Sima Guang objected strenuously to the very notion of 'individual', as opposed to 'family', property.[76] However, there was no doubt that in actual practice 'the household property in its entirety was the possession of the father' and all decisions as to its disposition rested with him.[77] Families, being themselves sites of inequality, cannot have 'interests' vested in property, and in Ming China it was adult males with no living fathers who were the real owners of property. This last qualification was important. In Confucian theory of the time, it was not possible for a man to own any property in the lifetime of his father, even if, like Wen Peng, he was into his early sixties before his father died.

With regard to gardens, we have seen how many of them are named with a formula such as 'The Garden of the X Family', usually using the words *jia* or *shi* for 'family'. Yet we have also seen how many of the most famous gardens were closely tied to an *individual* owner, and to that adult male's sense of personal identity and self-presentation in the wider world. The possibility that this was an unresolved area of tension in an age witnessing both a growing free market in land and philosophical and aesthetic addresses to the question of the integrity and nature of the individual personality, should not immediately be set aside, and has implications for the validity of C. B. Macpherson's classic theory of 'possessive individualism' as a mainspring in the development of European (specifically English Protestant) states.[78] It may have been the case that in some instances the creation of a garden acted as a focus of family solidarity, symbolizing its collective strength in an area and at a period when the formal attributes of a cohesive lineage, such as collective worship of ancestors and a printed genealogy, were relatively rare. Harriet Zurndorfer has shown how in sixteenth-century Huizhou the creation of a building acted as a way of focusing kinship feelings, rather than simply memorializing those that already existed, and she has drawn parallels between this and the building of *loggie* in Italy at the same period and for the same purposes.[79] A late sixteenth-century Jiangnan garden was situated fully within this area of tension, on the boundaries between theoretically collective property and the personality of the actually fully autonomous owner. Just how much authority that owner could enforce, even from beyond the grave, and how close the identification between individual and garden could on occasion be, is seen in another mid-Qing anecdote abut the Returning to the Fields Garden, laid out in Suzhou in the early seventeenth century by Wang Xinyi:

It is still lived in by the sons and grandsons of the Wang family, though it is said they have wished to sell it on several occasions. However there has suddenly appeared in the garden an indistinct figure in a red robe and gauze hat [i.e. Ming official dress], wailing and weeping until dawn, as if he could not bear to be separated from something he loved, so no one has dared to buy it.[80]

For every such case of filiality, there are several where the reverse is the case. Although there is no contemporary evidence for it, numerous later sources tell the story of how the Garden of the Unsuccessful Politician was gambled away by the improvident sons of its builder. Xie Zhaozhe commented on the phenomenon of once-great members of the bureaucracy turning to the construction of lavish mansions in their retirement, these serving only to act as a source of dissension among their descendants. For by tying up a great deal of the family wealth in a mansion or a garden, an individual was storing up considerable trouble against the day when it was time to divide the family 'property' in its widest sense. The principle of equal shares for all male heirs was never, it would seem, set aside, and ingenious solutions had to be adopted to keep a physical piece of property intact. The very rare survival of an entire village of Ming or early Qing dwellings virtually intact is ascribed to the practice of lineage leaders dividing property *horizontally* among heirs – the top and bottom halves of a building, for example – so that no brother could take his share without destroying that of the others.[81] An aesthetic garden was like a house, and not like a holding of large amounts of individually quite small fields, in that it could not be divided. Its creation by an individual therefore could not but lead to conflict with the normative methods of property transfer by inheritance, and in this respect it was less like real estate than it was like a painting, similarly valuable but similarly indivisible.

The very great mutability of gardens, as of all landed property, was recognized by Ming, and even more so by Qing, writers. One wrote despairingly of how a relative tried 'to build a property enduring for several hundred years for his descendants. But in less than five or six years his estates and mansions all had new owners, his sons were so poor that they could not maintain themselves'.[82] By the seventeenth century it seems to have been the rule, rather than the exception, for gardens to change hands at least once in a generation. The Garden of the Unsuccessful Politician, or sections of it, had at least fifteen changes of ownership over the three hundred years from the mid-sixteenth century to the mid-nineteenth. In Peking, the Yi Garden belonged to three separate aristocratic families within a century, while the Wu Family Garden in Nanjing changed hands 'several times' in fifty years. Given the rules of inheritance, which demanded the division of property, a given garden site stood a better chance of maintaining its physical integrity if sold in one piece to another family than it did if it passed to the builder's heirs, who may choose to carve it into smaller pieces.

Yet it might be argued that this very fragility and mutability did serve to inscribe the notion of 'property' even more firmly on the landscape of the garden. Separation and potential loss, Susan Stewart has argued, are central to the construction of the notion of 'ownership', which cannot exist without them.[83] As a piece of land that could be lost in memorable and recordable circumstances, the garden is constantly gesturing towards the wider realm of transfers of economic resources in land, on which the very existence of the Ming polity and the Ming elite depended.

Conclusion

The issue for June 1957 of *Wenwu cankao ziliao* ('Reference Materials on Cultural Relics'), the chief contemporary archaeological journal in China, is in some ways a poignant document. Devoted – uniquely in this journal's history – to the subject of gardens, it also includes the account of a meeting of workers in the field of culture, archaeology and art history called to address Mao Zedong's recently issued adjuration to 'Let a hundred flowers blossom, a hundred schools of thought contend.' Speaker after speaker accepts the implicit invitation the slogan extends to speak freely on questions concerning the political and professional issues of the day, and criticisms of the Communist Party's leading role are freely, if respectfully, given.[1] The subsequent history is well known: most of the critics whose opinions were voiced in that issue suffered at the least loss of employment, and at the other extreme imprisonment and persecution in the Party backlash that followed.[2] The poignancy is perhaps enhanced for the modern reader by the jarring juxtaposition of writing about gardens, supposedly sites of calm, peace and reclusion, with the most trenchant reminder of politics asserting and inserting itself in the field of scholarship. Gardens and strident controversy are not supposed to cohabit, even in the pages of a learned archaeological journal.

The poignancy is made possible by a particular view of 'the Chinese garden', which is historically specific. It can probably be located in time to the decades after the Taiping rebellion of the 1860s, and factors such as increased Western tourism in China and the accessibility of Suzhou by rail from the great port of Shanghai played a major role. It can be fairly easily demonstrated that, in the later Qing period, Suzhou, which is now the 'garden city' *par excellence* of the tourist brochures, was not particularly renowned for its gardens (as opposed to its other cultural delights) on an empire-wide scale. Its primacy was contested by Yangzhou to the north, one eighteenth-century source from which boasts: 'Hangzhou is famous for its lakes and hills, Suzhou is famous for its shops and markets, Yangzhou is famous for its gardens.'[3] When the Qianlong emperor visited Suzhou in the mid-eighteenth century he saw only two urban gardens in Suzhou, both of them distinguished more for their lengthy history than for their present condition (they were the Surging Waves Pavilion and the Lion Grove).[4] The Frenchman Isidore Hedde, who was in China from 1843 to 1846 in the immediate aftermath of the first Opium War, visited Suzhou and drew a map of it, on which gardens do not feature at all. His published catalogue of the goods he brought back from China does, however, contain a description of a sketch of a generalized 'Jardin occidental', which may or may not be the first European account of a Jiangnan garden since Matteo Ricci:

Grottoes. Islands of floating stone. Artificial mountains. Dwarf trees in the form of pagodas and animals. Crags of marble and fountains of fantastic design. Strange flowers. Houses of pleasure and relaxation.[5]

This terse fragment of orientalist stage-direction, reading almost like an account of the opening scene of an operetta set in far Cathay, yet contains all the elements that will resound through nineteenth- and early twentieth-century texts on 'the Chinese garden'. This is as yet not a localized phenomenon, and certainly Suzhou's paramountcy is not remarked on by early travel writers. The building of the railway connecting Suzhou to Shanghai in 1911,[6] by removing the need for a fairly length journey by boat, brought the city within range of day-trips, and possibly also made it a more attractive location to wealthy Chinese with business interests in the great port. By 1936 it was possible (for F. R. Nance) to write a detailed guidebook to Suzhou, naming it for the first time as 'the garden city', an appellation it retains in travel literature down to the present day.[7] Suzhou has an equally prominent role in Dorothy Graham's monograph of 1938.

But 'the gardens of Suzhou' remain a contested object at this period, contested from within learned Chinese circles. No less a figure than Liu Dunzhen, whose account of an investigation into the early architectural monuments of Suzhou was also published in 1936, goes out of his way to dismiss them as insignificant. He found only four sites to visit: the Yi Yuan, the Garden of the Unsuccessful Politician, the Lion Grove and the Wang Garden, and remarks that 'the first two are entirely commonplace in layout, and have no special features worth noting'.[8] This contrasts sharply with Nance's enthusiasm for the Garden of the Unsuccessful Politician, which 'even in its present state of dilapidation, has a lure and a beauty all its own'.[9] How can we explain this widely divergent perception of the same space? Surely the conflict is not an accident, but rather a reflection on Liu's refusal to accept the Western tourist appropriation of China's cultural heritage into a form fitting its own particular needs. Liu was prominent in the creation of a discourse of architectural history in China, the recoverer of early texts and surveyor of surviving early buildings, and it was these that engaged his attention. He is not ignorant of the enthusiasm with which writers like Nance and Graham embrace the gardens of Suzhou as a synecdoche for 'the Chinese garden', which is itself deployed in their writing as a synecdoche for 'Chinese culture' or 'China' as a whole. He simply rejects the ordering of cultural priorities it implies. The fact that after 1949 Liu was to be one of the most prominent scholars working on the history, restoration and architecture of garden sites in Suzhou is therefore quite easily explicable by the changing political context, in which the physical removal of Western systems of ordering and categorization allows gardens to be absorbed without conflict into the wider notion of a 'national heritage'. The gardens of Suzhou have remained there ever since, and have been the object of continuously growing enthusiasm and study, culminating recently in the opening of a museum in the city devoted to the subject.[10]

The insertion of the idea of the garden into rapidly shifting cultural and political contexts in this century may be particularly noticeable, but it would be wrong to contrast this with long centuries in which it sustained stable and unchanging meanings that were generally asserted to at all levels of 'Chinese society'. I have argued that, even within the relatively circumscribed group of the Jiangnan elite, the word yuan could evoke a wide range of actual practices and cultural constructs. It could not float transcendentally apart from, but was rather firmly imbricated in, discourses of property, social status, art, numerology and the understanding of plants. These were by no means its only areas of reference. If I have said relatively little about the cosmological connections of the garden as a microcosm, it is because this aspect of Chinese garden culture has been relatively well treated, but also because it has been treated in a rather ahistorical framework, with evidence gathered from widely different historical periods to support the thesis of the garden as a mysterious sacred landscape.[11] The sixteenth- and early seventeenth-century sources with which I have been concerned do not foreground these issues. That is not to say that they were not of importance at an earlier or a later date, or to deny that they have explicatory force for practitioners of garden design now.

There are yet more garden histories that could be written. For example, I have said nothing about the relationship of gardens with temples, or with the 'academies' (shu yuan) that were such important entities in the late Ming, though we know for example that the monk Shilian (1633–?1702) remodelled the gardens of several Buddhist institutions, and it has been recently shown that they were an intense focus of elite patronage at precisely the period I have been dealing with.[12] One other intriguing history is that of gardens in Chinese dreams. In the late Ming text *Zhou gong jie meng quan shu* ('The Duke of Zhou's Complete Book of the Interpretation of Dreams'), gardens feature as one of the twenty-seven categories into which dreams are categorized. They are equally a setting for the numerous dreams recorded in *biji* literature of the period, and potentially provide yet another point of departure for studying the role of gardens in the imaginative life of at least the literate class of the time.

What I have offered is largely an account of writing about gardens, and writing in early modern China was controlled by male members of the elite. A gendered reading of these texts is all that can be offered for now, but it is nevertheless important to consider the possibilities for a study of women's gardens in Ming China. We have seen how in the 'Treatise on Superfluous Things' certain flowers, certain birds and certain styles of ornament are deemed appropriate for women but not for men. The linkage between woman and flowers is regularly made in poetry and prose of the period. In the great Ming novel *Jin ping mei* ('The Golden Lotus' or 'The Plum in the Golden Vase'), women are often present in the garden of the mansion of the *nouveau riche* protagonist Ximen Qing, which incidentally contains a prominent rose arbour, deemed suitable only for women's quarters by the censorious Wen Zhenheng. But we might legitimately ask, *when* are they present, and in whose company are they present? Many of the most memorable 'garden scenes' in the book are ones of transgressive sexual and gastronomic excess. Was there a sense in which the garden was an acceptable site for behaviour deemed unfitting in the house? Were women allowed in the garden on their own? In mansions which had a garden, how did it fit into the rigorously segregated space of men's quarters and women's quarters, to which side did it 'belong', and how does that affect our understanding of layout? There is considerable evidence from the eighteenth century in the oft-cited sections of the novel *Hong lou meng* ('The Story of the Stone', or 'Dream of the Red Chamber'), but this must be treated exactly *as* eighteenth-century evidence, and not as something generally valid for previous or subsequent periods. No one has yet closely analysed the earlier euphuistic description of the garden in *Jin ping mei*, not as a document, but as a literary representation that can tell us something about the role of the garden in the Ming imaginary.[13]

There are yet more unexplored areas of deployment of the idea of the garden in specific historical circumstances in China. A study of

Cantonese shamanism in the third quarter of this century reveals a pervasive belief among its adherents in 'the Heavenly Flower Garden', where every living person is represented by a potted flowering plant.[14] Here is a distinctive non-elite appropriation of the very idea of a garden as an aesthetic site, but one whose history is obscure. Were such ideas current in Canton at the same time as Wen Zhenheng was subsuming the garden into a discourse of 'elegance' as a marker of social status? Have they ever been more widely distributed geographically within China? Further research would be needed before even a tentative answer could be given.

I have tried to see 'a garden' in the terms of the Ming textual record as something which is overdetermined, in the sense that it cannot be reduced to one single 'real' thing (property, the cosmos, the retreat) that it mimetically represents. This is the same as taking the garden for a discursive object, a site able to generate a multitude of readings. All the same, this multitude is not an infinity, but is rather bound by specific historical and geographical circumstances. These meanings have shifted over time, and remain contested, never at rest. In this respect, 'the garden' remains a site of negotiation and dissonance, symbolized by the shifting rankings, even within the short time-span of the last fifty years, of the gardens of Suzhou in terms of their fame, and by the fluctuating physical boundaries of the Garden of the Unsuccessful Politician over the same period.

In much recent cultural theory, the replacement of time by space is promoted as the key turn of the age, where, 'in a poetic condensation, history has been replaced by geography, stories by maps, memories by scenarios'.[15] Some of this theorizing is perhaps weakened by its juxtaposing against the post-modern condition of a stable 'past', when relations between signifier and signified were fixed, known and unproblematic. I have tried to show how the reduction in the number of meanings ascribed to the garden in China is an event of relatively recent times, not sustained by the multiplicity of meanings in which actual sites of the sixteenth and seventeenth centuries could find themselves enmeshed. I have tried deliberately to complicate the picture, and to point towards some of the ways in which the centrality of land in China in the early modern period gave these artefacts their power, while at the same their ability to slip across the margins of cultural categories lends them a richness that is paralleled by few other aspects of the material culture of that time and place.

References

Introduction

1 Ronald Inden, *Imagining India* (Oxford, 1990), p. 149.
2 James Cahill, *Three Alternative Histories of Chinese Painting* (Lawrence, KS, 1988), p. 9.
3 Robin Karson, *Fletcher Steele, Landscape Architect: An Account of the Gardenmaker's Life, 1885–1971* (New York, 1989), pp. 186–90.
4 Fletcher Steele, 'China Teaches: Ideas and Moods from Landscape of the Celestial Empire', *Landscape Architecture*, XXXVII (1946–47), pp. 88–93.
5 Fletcher Steele, *Gardens and People* (Boston, 1964).
6 Steele, 'China Teaches', p. 92, and Steele, *Gardens and People*, p. 205.
7 This is discussed more extensively in Craig Clunas, 'Nature and Ideology in Western Descriptions of the Chinese Garden', in J. Wolschke-Bulmahn, ed., *Nature and Ideology* (forthcoming).
8 J. C. Loudon, *An Encyclopaedia of Gardening . . .* (London, 1834), p. 388.
9 Dorothy Graham, *Chinese Gardens: Gardens of the Contemporary Scene, an Account of their Design and Symbolism* (New York, 1938), p. 3.
10 Wing-Tsit Chan, 'Man and Nature in the Chinese Garden', in Henry Inn, *Chinese Houses and Gardens*, ed. Shao Chang Lee, revd edn (New York, 1950). More recently, Benjamin Wai-Bun Ip, 'The Expression of Nature in Traditional Su Zhou Gardens', *Journal of Garden History*, VI (1986), pp. 125–40.
11 Osvald Sirén, *Gardens of China* (New York, 1949), p. 3; Jeffrey E. Meyer, *The Dragons of Tiananmen: Beijing as a Sacred City* (Columbia, SC, 1991), p. 168.
12 R. Keith Schoppa, *Xiang Lake – Nine Centuries of Chinese Life* (New Haven and London, 1989), p. 34.
13 Inden, p. 3.
14 Edward Said, *Culture and Imperialism* (New York, 1993).
15 Homi K. Bhabha, *The Location of Culture* (London, 1994), p. 66.
16 Mara Miller, 'Gardens as Works of Art: The Problem of Uniqueness', *British Journal of Aesthetics*, XXVI (1986), pp. 252–6, and Mara Miller, *The Garden as an Art* (Albany, 1993).
17 For example, the various essays dating from the mid-1970s on, collected in John Dixon Hunt, *Gardens and the Picturesque: Studies in the History of Landscape Architecture* (Cambridge, MA, 1992).
18 John Brinckerhoff Jackson, *The Necessity for Ruins, and Other Topics* (Amherst, 1980); James Westcoatt, 'Landscapes of Transformation: Lessons from the Earliest Mughal Gardens in India, 1526–1530 AD', *Landscape Journal*, X (1991), pp. 105–14.
19 Denis Cosgrove, *The Palladian Landscape* (University Park, PA, 1993).
20 Thomas Keirstead, *The Geography of Power in Medieval Japan* (Princeton, 1992), also his 'Gardens and Estates: Medievality and Space', *Positions: East Asia Cultures Critique*, I (1993), pp. 289–320.
21 Nicholas Green, 'Rustic Retreats: Visions of the Countryside in Mid-nineteenth-century France' in *Reading Landscape*, ed. Simon Pugh (Manchester and New York, 1990), pp. 161–76 (163).

1 The Fruitful Garden

1 Alfred Schinz, *Cities in China: Urbanization of the Earth / Urbanisierung der Erde*, ed. Wolf Tietze (Berlin and Stuttgart, 1989), p. 192. The larger figure of 23.4 square kilometres appears in Michael Marmé, 'Population and Possibility in Ming (1368–1644) Suzhou: A Quantified Model', *Ming Studies*, XII (1981), pp. 29–64 (57 n.34). For an overview of the city's development see Gao Yongyuan, 'Gudai Suzhou chengshi jingguan de lishi dili toushi, *Lishi dili*, VII (1990), pp. 62–71.

2 Frederick W. Mote and Dennis Twitchett, eds, *The Cambridge History of China*, VII: *The Ming Dynasty, 1368–1644: Part I* (Cambridge, 1988), p. 34 (the siege), p. 123 (the forced emigration of 1370), p. 310 (the flood of 1440), p. 337 (the winter flood of 1454).

3 Wang Qi, *Yu yuan za ji* (preface dated 1500), Yuan Ming biji shiliao congkan edn (Beijing, 1984), *juan* 5, p. 42.

4 F. W. Mote, 'The Transformation of Nanking, 1350–1400', in *The City in Late Imperial China*, ed. G. William Skinner (Stanford, 1977), pp. 101–53 (141–2).

5 Marmé, pp. 36–7.

6 On a first reference to figures mentioned, the page numbers of their entry in the *Dictionary of Ming Biography*, cited as DMB, or failing that in the *Mingren zhuanji ziliao suoyin*, 'Index to Ming Biographical Materials', cited as MRZJ, are given. In cases where an individual's dates of birth or death are not known I have given the year in which they passed the *jinshi*, the highest level of the imperial examination system.

7 A *mu* was the unit of measurement, equivalent in the Ming to approximately one-seventh of an acre.

8 Wang Ao, ed., *Gusu zhi* (1506), Zhongguo shixue congshu facsimile edn (Taibei, 1965), *juan* 32, p. 25a.

9 Marmé, p. 41.

10 The most obvious examples are the estates of Wang Ao himself, and of his brother Wang Quan, which are included in the *Yuan lin*, 'Garden Grove' section of the 1642 Wu county gazetteer. Perhaps convention compelled the compiler not to vaunt his own property, though no such restraint was applied to that of friends and connections. Niu Ruolin and Wang Huanru, eds, *Wu xian zhi*, preface dated 1642, 54 *juan* plus 1 *juan* of illustrations, *juan* 23, pp. 26b–28a. Here are listed Wang Ao's *Xi yuan* and *Zhen shi yuan* and his brother's *Qie shi yuan*, 'where the owner both ploughed and studied', and which was famed for its groves of oranges.

11 On this basis, the most prominent sites are: the 'Splendid Hermitage' (*Yao an*) on the banks of the Songjiang River in Wujiang county (fifteen citations); the Stone Lake Detached Villa (*Shi hu bie shu*) of Fan Chengda (1120–93) (twelve citations); the 'Pleasure Plot' (*Le pu*), the 'Southern Garden' (*Nan yuan*) and the 'Surging Waves Pavilion' (*Cang lang ting*) (all with eleven).

12 *Gusu zhi*, 32, 16a (p. 448).

13 The tomb inscription for his father's first wife (not Wen Zhengming's mother) was provided by Li Dongyang. Wen Zhengming's wife was a granddaughter of Xia Chang. Masahiro Sawada, 'Mindai Soshū Bun-shi no inseki. Gochū bun-en kōsatsu e no tekakari', *Daitō bunka daigaju kiyō (jimbun kagaku)*, XXII (1984), pp. 55–71 (60 and 58).

14 James Cahill, *Parting at the Shore: Painting of the Early and Middle Ming Dynasty, 1368–1580* (New York and Tokyo, 1978), pp. 78–9.

15 *Wen Zhengming ji*, ed. Zhou Daozhen, Shanghai guji chubanshe edn, 2 vols (Shanghai, 1987), I, p. 205. Hereafter cited as WZMJ.

16 Lu Rong, *Shu yuan za ji*, quoted in Ye Jingyuan , *Zhongguo nongxue yichan xuan ji, jia lei di shisi zhong: Gan ju I* (Beijing, 1958), p. 221.

17 John W. Dardess, 'Settlement, Land Use, Labor and Estheticism in T'ai-ho County, Kiangsi', *Harvard Journal of Asiatic Studies*, IL (1990), pp. 295–364.

18 The alternative of 'Garden of the Artless Official', proposed by Jan Stuart, 'Ming Dynasty Gardens Reconstructed in Words and Images', *Journal of Garden History*, X (1990), pp. 162–72, is in many ways superior, but I retain 'Unsuccessful Politician' after some consideration, for the sake of congruence with modern Chinese guidebook usage.

19 Qian Yun, ed., *Classical Chinese Gardens* (Hong Kong and Beijing, 1982), p. 90.

20 Zhang Tingyu, *Ming shi*, Zhonghua shuju edn, 28 vols (Beijing, 1974), XVIII, pp. 4801–3. Hereafter cited as MS.

21 WZMJ, I, pp. 488–9.

22 WZMJ, I, pp. 438–40.

23 Charles O. Hucker, *The Censorial System of Ming China* (Stanford, 1966), p. 59, points out that censorial jobs in general were not given to men with less than three years experience in a lower post, and that Supervising Secretaries (*Ji shi zhong*; also Rank 7a) were not supposed to be under thirty. If Wang Xianchen was thirty in 1490, when first a censor, he was born around 1460.

24 WZMJ, I, p. 392.

25 WZMJ, I, p. 195.

26 The irrevocability of Wang Xianchen's retirement is attested by the important ritual gesture of literally 'tearing his [official] hat': WZMJ, II, p. 1212. On this ritual see Chen Guodong, 'Ku miao yu fen Ru fu – Ming mo Qing chu shengyuan ceng de shehuixing dongzuo', *Xin shixue*, III (1992), pp. 69–94.

27 *Gusu zhi*, juan 29, p. 13a. There are later stories, unsupported by contemporary evidence, that Wang Xianchen forcibly dispossessed the monks to take possession of the site.

28 Liu Dunzhen, *Suzhou gudian yuanlin* (n.p., 1979), p. 53 n. 1. The introduction is translated by Frances Wood in *Garden History*, Journal of the Garden History Society, X (1982), pp. 108–41.

29 WZMJ, II, pp. 896–7, and WZMJ, II, p. 906.

30 WZMJ, II, pp. 800, 910, 912.

31 WZMJ, II, pp. 1095–6, 963.

32 WZMJ, I, pp. 513–4.

33 This album, the current whereabouts of which is not known, is reproduced in full in *An Old Chinese Garden: A Three-fold Masterpiece of Poetry, Calligraphy and Painting, by Wen Chen Ming, Famous Landscape Artist of the Ming Dynasty. Studies Written by Kate Kerby, Translations by Mo Zung Chung*, Chung Hwa Book Company (Shanghai, 1922). I have used the text of 'Zhuo zheng yuan ji' in WZMJ, II, pp. 1275–8, comparing it to the photographs in Kerby. The texts of the poems are WZMJ, II, pp. 1205–13. There is another extant version, in a private collection, of the 'Record' purporting to be in Wen's calligraphy, also dated 1533. *Anthology of Chinese Art: Min Chiu Society Silver Jubilee Exhibition*, Hong Kong Museum of Art (Hong Kong, 1985), pp. 108–11.

34 This album, now in the Metropolitan Museum of Art in New York, is reproduced, together with translations of the poems, in Roderick Whitfield, with an Addendum by Wen Fong, *In Pursuit of Antiquity: Chinese Paintings of the Ming and Ch'ing Dynasties From the Collection of Mr and Mrs Earl Morse* (Rutland, VT, and Tokyo, 1969), pp. 66–70. It does not seem to have been remarked that Wang Xianchen would, if still alive, have been well into his nineties when this second album was painted, given that he cannot have been born after 1460.

35 Wang Jiacheng, 'Wen Zhengming ji qing yuanlin de xinlu licheng', *International Colloquium on Chinese Art History: Painting and Calligraphy*,

2 vols, National Palace Museum (Taipei, 1992), I, pp. 359–76, Appendix, lists three in addition to the albums.

36 Liu Dunzhen, p. 53, n. 4.

37 The wisteria supposedly planted by Wen Zhengming is mentioned in Nance, p. 41, and is still pointed out to visitors, but there is no early evidence for the existence of the plant in the garden. It is not mentioned in Wen Zhengming's 1533 record of the site.

38 Listed in Frances Ya-sing Tsu (Zhu Ya-xin), *Landscape Design in Chinese Gardens* (New York, 1988), p. 248.

39 They are (Zhu Yaxin's translations): Truth-Winning Pavilion (*De zhen ting*), Little Surging Wave (*Xiao cang lang*), Little Flying Rainbow (*Xiao fei hong*) and Leaning Jade Studio (*Yi yu xuan*).

40 Stuart, p. 167.

41 Liu Dunzhen, p. 53, n. 6.

42 Maggie Keswick, *The Chinese Garden: History, Art and Architecture* (London, 1978), p. 108.

43 The phrase is Lui Dunzhen, p. 53.

44 Qian Yong's colophon, dated 1833, to the 1533 Wen Zhengming album, reproduced in Kerby. This passage is omitted from the same author's published account of the garden.

45 None of them appears in the very comprehensive Zhang Jianhua, *Ming Qing Jiangsu wen ren nian biao* (Shanghai, 1986).

46 The fullest English discussion of this literature is Francesca Bray, *Science and Civilisation in China: Volume 6, Biology and Biological Technology. Part II: Agriculture* (Cambridge, 1984).

47 Craig Clunas, *Superfluous Things: Material Culture and Social Status in Early Modern China* (Cambridge, 1991), pp. 166–8.

48 WZMJ, II, p. 1212.

49 The poem is WZMJ, II, p. 1205, translated by Whitfield, p. 66.

50 Bray, pp. 539–51; Dardess, pp. 311–31.

51 Wang Zhen, *Nong shu*, Zhonghua shuju edn (Beijing, 1956), p. 134. On this text, dated 1313, see Bray, pp. 59–64. The relevant passage is also translated in ibid., p. 542.

52 Chen Hengli and Wang Dacan, '*Bu nong shu*' yanjiu (Beijing, 1958), p. 275. Hilary J. Beattie, *Land and Lineage in China: A Study of T'ung-ch'eng county, Anhwei, in the Ming and Ch'ing Dynasties* (Cambridge, 1979), p. 98.

53 S. L. Kline, *Colonial Culhuacan, 1580–1600: A Social History of an Aztec Town* (Albuquerque, 1986), p. 132.

54 Joseph Needham, with the collaboration of Lu Gwei-djen and a special contribution by Huang Hsing-tsung, *Science and Civilisation in China: Volume 6, Biology and Biological Technology. Part I: Botany* (Cambridge, 1986), p. 365.

55 Bray, p. 545.

56 Sun Yunwei, ed., *Zhongguo guoshi shi yu guoshu ziyuan* (Shanghai, 1983), p. 5; Sun identifies it on p. 6 as *Malus Asiatica* Nakai.

57 Xu Guangqi, *Nong zheng quan shu jiao zhu*, commentary by Shi Shenghan, edited by Xibei nongxueyuan gu nongxue yanjiushi, 3 vols (Shanghai, 1983), p. 778, and Sun Yunwei, p. 36.

58 Maggie Bickford, et al., *Bones of Jade, Soul of Ice: The Flowering Plum in Chinese Art*, Yale University Art Gallery (New Haven, 1985).

59 Bickford, et al., pp. 31–3 and pp. 245–50.

60 Xu Guangqi, p. 770, also Sun Yunwei, pp. 35–7.

61 C. R. Boxer, ed., *South China in the Sixteenth Century*, The Hakluyt Society, 2nd series, vol. 106 (London, 1953), p. 132.

62 It remains an important economic crop; Woon Young Chun, BSF, MF, *Chinese Economic Trees* (Shanghai, 1921), p. 164; Tong Bingya, *Guoshu shihua* (Beijing, 1983), pp. 198–206; Wang Dongfeng, ed., *Jianming Zhongguo pengren cidian* (Taiyuan, 1987), p. 222; Kong Xu, ed., *Zhongguo guoshu zaipei xue* (Beijing, 1978), pp. 545–77.

63 Ping-ti Ho, 'The Introduction of American Food Plants into China', *American Anthropologist*, LVII (1955), pp. 191–201 (192).

64 Xu Guangqi, p. 1071, and Sun Yunwei, p. 36.

65 Xu Guangqi, p. 1045–56.

66 Xu Guangqi, p. 1174–8. For an earlier situation see Stephen H. West, 'Cilia, Scale and Bristle: The Consumption of Fish and Shellfish in the Eastern Capital of the Northern Song', *HJAS*, XLVII (1990), pp. 595–634.

67 WZMJ, II, p. 1207. The translation is that in Kerby.

68 West, p. 623.

69 Bray, p. 98.

70 Bray, p. 608.

71 Michel Cartier, *Une réforme locale en Chine au XVIe siècle. Hai Rui à Chun'an, 1558–1562* (Paris, 1973), p. 83.

72 Joseph P. McDermott, 'Bondservants in the T'ai-hu Basin During the Late Ming: A Case of Mistaken Identities', *JAS*, XL (1981), pp. 675–701 (697).

73 David R. Coffin, *The Villa in the Life of Renaissance Rome* (Princeton, 1979) is the source for my understanding of this.

74 Claudia Lazzaro, *The Italian Renaissance Garden: From the Conventions of Planting, Design and Ornament to the Grand Gardens of Sixteenth-century Central Italy* (New Haven and London, 1990), p. 12.

75 Robert Williams, 'Rural Economy and the Antique in the English Landscape Garden', *Journal of Garden History*, VII (1987), pp. 73–96.

76 Christopher K. Currie, 'Fishponds as Garden Features, c. 1550–1750', *Garden History*, Journal of the Garden History Society, XVIII (1990), pp. 22–46 (24–5).

77 Clunas, *Superfluous Things*, p. 139.

78 Craig Clunas, 'Regulation of Consumption and the Institution of Correct Morality by the Ming State', in *Norms and the State in China*, ed. Chün-chieh Huang and Erik Zürcher (Leiden, New York and Cologne, 1993), pp. 39–49.

79 Wang Zhen, p. 134.

80 Xu Guangqi, p. 114.

81 For example, *zhuo hua*, 'my clumsy picture', *zhuo wen*, 'my clumsy writing', *zhuo bi*, 'my clumsy brush': WZMJ, pp. 1040, 1446 and 1453.

82 Clunas, *Superfluous Things*, pp. 85–6.

83 *Gusu zhi*, juan 32, p. 25b (p. 453).

84 Helmut Wilhelm, 'Shih Ch'ung and his Chin-ku-yüan', *Monumenta Serica*, XIX (1959), pp. 314–27. See also Ellen Johnston Laing, 'Ch'iu Ying's Two Garden Paintings Belonging to the Chion-in, Kyoto', *Proceedings of the International Colloquium on Chinese Art History: Painting and Calligraphy*, 2 vols, National Palace Museum (Taipei, 1992), I, pp. 331–58.

85 Coffin, p. 187; Cosgrove, *The Palladian Landscape*, p. 103, pp. 110–13.

86 Ralph Austen, *A Treatise of Fruit-Trees together with The Spirituall Use of an Orchard* (Oxford, 1653), The English Landscape Garden reprint edn, edited with introductory notes by John Dixon Hunt, Garland Publishing (New York and London, 1982).

87 Michel Foucault, 'Of Other Spaces', *Diacritics*, XVI (1981), pp. 22–7 (24).

88 Bray, p. 542, operating from within the discourse of agriculture, makes the identification *yuan* = 'orchard'. 'Gardens' are to be dealt with in a separate volume of *Science and Civilisation in China*.

89 Sun Yunwei, p. 27.

90 Bray, p. 550.
91 Wang Yuhu, *Zhongguo nongxue shulu*, 2nd edn (Beijing, 1979), p. 129.
92 Xu Guangqi, p. 769.
93 Quoted by Sun Yunwei, p. 23. Shen Lianchuan, in his early seventeenth-century *Bu nong shu*, and writing from the point of view of the small scale landholder, rather spoils the ideal of detachment by adding that fruit trees 'can save you from spending money in the market-place'. Chen Hengli and Wang Dacan, p. 268.
94 Williams, p. 94, Currie p. 22. The English ruling class went further by banning game meat from commercial trade, reinforcing its role as a symbolic commodity of giftgiving.
95 This was one of the major sights of Peking and its environs. Kathlyn Liscomb, 'The Eight Views of Beijing: Politics in Literati Art', *Artibus Asiae*, IL (1988–89), pp. 127–52 (140).
96 WZMJ, II, p. 1213.
97 Keith Tribe, *Land, Labour and Economic Discourse* (London, Henley and Boston, 1978), p. 26.

2 The Aesthetic Garden

1 Gui Youguang, *Zhenchuan xiansheng ji*, Zhongguo gudian wenxue congshu, 2 vols, Shanghai guji chubanshe edn (Shanghai, 1981), p. 387.
2 Wu Changyuan, *Chen yuan shi lüe* (preface dated 1788), Beijing guji chubanshe edn (Beijing, 1981), p. 230.
3 Liu Ce, *Zhongguo gudai yuan you* (Ningxia, 1979); Edward S. Schafer, 'Hunting Parks and Animal Enclosures in Ancient China', *Journal of the Economic and Social History of the Orient*, XI (1968), pp. 318–43.
4 Shen Shixing, *Da Ming huidian*, Zhonghua shuju edn (Beijing, 1989), pp. 1108–9.
5 Dan Shiyuan, *Mingdai jianzhu dashi nianbiao*, photographic reprint of original 1926 Zhongguo yingzao xueshe edn (Taibei, 1976), p. 138.
6 For a map, see Hou Renzhi, ed., *Beijing lishi dituji* (Beijing, 1985), pp. 33–4.
7 Dan Shiyuan, pp. 64, 106, 110,. 111, 119.
8 Zhang Jiaji, *Zhongguo zao yuan shi* (Taibei, 1990), pp. 189–90.
9 Boxer, p. 186.
10 Zhang Jiaji, p. 191.
11 Gui Youguang, p. 963.
12 *Wu xian zhi*, juan 23, pp. 26b–27a.
13 WZMJ, I, pp. 23–8.
14 WZMJ, I, p. 236.
15 Anne de Coursey Clapp, *The Painting of T'ang Yin* (Chicago, 1991), pp. 30–1.
16 WZMJ, I, pp. 298–9, p. 299, pp. 299–304.
17 WZMJ, I, p. 304.
18 WZMJ, I, p. 299.
19 Alice R. M. Hyland, *Deities, Emperors, Ladies and Literati: Figure Paintings of the Ming and Qing Dynasties* (Seattle and London, 1987), pp. 15–16, fig. 1, colour plate II. Cahill, *Parting*, pp. 24–5.
20 Anon., 'Social Gatherings in the Ming Period', *Annual Report of the Librarian of Congress for 1940*, 1974 reprint edn, compiled by P. K. Yu, vol. II, pp. 648–50.
21 Craig Clunas, 'Ideal and Reality in the Ming Garden', in *The Authentic Garden*, ed. L. Tjon Sie Fat and E. de Jong (Leiden, 1991), pp. 197–206.
22 Chen Zhi and Zhang Gongshi, eds, *Zhongguo lidai mingyuanji xuan zhu* (Hefei, 1983), pp. 157–73.

23 Gu Qiyuan, *Ke zuo zhui yu*, Yuan Ming shiliao biji congkan edn (Beijing, 1987), pp. 161–2.

24 Gao Jin, ed., *Nan xun sheng dian*, preface dated 1771, 120 *juan* edn, *juan* 98, pp. 16a–18a; Tong Jun *Jiangnan yuanlin kao*, 2nd edn (Beijing 1984), p. 24.

25 Joanna F. Handlin Smith, 'Gardens in Ch'i Piao-chia's Social World: Wealth and Values in Late Ming Kiangnan', *Journal of Asian Studies*, LI (1992), pp. 55–81 (68).

26 Chen Zhi and Zhang Gongshi, op. cit.

27 Jin Xuezhi, p. 32.

28 Gao Jin, *juan* 99, pp. 4a–5b.

29 See the detailed map in Marmé, pp. 30–31.

30 Huangfu Fang, ed., *Changzhou xian zhi*, 14 *juan*, preface dated 1571, published 1598.

31 *Changzhou xian zhi*, *juan* 13, pp. 13a–16b. (The rhetoric of a gazetteer makes it hard to tell if statements should be read in the present or the past; grammatically there is no distinction between 'X Garden is outside Y Gate' and 'X Garden *was* outside Y Gate').

32 *Wu xian zhi*, *juan* 23, p. 35b.

33 *Wu xian zhi*, *juan* 23, pp. 34b–35a.

34 Clunas, *Superfluous Things*, pp. 20–25, 176.

35 *Wu xian zhi*, *juan* 23, pp. 50b–52a.

36 Zhang Han, *Song chuang meng yu*, cited in Clunas, *Superfluous Things*, p. 145.

37 Xie Zhaozhe, *Wu za zu*, Guoxue zhenben wenku edn, 1st series, no 13, 2 vols (Shanghai, 1935), I, p. 102.

38 Shen Defu, p. 654.

39 One attempt to describe this change is Wang Juyuan, 'Suzhou Ming Qing zhai yuan fengge de fenxi', *Yuanyi xuebao / Acta Horticulturalia* 11/2 (1963), pp. 177–94.

40 Gu Qiyuan, p. 17.

41 Ibid.

42 Handlin Smith, p. 69.

43 Lazzaro, *The Italian Renaissance Garden*, p. 28.

44 The 'culture of flowers' was established in China well before this time, and an interest in rare varieties was well attested in the Song period. Jack Goody, *The Culture of Flowers* (Cambridge, 1993), pp. 347–86. Needham, VI. 1, pp. 409 and 412 shows that very few new varieties are recorded in the botanical literature between about 1200 and 1600, so the Ming expansion may have been mostly a matter of disseminating existing rarities.

45 John Hay, *Kernels of Energy, Bones of Earth: The Rock in Chinese Art* (New York, 1985), supplemented by John Hay, 'Structure and Aesthetic Criteria in Chinese Rocks and Art', *Res*, XIII (1987), pp. 6–22.

46 Edward H. Schafer, *Tu Wan's Stone Catalogue of Cloudy Forest* (Berkeley and Los Angeles, 1961), pp. 5–6. Schafer argues that the use of heaps of stones in the Six Dynasties was replaced by single stones in the Tang. He dates the connoisseurship of rocks to the ninth century.

47 James M. Hargett, 'Huizong's Magic Marchmount: The Genyue Pleasure Park of Kaifeng', *Monumenta Serica*, XXXVIII (1989–90), pp. 1–48 (5).

48 Tong Jun, *Jiangnan yuanlin kao*, 2nd edn (Beijing, 1984), p. 9.

49 Mote, 'Millenium', p. 49.

50 Huang Xingzeng, *Wu feng lu*, 1 *juan*, Xue hai lei bian, Han fen lou reprint edn (Shanghai, 1920), p. 3b.

51 Qian Yong, *Lü yuan cong hua*, Qingdai shiliao biji congkan edn, 2 vols (Beijing, 1979), pp. 522–3.

52 Lang Ying, *Qi xiu lei gao*, Shijie shuju edn, 2 vols (Taibei, 1984), *juan* 2, p. 48.

53 Xie Zhaozhe, *Wu za zu*, p. 103.

54 Xie Zhaozhe, I, pp. 103, 116.

55 Xie Zhaozhe, I, p. 116.

56 Zhu Mian was the chief collector of stones for Song Huizong; see Schafer, *Stone Catalogue*, p. 8.

57 Yuan Hongdao, 'Yuan Zhonglang you ji' in Yuan Hongdao, *Yuan Zhonglang quan ji*, Guang zhi shuju edn (Hong Kong, n.d.), pp. 10–11.

58 Wen Zhenheng. *Zhang wu zhi jiao zhu*, Jiangsu kexue chubanshe edn, annotations by Chen Zhi, Yang Zhaobo, ed. (Nanjing, 1984), p. 41.

59 Wen Zhenheng, p. 391.

60 Boxer, pp. 132–3 and 99. Da Cruz's 'little fountains' are presumably ponds, since hydraulics were not used at this period.

61 Handlin Smith, pp. 58, 60, 69.

62 Chen Zhi and Zhang Gongshi, pp. 228–33.

63 *Bian min tu zuan*, Zhongguo gudai keji tulu congbian chu ji 2, Zhonghua shuju facsimile of 1593 edn, 4 vols (Beijing, 1959), *juan* 15, 'Manufactures' (*Zhi zao lei*).

64 Clunas, *Superfluous Things*, pp. 37–8 and 114.

65 Chen Hengli and Wang Dacan, p. 268.

66 The contents are listed in *Zhongguo congshu zong lu*, revd edn, 3 vols (Shanghai, 1982), I, pp. 48–50.

67 Yu Zongben, ed., *Zhong shu shu*, I *juan*, contained in Hu Wenhuan, ed., *Ge zhi cong shu*, han 19, ce 103, unpaginated preface.

68 *Zhong shu shu*, pp. 12a, 13b.

69 Bray, pp. 65–70.

70 Xu Guangqi, p. 114.

71 Pierre Bourdieu, *Distinction: A Social Critique of the Judgement of Taste*, trans. Richard Nice (London 1984), passim.

72 Dardess, p. 296.

73 Dardess, pp. 366–63.

74 Wang Daokun (1525–93), *Tai han ji*, cited in Zhang Haipeng and Wang Yanyuan, eds, *Ming Qing Anhui shang ziliao xuan bian* (Hefei, 1985), pp. 359–60.

75 Pan Yongyin, *Xu shu tang Ming bai lei chao* (compiled 1662), *juan* 10, quoted in Xie Guozhen, III, p. 353.

76 Clunas, *Superfluous Things*, pp. 138–9, for two examples.

77 Handlin Smith, p. 69, argues: 'Shared aesthetic values overshadowed any distinctions in wealth that garden size suggested and provided a basis for social solidarity with the local elite.' On the *Ban mu yuan* see J. L. van Hecken, CICM and W. A. Grootaers, CICM, 'The Half Acre Garden, *Pan-mou Yuan*', *Monumenta Serica*, XVIII (1956), pp. 360–87.

78 Susan Stewart, *On Longing: Narratives of the Miniature, the Gigantic, the Souvenir, the Collection* (Durham, NC, and London, 1993), p. 70.

79 Stewart, p. 35.

80 On the concept of 'reclusion', see Alan J. Berkowitz, 'The Moral Hero: A Pattern of Reclusion in Traditional China', *Monumenta Serica*, XL (1992), pp. 1–32, also idem, 'Reclusion in Traditional China: A Selected List of References', *Monumenta Serica*, XL (1992), pp. 33–46.

81 Cahill, *Three Alternative Histories*, p. 63.

82 Chu-tsing Li and James C. Y. Watt, eds, *The Chinese Scholar's Studio: Artistic Life in the Late Ming Period* (New York, 1987), p. 33, citing the late Yuan writer Kong Qi.

83 Mori Masao, p. 36.

84 Tong Jun, p. 43.

85 Xie Zhaozhe, I, p. 118. See also Cahill, *Three Alternative Histories*, pp. 26–7.

86 Quoted in Tong Jun, p. 44.

87 Yu Zhenmu, *Shen cui xuan ji*, cited in Liu Jiuan, 'Wumen huajia zhi biehaotu ji jian bie ju li', *Gugong bowuyuan yuankan* 1L/3 (1990), pp. 54–61 (55–6).

88 Quoted in Tong Jun, p. 43. The context is a letter to Chen Jiru.

89 Wen Zhenheng, p. 18.

90 Timothy Brook, *Praying for Power: Buddhism and the Formation of Gentry Society in Late-Ming China*, (Cambridge and London, 1993), p. 28.

91 Jin Xuezhi, *Zhongguo yuanlin meixue* (Nanjing, 1990), pp. 40–45. On the Song imperial gardens see also West, pp. 608–9. The Fan Zhongyan story is cited by Handlin Smith, p. 76; the Shao Yong poem is quoted in Tong Jun, p. 46.

92 Shen Defu, p. 606.

93 Craig Clunas, 'Ideal and Reality in the Ming Garden', pp. 197–205.

94 Pasquale M. D'Elia, sJ, ed., *Fonti Ricciane . . .*, 3 vols (Rome, 1942). II, p. 64.

95 Handlin Smith, p. 65.

96 Text in Du Lianzhe, ed., *Mingren zizhuan wenchao* (Taibei, 1977), pp. 256–7.

97 Shen Zan, *Jin shi cong can*, quoted in Xie Guozhen, III, pp. 245–6. Shen Zan (1558–1612, *jinshi* 1586) was a native of Wujiang.

98 Peter Burke, '*Res et verba*: Conspicuous Consumption in the Early Modern World', in J. Brewer and R. Porter, eds, *Consumption and the World of Goods* (London, 1993), pp. 148–61 (152). I have revised the position in Clunas, *Superfluous Things*, p. 159. where I underestimated the accessibility of gardens, and hence their role in conspicuous display.

99 David R. Coffin, 'The "Lex Hortorum" and Access to Gardens of Latium During the Renaissance', *Journal of Garden History*, II (1982), pp. 210–32.

100 From Wang's 'Autobiography', as translated in Pei-yi Wu, *The Confucian's Progress: Autobiographical Writings in Traditional China* (Princeton, 1990), p. 260.

101 See the very fine article by Judith Zeitlin, 'The Petrified Heart: Obsession in Chinese Literature, Art and Medicine', *Late Imperial China*, XII (1991), pp. 1–26.

102 Wang Xinyi, *Gui tian yuan ju ji*, quoted in Chen Zhi and Zhang Gongshi, p. 288.

103 Wang Yaoting, 'Tao hua yuan yu Hua xi yu yin', *Proceedings of the International Colloquium on Chinese Art History, 1991: Painting and Calligraphy*, National Palace Museum, 2 vols (Taipei, 1992), pp. 279–305 (286), citing the *Ni gu lu* by Chen Jiru, Dong's close friend.

104 Tong Jun, p. 45, citing Dong Qichang, *Tu chai ji*.

105 Rolf A. Stein, *The World in Miniature: Container Gardens and Dwellings in Far Eastern Religious Thought*, translated by Phyllis Brooks, with a new Foreword by Edward H. Schafer (Stanford, 1990), pp. 25–42. My reservations about the general orientation of this magisterial work are expressed in a review in *Journal of the Economic and Social History of the Orient*, XXXV (1993), pp. 370–72.

106 This quotation from *Gusu zhi* is from Gu Lu, *Qing jia lu* (published 1830), *juan* 6, quoted in Xie Guozhen, I, p. 73.

107 Huang Xingzeng, p. 3b.

108 Quoted in Xie Guozhen, I, p. 70.

109 The *hu ci*, or *Damnacanthus indicus*, is an evergreen shrub native to Asia, with lustrous leaves, four-petalled flowers and longlasting bright red berries. It naturally grows to about five feet in height. Thomas H. Everett, *The New York Botanical Garden Illustrated Encyclopaedia of Horticulture*, 10 vols

(New York and London, 1981), III, p. 1008. For modern dwarfed examples see Fu Shanyi and Liu Shanghua, eds, *Panjing yishu zhanlan* (Beijing, 1979), pp. 102, 105.

110 Gu Qiyuan, pp. 17–18.

111 Liu Zongzhou, [*Zeng ding*] *Ren pu lei ji*, Shanghai Daxing tushu gongsi edn (Shanghai, 1935), pp. 113–5. On this text see Cynthia J. Brokaw, *The Ledgers of Merit and Demerit: Social Change and Moral Order in Late Imperial China* (Princeton, 1991), p. 134.

112 Handlin Smith, p. 75.

113 Ibid.

114 Shuzo Shiga, 'Family Property and the Law of Inheritance in Traditional China', in *Chinese Family Law and Social Change in Historical and Comparative Perspective*, ed. David C. Buxbaum (Seattle and London, 1978), pp. 109–50.

3 The Gardens of the Wen Family

1 Wen Zhengming, *Futian ji*, Mingdai yishujia ji huikan, 2 vols (Taibei, 1968) reproduces the posthumous thirty-five *juan* edition, which is the main contemporary source of his writings.

2 Wen Han, *Wen shi zu pu*, in *Qu shi cong shu*, cited hereafter as WSZP: see also Ellen Johnston Laing, 'Wen Tien and Chin Chün-ming', *Journal of the Institute of Chinese Studies of the Chinese University of Hong Kong*, VIII (1976), pp. 411–22.

3 Quoted in Clunas, *Superfluous Things*, p. 164. On Shen Chunze see ibid., p. 25.

4 Gao Jin, *juan* 32, p. 2b and *juan* 94, pp. 4a–5b.

5 Works on Wen as a painter includes: Marc F. Wilson and Kwan S. Wong, *Friends of Wen Cheng-ming: A View from the Crawford Collection*, China House Gallery (New York, 1974); Anne de Coursey Clapp, *Wen Cheng-ming: The Ming Artist and Antiquity*, Artibus Asiae Supplementum 34 (Ascona, 1975); Richard Edwards, *The Art of Wen Cheng-ming (1470–1559)* (Ann Arbor, 1976); Jiang Zhaoshen, *Wen Zhengming yu Suzhou huatan*, Gu gong congkan jia zhong (Taibei, 1977); Cahill, *Parting*, pp. 211–39.

6 Wen Jia, 'Account of the Conduct of my Late Father', in WZMJ, II, pp. 1618–24.

7 Peter Brown, *Society and the Holy in Late Antiquity* (Berkeley, Los Angeles and Oxford, 1989), pp. 131, 182–3.

8 Berkowitz, 'The Moral Hero', pp. 1–2.

9 Xu Jiandeng, *Chu xue ji*, quoted in Sun Yunwei, p. 23. The importance of impermeable boundaries is stressed by all the agronomic writers, e.g. Xu Guangqi, p. 1021, where the main purpose of the seven-feet-tall structure specified is to 'keep out robbers'.

10 Ann van Erp-Houtepen, 'The Etymological Origins of the Garden', *Journal of Garden History*, VI (1986), pp. 227–31.

11 Mori, p. 46.

12 Wen Zhaozhi, ed., *Wen shi wu jia ji*, 4 *juan*, Qinding si ku quan shu zhen ben chu ji edn (Shanghai, 1934–5), pp. 1, 16b–23a. Cited hereafter as WSWJJ.

13 Cahill, *Parting*, p. 78 & pl. 25.

14 WZMJ, I, p. 95.

15 WZMJ, I, p. 127.

16 WZMJ, I, p. 165.

17 Sawada, p. 63. On Qian Tongai, a member of a family of imperial physicians who like Wen failed the examinations repeatedly, and went on to be a major

calligraphy collector, see also Clapp, *T'ang Yin*, p. 60. Wen provided his tomb inscription.

18 WZMJ, I, p. 177. Mme Gu (1433–63) was the second wife of Wen's paternal grandfather, Wen Hong, but was in fact no blood-relation of his, as he was descended from the first wife, Mme Chen. Sawada, pp. 60–61.

19 WZMJ, I, pp. 176, 183. 'Yike' is not identified, but WZMJ, I, p. 210 reveals he is Chen Yike, whose sacrificial eulogy is WZMJ, I, pp. 572–3.

20 WZMJ, I, pp. 12, 13–15. Chen Guinan is not identified.

21 WZMJ, I, p. 205.

22 WZMJ, I, p. 207.

23 WZMJ, I, p. 212.

24 WZMJ, I, pp. 23–8.

25 WZMJ, I, p. 222. Tang Zizhong is Tang Zhen (MRZJ, 628).

26 WZMJ, I, pp. 236, 237.

27 WZMJ, I, pp. 236, 240.

28 WZMJ, I, pp. 254–5.

29 WZMJ, I, p. 268. The manuscript of Wen's collected works has *yuan*, 'garden', instead of *zhuang*, 'estate', suggesting something of their interchangeability.

30 WZMJ, II, pp. 862–3, 865–7. The former is almost certainly Bai Ang (1435–1503; MRZJ 113–14), President of the Board of Punishments and colleague of Wang Ao. The latter is Wang's son-in-law, Xu Jin (*jinshi* of 1505; MRZJ, 471), later Vice-President of the Board of Civil Office.

31 WZMJ, II, pp. 1199, 929.

32 WZMJ, I, p. 344.

33 WZMJ, II, p. 878, I, p. 346 and II, p. 987.

34 WZMJ, II, p. 991.

35 WZMJ, II, p. 993.

36 WSZP, pp. 35a–38a. This was not the first genealogy of the Wen family, since it attributes a now-lost earlier version to Wen Lin.

37 McDermott, 'Bondservants', p. 700.

38 WZMJ, I, pp. 466–7.

39 *Wu xian zhi*, juan 22, p. 24b.

40 WSZP, p. 6b.

41 Gu Ling was the great-grandson of Wen Zhaozhi's nephew, Wen Zhenheng. Clunas, *Superfluous Things*, pp. 23–4.

42 WSWJJ, juan 10, pp. 6a–b, 7b.

43 WSWJJ, juan 12, pp. 5a–b, 5b, juan 13, pp. 3a–b.

44 WSWJJ, juan 13, pp. 22a, 24a.

45 WSWJJ, juan 12, p. 11b, juan 13, pp. 18a–b, 25b, juan 14, pp. 12b–13a.

46 WSZP, p. 6b.

47 The text of Wen Yuanfa, *Qingliang ju shi zi xu*, is in Du Lianzhe, pp. 5–10; Zhang Jianhua, p. 385.

48 Jerry Dennerline, *The Chia-ting Loyalists: Confucian Leadership and Social Change in Seventeenth-century China* (New Haven and London, 1981), p. 51, describes him as 'the acknowledged leader of the Tung-lin faction within the Han-lin network'.

49 WSZP, p. 8b. The use of *hong* was prescribed by Zhu Xi's *Jia li*. Ebrey, *Chu Hsi's Family Rituals*, p. 100.

50 *Wu xian zhi*, juan 22, p. 44b. Note that this is the chapter on 'Residences' (*Di zhai*), not the one on 'Gardens' (*Yuan lin*). The 'Herb Patch' receives no mention in the latter, despite its description as the 'most splendid' of Suzhou's gardens. This should reinforce our caution in taking gazetteers as reliable total surveys.

51 See Liu Dunzhen, p. 71.

52 Wen was a sponsor/editor, along with Gu Xichou, Wang Daokun and the garden-builder Qi Biaojia, of Yan Maoyou's 'Record for Gaining Good Fortune' (*Di ji lu*, preface dated 1631); Brokaw, p. 159.

53 Chen Guodong, p. 88.

54 *Wu xian zhi*, juan 23, p. 38b.

55 *Wu xian zhi*, juan 23, p. 50b.

56 *Tian shui bing shan lu* (prefaced dated 1562), in *Ming Wuzong wai ji*, Zhongguo lishi yanjiu ziliao congshu edn, reprint of 1951 Shanghai Shenzhou guoguang she edn (Shanghai, 1982), p. 165.

57 Frederic Wakeman Jr, *The Great Enterprise: The Manchu Reconstruction of Order in Seventeenth-century China*, 2 vols (Berkeley, Los Angeles and London, 1985), p. 978.

58 *Li shi qiu mu zhi*, wszp, pp. 29a–32b.

59 Ebrey, *Chu Hsi's Family Rituals*, pp. 10–11.

60 Quoted in Du Lianzhe, p. 9.

61 Zhu Wenjie, 'Wuxi xin faxian Mingdai Gao Panlong shou shu jia xin', *Wenwu*, 1986.4: 75–6 shows a holding of 400 *mu* each by Gao and his three brothers.

62 Ibid.

63 Craig Clunas, 'Some Literary Evidence for Gold and Silver Vessels in the Ming Period (1368–1644)', in *Pots and Pans: A Colloquium on Precious Metals and Ceramics*, ed. Michael Vickers and Julian Raby, Oxford Studies in Islamic Art 3 (Oxford, 1987), pp. 83–7.

64 Qian Yong, *Deng lou za ji*, cited by Xie Guozhen, III, pp. 341–2.

65 C. K. Yang, *Religion in Chinese Society: A Study of Contemporary Social Functions of Religion and Some of their Historical Factors* (Berkeley and Los Angeles, 1967), pp. 167–75.

66 The 'Monograph on Sacrificial Rites of Successive Generations' (*Li shi si dian zhi*) is wszp, pp. 33a–34b.

67 When their standing declined in the Qing period, the shrine of Wen Tianxiang declined with it. It was unsatisfactorily restored in 1710, and by 1730, when the genealogy was written, was in danger of imminent collapse.

68 Boxer, p. 103.

69 The material on arches (*fang biao*) is wszp, pp. 27a–b.

70 wszp, pp. 27b–28a.

71 Mote, 'Millenium', p. 59.

72 Suzhou shi wenwu baoquan weiyuanhui, *Suzhou Huqiu ta chutu wenwu* (Beijing, 1958), p. 1.

73 An essay by Grand Secretary Yang Shiqi dated 1424, commemorating the restoration, is in *juan* 2 of Wen Zhaozhi, *Hu qiu shan zhi*.

74 Yuan Hung-tao, *Pilgrim of the Clouds: Poems and Essays from Ming China*, translated by Jonathan Chaves (New York and Tokyo, 1978), p. 93.

75 Wang Chongmin, *Zhongguo shanben shu tiyao* (Shanghai, 1983), pp. 206–7. Timothy Brook, *Geographical Sources of Ming-Qing History*, Michigan Monographs in Chinese Studies 58 (Ann Arbor, 1988), p. 96. There is an earlier gazetteer of Tiger Hill, no longer extant, produced in the Hongwu reign by Wang Bin, and re-edited in Chenghua by Liu Hui. Both of these versions were simply collections of writings about Tiger Hill, with none of the topographical or historical material proper to the gazetteer form. I have examined the copy of *Huqui shan zhi* in the Library of Congress (Loc v.B131.1 H86 w), which is a Ming edition, though not the earliest one, as it includes transcripts of imperial decrees of 1445 and 1600 concerning the installation of complete texts of the Buddhist canon at the Tiger Hill monastery.

76 Wen Zhaozhi, *Huqiu shan zhi*, juan 1, pp. 20b–25a.

4 The Represented Garden

1 Michel Foucault, *The Archaeology of Knowledge*, trans. A. M. Sheridan-Smith (New York, 1972), p. 47.
2 Lothar Ledderose, 'Subject Matter in Early Chinese Painting Criticism', *Oriental Art*, n.s. XIX (1972), pp. 1–5.
3 Foucault, *Archaeology of Knowledge*, p. 49.
4 Jin Xuezhi, pp. 53–60.
5 Joseph Needham, with the collaboration of Wang Ling, *Science and Civilization in China. Volume 3: Mathematics and the Sciences of the Heavens and the Earth* (Cambridge, 1959), pp. 645, 647. The text also includes important early speculation on the formation of fossils.
6 Wang Shizhen, *Yizhou shan ren xu gao*, 18 vols, edited by Shen Yunlong, Ming ren wen ji congkan di 1 qi, no 22, Wenhai chubanshe edn (Taibei, 1970), pp. 2405–12.
7 WZMJ, II, pp. 1275–8, and WZMJ, II, pp. 497–502.
8 Pei-yi Wu, p. 117.
9 Michel de Certeau, *The Practice of Everyday Life* (Berkeley, Los Angeles and London, 1984), p. 117.
10 De Certeau, pp. 118–22.
11 Michel Cartier, 'Une nouvelle historiographie chinoise. La formation d'un marché national vue par Wu Chengming', *Annales*, XXXXI (1986), pp. 1303–12.
12 On cartography see Needham, *Volume 3*, pp. 497–590. This is superceded by the relevant volume of the Chicago University Press *History of Cartography*, some of the arguments of which are prefigured in Cordell D. K. Yee, 'A Cartography of Introspection: Chinese Maps as Other than European', *Asian Art*, V/4 (1992), pp. 29–47.
13 *Bian min tu zuan*, juan, 1.
14 De Certeau, p. 123.
15 Cao Xueqin, *The Story of the Stone*, translated by David Hawkes and John Minford, 5 vols (Harmondsworth, 1972–86), I, pp. 324–5, quoted in Yi-fu Tuan, 'Language and the Making of Place: A Narrative–Descriptive Approach', *Annals of the Association of American Geographers*, LXXXI (1991), pp. 684–96 (691).
16 Coffin, *The Villa*, p. 187; Williams, 'Rural Economy', p. 74.
17 There is a full list of the sites in John C. Ferguson, 'Wang Ch'uan', *Ostasiatische Zeitschrift*, III (1914–15), pp. 51–60 (54), and the poems on them are given in *Poems of Wang Wei*, translated with an introduction by G. W. Robinson (Harmondsworth, 1973), pp. 27–33. On Ming dynasty rubbings believed to be copies of Wang Wei's lost handscroll see Berthold Laufer, 'The Wang Ch'uan T'u, a Landscape of Wang Wei', *Ostasiatische Zeitschrift*, I (1912–13), pp. 28–55.
18 Robert E. Harrist Jr, 'Site Names and their Meanings in the Garden of Solitary Enjoyment', *Journal of Garden History*, XIII (1993), pp. 199–212. The same point is made by Jin Xuezhi, pp. 49–50.
19 WZMJ, II, 1205–13.
20 Seen by Stuart as the programmatic heart of the garden, p. 170.
21 Richard Edwards, *The Field of Stones: A Study of the Art of Shen Chou (1427–1509)* (Washington, DC, 1962), cat. no. XLIII, pl. 36, pp. 59–61, discusses and illustrates a handscroll of Lord Zhang's Cavern by Shen dated 1499. Richard M. Barnhart, *Peach Blossom Spring: Gardens and Flowers in Chinese Painting* (New York, 1983), pp. 101–04 illustrates a later version of this composition by Shitao (1642–1707), now in the Metropolitan Museum of Art, New York.
22 Chen Zhi and Zhang Gongshi, p. 105, quoting the gazetteer, *Yixing Jingxi xian zhi*.

23 These included one of Wang Shouren's closest disciples Wang Ji (1498–1563; DMB 1351–5), who shared the interest in Daoism, Fan Qin (also *jinshi* of 1532; MRZJ 363), builder of the famous Tianyi ge library, and Huangfu Fang, already encountered as a friend and contact of Wen Zhengming's grandson Wen Zhaozhi. His tomb inscription was to be provided by Li Chunfung (1511–85; DMB 818–9), a chief Grand Secretary who also had Daoist connections, as the author of 'blue paper invocations' (*qing ci*) at the court of the Jiajing emperor. Liu Ts'un-yan, 'The Penetration of Taoism into the Ming Neo-Confucian Elite', T'oung Pao, 57 (1971), pp. 31–102 (57–8). Another Grand Secretary author of these Daoist prayers, Yan Na (1511–84; MRZJ 946) also wrote an obituary, as did Wan Shihe (1516–86), President of the Board of Rites.

24 The former is illustrated in Stuart, p. 167 and fig. 7, the latter is Li and Watt, cat. no. 6, pp. 147–8.

25 Alice R. M. Hyland, 'Colophons Written by Wen Jia (1501–1583)', *Oriental Art*, n.s. XXXVIII (1992), pp. 134–44 (p. 141 and fig. 11). An album of twenty-one leaves, purporting to be the lost original but possibly a good early copy, is in the Nanjing Museum.

26 *Eight Dynasties of Chinese Painting: The Collections of the Nelson Gallery – Atkins Museum of Art, Kansas City, and the Cleveland Museum of Art*, with essays by Wai-kam Ho, Sherman E. Lee, Laurence Sickman and Marc F. Wilson (Cleveland, 1980), no. 155, pp. 187–90.

27 John Barrell, 'The Public Prospect and the Private View: The Politics of Taste in Eighteenth-century England', in Simon Pugh, ed., *Reading Landscape*, pp. 19–40.

28 The line is by Wang Zhihuan, see *Quan Tang shi*, 12 vols, Zhonghua shuju edn (Beijing, 1960), p. 2849.

29 Wen Zhaozhi, *Huqiu shan zhi, juan* 1, p. 5a.

30 Cahill, *Parting*, p. 217 and colour pl. 13.

31 Ellen Johnston Laing, 'Qiu Ying's Depiction of Sima Guang's Duluo [sic] Yuan and the View from the Chinese Garden', *Oriental Art*, n.s. XXXIII (1987), pp. 375–80. The scroll is no. 166 in *Eight Dynasties of Chinese Painting*, pp. 206–9.

32 Laing, 'Qiu Ying's Depiction', p. 379, citing Hans H. Frankel, 'The Contemplation of the Past in T'ang Poetry', in *Perspectives on the T'ang*, ed. Arthur F. Wright and Denis Twitchett (New Haven and London, 1973), pp. 345–66 (346).

33 *Eight Dynasties*, p. 206. The exact relationship of Xiang Miaomo, *zi* Yukui remains unclear; see the family tree in Wang Shiqing, 'Dong Qichang de jiaoyou', in Wai-kam Ho and Judith G. Smith, eds, *The Century of Tung Ch'i-ch'ang, 1555–1636*, 2 vols (Seattle and London, 1992), II, pp. 461–83 (470).

34 Gui Youguang, p. 369: Chen Zhi and Zhang Gongshi, pp. 228–33.

35 Zhang Chou, *Qing he shu hua fang*, quoted in Liu Jiuan, p. 55.

36 Elucidations of the often arcane references behind these names frequently appear in Ming *biji*, e.g. Shen Defu, II, pp. 584–5.

37 Cahill, *Parting*, p. 78.

38 Richard Vinograd, 'Family Properties: Personal Context and Cultural Pattern in Wang Meng's *Pien Mountains* of 1366', *Ars Orientalis*, XIII (1982), pp. 1–29 (11). The importance of paintings of the 'family mountain' (*jia shan*) is pointed out in A. J. Hay, *Huang Kung-wang's 'Dwelling in the Fu-ch'un Mountains': Dimensions of a Landscape*, PhD diss., Princeton University, 1978, p. 224. For the continued vitality of this sort of understanding of mountain property in the seventeenth century, see J. P. McDermott, 'The Making of a Chinese Mountain, Huangshan: Politics and Wealth in Chinese Art', *Art and Power in Japan and China*, special number of *Asian Cultural Studies*,

International Christian University Publications III-A (Tokyo, 1989), pp. 145–76 (163).

39 A point made in Kong Zhen, 'Liao yi hua tu xie qing ju – Tan yuanlin, tingyuan wei ticai de Wumen huihua' ('Simple Pictures of Pure Dwellings – On Wu School Paintings of Gardens and Estates', *Gugong bowuyuan yuankan*, IL (1990), pp. 87–91 (89).

40 Dardess, p. 352.

41 Clapp, *T'ang Yin*, pp. 27, 32.

42 Clapp, *T'ang Yin*, p. 57.

43 Liu Jiuan, pp. 55–6.

44 Discussed in Xu Zhongling, 'Du Qiong he ta de liang fu shanshui hua', *Wenwu* (1991.9), pp. 74–7.

45 Clapp, *T'ang Yin*, p. 56.

46 Wang Jian, 'Wen Zhengming "Zhen shang zhai tu"', *Wenwu* (1978.6), pp. 89–90. For Hua Xia's dates see Zhang Huijian, pp. 157, 229.

47 Nicholas Thomas, *Entangled Objects: Exchange, Material Culture and Colonialism in the Pacific* (Cambridge, MA, and London, 1991), p. 63.

48 Shuzo Shiga, 'Family Property', p. 146.

49 Arjun Appadurai, 'Introduction: Commodities and the Politics of Value', in Arjun Apadurai, ed., *The Social life of Things: Commodities in Cultural Perspective* (Cambridge, 1986), pp. 3–63 (5), quoted in Clunas, *Superfluous Things*, p. 2.

50 James Cahill, 'Types of Artist-Patron Transactions in Chinese Painting', in Chu-tsing Li, ed., *Artists and Patrons: Some Social and Economic Aspects of Chinese Painting* (Lawrence, KS, 1989), pp. 7–20 (8).

51 Zhang Jianhua, pp. 265, 288.

52 Quoted in Jin Xuezhi, p. 51.

53 Jin Xuezhi, p. 51.

54 Handlin Smith, p. 64.

55 Quoted in Tong Jun, p. 45.

56 Qian Yong, pp. 522–3, compares the crowds in the Lion Grove in the second and third months to Zhang Zeduan's famous handscroll, 'Going up the River in a Time of Peace and Prosperity'.

57 On this literature see Clunas, *Superfluous Things*, chapter 1, passim.

58 Wen Zhenheng, p. 20.

59 Ibid., p. 41.

60 Ibid., p. 46.

61 Ibid., p. 50.

62 Ibid., p. 53.

63 Clunas, *Superfluous Things*, pp. 54–6.

64 Wen Zhenheng, p. 68.

65 Ibid., pp. 80–81, 360, 391.

66 Ibid., pp. 56, 62.

67 For this term, and its use in late Ming discourse on taste, see Clunas, *Superfluous Things*, pp. 86–7.

68 Wen Zhenheng, p. 78.

69 Ibid., pp. 96–7.

70 Ibid., p. 95.

71 Ibid., p. 102.

72 Ibid., pp. 102–3.

73 Ibid., pp. 109–10.

74 Ibid., pp. 112–13.

75 Ibid., p. 113.

76 Ibid., pp. 113–14.

77 Ibid., p. 121; This avine cottage industry is mentioned also in Gui Youguang, p. 381.
78 Ibid., p. 364.
79 Ji Cheng, *The Craft of Gardens*, translated by Alison Hardie , photographs by Zhong Ming, with a foreword by Maggie Keswick (New Haven and London, 1988). See also the reviews of this work by Jan Stuart in *Journal of the Society of Architectural Historians*, IL (1990), pp. 213–14, and by Joe McDermott in *Garden History*, Journal of the Garden History Society, XVIII (1990), pp. 70–74. The Chinese edition I have used is Ji Cheng, *Yuan ye zhu shi*, notes and commentary by Chen Zhi, Yang Bozhao and Chen Congzhou, Zhongguo jianzhu chubanshe (Beijing, 1988). The text forms the point of departure for an important dissertation by Stanislaus Fung, of the Department of Architecture, University of Adelaide, which stresses the importance of going beyond a documentary reading, and which will enlarge understanding of its positioning as a 'classic' within Chinese discourses of the garden.
80 McDermott, review of *The Craft of Gardens*, p. 72.
81 Ji Cheng (Hardie translation), p. 35.

5 The Landscape of Number

1   Ho Peng Yoke, 'Chinese Science: The Traditional Chinese View', *Bulletin of the School of Oriental and African Studies*, LIV (1991), pp. 506–19. Ho Peng Yoke, *Li, Qi and Shu: An Introduction to Science and Civilization in China* (Seattle and London, 1985), pp. 6–7.
2   Smith, p. 123.
3   For example Andrew March, 'An Appreciation of Chinese Geomancy', *Journal of Asian Studies*, XXVII (1968), pp. 253–67; Stephen D. R. Feuchtwang, *An Anthropological Analysis of Chinese Geomancy* (Vientiane, 1974, reprinted Taipei 1982); Smith, pp. 131–72; Fan Wei, 'Village *Fengshui* Principles', in *Chinese Landscapes: The Village as Place*, ed. Roland G. Knapp (Honolulu, 1992), pp. 35–45.
4   Smith, p. 131, shows that the same was true in the Qing. For a Ming usage by an elite writer of the term *feng shui*, very rare in the titles of geomantic treatises, see Lang Ying, II, p. 823, also Harriet T. Zurndorfer, *Change and Continuity in Chinese Local History: The Development of Hui-chou Prefecture 800 to 1800* (Leiden, 1989), p. 240.
5   Gu Qiyuan, p. 311.
6   Feuchtwang, pp. 17–18. Smith, p. 133, quotes a Ming account in which the Fujian School is called the 'Ancestral Temple method', and described as 'very rare'.
7   Patricia Buckley Ebrey, *Confucianism and Family Rituals in Imperial China: A Social History of Writing about Rites* (Princeton, 1991), pp. 114–15, 138–41.
8   Zurndorfer pp. 239–41, discusses the ambiguous status of geomantic practice in Huizhou.
9   D'Elia, *Fonti Ricciane*, I, p. 96.
10 Xie Zhaozhe, pp. 242–6.
11 Xie uses the term *shi shi*, literally 'masters of time', commonly used to mean 'geomancer' in Ming texts; see Klaas Ruitenbeek, *Carpentry and Building in Late Imperial China: A Study of the Fifteenth-century Carpenter's Manual 'Lu Ban Jing'* (Leiden, New York and Cologne, 1993), p. 16.
12 Also partially translated in Eduard B. Vermeer, 'The Decline of Hsing-hua Prefecture in the Early Ch'ing', in *Development and Decline of Fukien Province in the 17th and 18th Centuries*, ed. E. B. Vermeer (Leiden, 1990), pp. 101–61 (154–5).

13 Xie Zhaozhe, pp. 246–7.

14 Dardess, pp. 345–6.

15 Gu Qiyuan, pp. 161–2.

16 Lang Ying, II, pp. 824–5.

17 More examples of Ming critique of geomancy are in Ebrey, *Confucianism and Family Rituals*, p. 172, and Ebrey, trans., *Chu Hsi's Family Rituals*, p. 106, n. 118.

18 WZMJ, I, p. 299. The hill's geomantic connections are also noted in Zhang Jiaji, p. 189, and the geomancy of Peking is discussed in Smith, p. 147. The flourishing of trees is always in Ming literature a sign of a geomantically favourable spot, a topic that might be explored with regard to garden description.

19 Hargett, p. 7.

20 WZMJ, II, p. 498.

21 Smith, pp. 371–2.

22 Joan Hornby, 'China', in *Ethnographic Objects in the Royal Danish Kunstkammer*, ed Bente Dam-Mikkelsen and Torben Lundbaek (Copenhagen, 1980), pp. 155–219 (216).

23 WZMJ, II, p. 500.

24 Smith, p. 159, accepts all three as being closely related through 'yinyang complementarity'.

25 Roger Goepper, *The Essence of Chinese Painting* (London, 1963), pp. 147–74.

26 Hay, *Huang Kung-wang's 'Dwelling in the Fu-ch'un Mountains'*, p. 239.

27 Susan Bush, 'Long-mo, Kai-ho and Ch'i-fu: Some Implications of Wang Yuan-ch'i's Three Compositional Terms', *Oriental Art*, n.s. VIII (1962), pp. 120–27; John B. Henderson, *The Development and Decline of Chinese Cosmology* (New York, 1984), pp. 196–7, 228–37.

28 *Wu xian zhi, juan* 23, p. 43b.

29 Ruitenbeek, pp. 38, 61.

30 *The Plum in the Golden Vase, or Chin P'ing Mei: Volume One: The Gathering*, trans. David Tod Roy (Princeton, 1994), p. 295.

31 For a demonstration of this, in a context where collective memory ascribes geomantic considerations to landscape features, but it would be difficult to intuit them from observing the lie of the land now, see Patrick H. Hase and Lee Man-yip, 'Sheung Wo Hang Village, Hong Kong: A Village Shaped by Fengshui', in *Chinese Landscapes: The Village as Place*, ed. Roland G. Knapp (Honolulu, 1992), pp. 79–94.

32 Ruitenbeek, pp. 278–88 (reproduced are quatrains nos 63 and 67).

33 Quoted in Ruitenbeek, p. 38.

34 Wen Zhenheng, pp. 36–7.

35 Xie Zhaozhe, p. 245.

36 Wen Zhenheng, pp. 36–7, is a list of such 'taboos'.

37 For example, Ruitenbeek, p. 70.

38 Wen Zhenheng, p. 118.

39 Wen Zhenheng, p. 111.

40 Ruitenbeek, p. 288 (quatrain no. 64).

41 On linkages between the human countenance and the landscape see Mette Siggstedt, 'Forms of Fate: An Investigation of the Relationship Between Formal Protraiture, Especially Ancestor Portraits, and Physiognomy (*xiangshu*) in China', *Proceedings of the International Colloquium on Chinese Art History: Painting and Callligraphy*, 2 vols, National Palace Museum (Taipei, 1992), II, pp. 713–48.

42 Ji Cheng (Hardie translation), pp. 45, 54.

43 Beattie, pp. 5–7.

44 Frank Leeming, 'Official Landscapes in Traditional China', *Journal of the Economic and Social History of the Orient*, XXIII (1980), pp. 153–204.

45 The impulse was always there to regularize. In 1432 the Prefect of Suzhou proposed splitting fields into uniform sections of 500 *mu*. Hamashima Atsutoshi, 'The Organization of Water Control in the Kiangnan Delta in the Ming Period', *Acta Asiatica*, XXXVIII (1980), pp. 69–92 (81).

46 Timothy Brook, 'The Spatial Structure of Ming Local Administration', *Late Imperial China*, VI (1985), pp. 1–55.

47 Ray Huang, *Taxation and Governmental Finance in Sixteenth-century Ming China* (Cambridge, 1974), pp. 99–100.

48 Wei Qingyuan, *Mingdai huang ce zhidu* (Beijing, 1961), pp. 111–20.

49 Peter H. Lee, *A Korean Storyteller's Miscellany: The 'P'aegwan chapki' of Ŏ Sukkwŏn* (Princeton, 1989), pp. 74–6.

50 For example, the representations of the property of the thinker Wang Gen, in *Chong xi Xinzhai Wang xian sheng quan ji*, 8 juan (1631 edn). A map in the manuscript genealogy of the Wu family of Huizhou is cited in Harriet T. Zurndorfer, *Change and Continuity in Chinese Local History: The Development of Hui-chou Prefecture 800 to 1800*, Sinica Leidensia 20 (Leiden, 1989) p. 135, n. 75.

51 Chaso Kang, 'New Data on Land Ownership in Ming-Ch'ing China: A Research Note', *Journal of Asian Studies*, XL (1981), pp. 719–34 (733).

52 Kang Chao, *Man and Land in Chinese History: An Economic Analysis* (Stanford, 1986), p. 96, discounts the more usual explanation of equal division among heirs as the chief cause of fragmentation of landholdings.

53 Huang, pp. 98–99.

54 Hamashima, p. 77.

55 Ibid., pp. 73–4, 81, 84.

56 Du Shiran, 'Mingdai shuxue ji qi shehui beijing', *Ziran kexueshi yanjiu*, VIII (1989), pp. 9–16 (10).

57 Needham, *Science and Civilisation in China*, III, p. 25; Frank J. Swetz, *The Sea Island Mathematical Manual: Surveying and Mathematics in Ancient China* (University Park, PA, 1992), p. 9.

58 Kang Chao, *Man and Land*, pp. 70–71.

59 Ibid., pp. 71–3. More detail is given by the same author in Zhao Gang, 'Ming Qing diji yanjiu', *Zhongyang yanjiuyuan jindaishi yanjiusuo jikan*, XIX (1980), pp. 37–59 (46–51).

60 But see Ray Huang, *1587, A Year of No Significance: The Ming Dynasty in Decline* (New Haven and London, 1981), pp. 138–41, where a significantly different point is argued.

61 Hai Rui, *Hai Rui ji*, 2 vols (Beijing, 1962), pp. 190–201.

62 He Liangjun, *Si you zhai cong shuo*, Yuan Ming shiliao biji congkan, Zhonghua shuju edn (Beijing, 1983), pp. 113, 121.

63 Du Lianzhe, p. 7.

64 Michael Baxandall, *Painting and Experience in Fifteenth-century Italy: A Primer in the Social History of Pictorial Style* (Oxford and New York, 1972), pp. 86–93.

65 Needham, III, pp. 75–6.

66 Cosgrove, p. 111.

67 H. F. Schurman, 'Traditional Property Concepts in China', *Far Eastern Quarterly*, XV (1956), pp. 507–16.

68 G. E. Aylmer, 'The Meaning and Definition of "Property" in Seventeenth-century England', *Past and Present*, LXXXVI (1980), pp. 87–97.

69 For example Inden, p. 144.

70 Mote, 'A Millenium', p. 64, n. 20.

71 Burke, p. 152.

72 Cosgrove, p. 71.

73 Qian Yong, p. 17. Wu Sangui's son-in-law was the owner and restorer of the derelict Garden of the Unsuccessful Politician.

74 Romeyn Taylor, 'Official and Popular Religion and the Political Organization of Chinese Society in the Ming', in *Orthodoxy in Late Imperial China*, ed. Kwang-ching Liu (Berkeley, Los Angeles and Oxford, 1990), pp. 126–57 (151).

75 Ebrey, *Chu Hsi's Family Rituals*, p. 109, n. 130. For examples of Ming *mai di juan* see Chen Boquan, 'Jiangxi chutu dijuan zong shu', *Wenwu* (1987.3), pp. 223–31, also Ikeda On, 'Chugoku rekidai boken rakkyo', *Toyo bunka kenkyujo kiyo*, LXXXVI (1981), pp. 193–278.

76 Ebrey, *Confucianism and Family Ritual*, p. 84.

77 Shuzo, p. 149.

78 C. B. McPherson, *The Political Theory of Possessive Individualism from Hobbes to Locke* (Oxford, 1962).

79 Zurndorfer, pp. 83–4.

80 Qian Yong, p. 524.

81 Tao Fuhai, 'Shanxi Xiangfen Dingcun minju', *Wenwu* (1992.6), pp. 63–62 (62).

82 He Liangjun, p. 312.

83 Stewart, p. 127.

Conclusion

1 Anon, 'Jielu maodun, chang suo yu yan – Wenhua bu yaoqing zai jing wenwu zhuanjia juxing zuotan', *Wenwu cankao ziliao* (1957.6), pp. 3–7.

2 The next issue opened with a savage attack signed by Li Wenxin, 'Quanguo wenwu gongzuozhe tuanjieqilai, zai dang de qizhi xia fencui youpai fenzi de jingong – su Chen Mengjia deng de miulun', *Wenwu cankao ziliao* (1956.8), pp. 1–2.

3 *Yangzhou hua fang ku*, cited in Tong Jun, p. 28.

4 Gao Jin, *juan* 99, pp. 4a–5b, 6a–7b.

5 Jean Claude Philippe Isidore Hedde, *Déscription méthodique des produits divers recueillis dans un voyage en Chine* (St Etienne, 1848), p. 81, cat. no. 388. The map of Suzhou is on p. 77.

6 Mote, 'Millenium', p. 47, quoting Hampden C. Du Bose, *'Beautiful Soo': A Handbook to Soochow* (Shanghai, 1911).

7 F. R. Nance, *Soochow, The Garden City* (Shanghai, 1936).

8 Liu Dunzhen, *Suzhou gu jianzhu diaocha ji*, Zhongguo yingzao xueshe (Beijing, 1936), p. 3.

9 Nance, p. 42.

10 The layout of the museum is extensively described in Suzhou yuanlin bowuguan, *Suzhou yuanlin bowuguan jian guan jinian* (Suzhou, 1992). See also *Suzhou yuanlin bowuguan jian guan ziliao huibian* (Collected Materials on the Opening of the Suzhou Garden Museum) (Suzhou, 1992).

11 For example Kiyohiko Munakata, 'Mysterious Heavens and Chinese Classical Gardens', *Res*, XV (1988), pp. 61–88.

12 Pei-yi Wu, pp. 201–3: Brook, *Praying for Power* is richly suggestive, e.g. his notice (p. 255) of the building of a garden for a Ningbo monastery in 1631.

13 *The Plum in the Golden Vase*, pp. 377–9.

14 Jack M. Potter, 'Cantonese Shamanism', in *Religion and Ritual in Chinese Society*, ed. Arthur P. Wolf (Stanford, 1974), pp. 207–31 (213).

15 Celeste Olalquiaga, *Megalopolis: Contemporary Cultural Sensibilities* (Minneapolis and Oxford, 1992), p. 93.

Bibliography

Anon., 'Social Gatherings in the Ming Period', *Annual Report of the Librarian of Congress for 1940*, 1974 reprint edn, compiled by P. K. Yu, vol. II, pp. 648–50

Anon., 'Jielu maodun, chang suo yu yan – Wenhua bu yaoqing zai jing wenwu zhuanjia juxing zuotan' (Reveal contradictions and speak out freely – The Ministry of Culture invites cultural relics specialists in the capital to participate in a conference), *Wenwu cankao ziliao* (1957.6), pp. 3–7

Appadurai, Arjun, 'Introduction: Commodities and the Politics of Value', in Arjun Appadurai, ed., *The Social life of Things: Commodities in Cultural Perspective* (Cambridge, 1986), pp. 3–63

Austen, Ralph, *A Treatise of Fruit-Trees together with The Spirituall Use of an Orchard* (Oxford, 1653), The English Landscape Garden reprint edn, edited with introductory notes by John Dixon Hunt (New York and London, 1982)

Aylmer, G. E., 'The Meaning and Definition of "Property" in Seventeenth-century England', *Past and Present*, LXXXVI (1980), pp. 87–97

Barnhart, Richard M., *Peach Blossom Spring: Gardens and Flowers in Chinese Painting* (New York, 1983)

Barrell, John, *The Idea of Landscape* (Cambridge, 1972)

– *The Dark Side of the Landscape* (Cambridge, 1983)

– 'The Public Prospect and the Private View: The Politics of Taste in Eighteenth-century Britain', in Simon Pugh, ed., *Reading Landscape*, pp. 19–40

Baxandall, Michael, *Painting and Experience in Fifteenth-century Italy: A Primer in the Social History of Pictorial Style*, 2nd edn (Oxford and New York, 1988)

Beattie, Hilary J., *Land and Lineage in China: A study of T'ung-ch'eng county, Anhwei, in the Ming and Ch'ing dynasties*, Cambridge Studies in Chinese History Literature and Institutions (Cambridge, 1979)

Berkowitz, Alan J., 'The Moral Hero: A Pattern of Reclusion in Traditional China', *Monumenta Serica*, XL (1992), pp. 1–32

– 'Reclusion in Traditional China: A Selected List of References', *Monumenta Serica*, XL (1992), pp. 33–46

Bian min tu zuan (Illustrated Epitome to Benefit the People), Zhongguo gudai keji tulu congbian chu ji 2, Zhonghua shuju fascimile of 1593 edn, 4 vols (Beijing, 1959)

Bickford, Maggie et al., *Bones of Jade, Soul of Ice: The Flowering Plum in Chinese Art*, Yale University Art Gallery (New Haven, 1985)

Bourdieu, Pierre, *Distinction: A Social Critique of the Judgement of Taste*, trans. Richard Nice (London, 1984)

Boxer, C. R., ed., *South China in the Sixteenth Century*, The Hakluyt Society, 2nd series, vol. 106 (London, 1953)

Bray, Francesca, *Science and Civilisation in China: Volume 6, Biology and Biological Technology. Part II: Agriculture* (Cambridge, 1984)

(British Museum), *Chinese and Associated Lacquer from the Garner Collection* (London, 1973)

Brokaw, Cynthia J., *The Ledgers of Merit and Demerit: Social Change and Moral Order in Late Imperial China* (Princeton, 1991)

Brook, Timothy, 'The Spatial Structure of Ming Local Administration', *Late Imperial China*, 6/1 (1984), pp. 1–55

– *Geographical Sources of Ming-Qing History*, Michigan Monographs in Chinese Studies 58 (Ann Arbor, 1988)

Brown, Peter, *Society and the Holy in Late Antiquity* (Berkeley, Los Angeles and Oxford, 1989)

Burke, Peter, '*Res et verba*: Conspicuous Consumption in the Early Modern World', in J. Brown and R. Porter, eds, *Consumption and the World of Goods* (London, 1993)

Bush, Susan, 'Lung-mo, K'ai-ho and Ch'i-fu: Some Implications of Wang Yuan-ch'i's Three Compositional Terms', *Oriental Art*, n.s. VIII (1962), pp. 120–27

Cahill, James, *Parting at The Shore: Chinese Painting of the Early and Middle Ming Dynasty, 1368–1580* (New York and Tokyo, 1978)

– *Three Alternative Histories of Chinese Painting*, The Franklin D. Murphy Lectures, Spencer Museum of Art, The University of Kansas (Lawrence, KS, 1988)

– 'Types of Artist-Patron Transactions in Chinese Painting', in Chu-tsing Li, ed., *Artists and Patrons: Some Social and Economic Aspects of Chinese Painting* (Lawrence, KS, 1989)

Cao Xueqin, *The Story of the Stone*, trans. David Hawkes and John Minford, 5 vols (Harmondsworth, 1972–1986)

Cartier, Michel, *Une réforme locale en Chine au XVIe siecle. Hai Rui à Chun'an, 1558–1562*, Le Monde d'outre-mer passe et present, Première série, Etudes, 39 (Paris, 1973)

– 'Une nouvelle historiographie chinoise. La formation d'un marché national vue par Wu Chengming', *Annales*, XLI/6 (1986), pp. 1303–12

Chan, Wing-Tsit, 'Man and Nature in the Chinese Garden', in Henry Inn, *Chinese Houses and Gardens*, ed. Shao Chang Lee, revd edn (New York, 1950)

Chao Kang, 'New Data on Land Ownership in Ming-Ch'ing China: A Research Note', *Journal of Asian Studies*, 40 (1981), pp. 719–34

– *Man and Land in Chinese History: An Economic Analysis* (Stanford, 1986)

Chen Boquan, 'Jiangxi chutu dijuan zong shu' (A general account of land deeds excavated in Jiangxi), *Wenwu* (1987.3), pp. 223–31

Chen Congzhou, *Suzhou yuanlin* (Gardens of Suzhou) (Shanghai, 1956)

Chen Guodong, 'Ku miao yu fen Ru fu – Ming mo Qing chu shengyuan ceng de shehuixing dongzuo' (Weeping in the temple and burning the Confucian garments – A social gesture of the *shengyuan* stratum in the late Ming and early Qing), *Xin shixue* 3/1 (1992), pp. 69–94

Chen Hengli and Wang Dacan, '*Bu nong shu*' yanjiu (A Study of 'The Supplementary Book of Agriculture') (Beijing, 1958)

Chen Zhi and Zhang Gongshi, eds, *Zhongguo lidai mingyuanji xuan zhu* (A Selection of Writings on Famous Gardens in Chinese History) (Hefei, 1983)

Chong xi Xinzhai Wang xian sheng quan ji (Re-cut Complete Works of Master Wang Xinzhai [Wang Gen]), 8 *juan* (1631)

Chun, Woon Young, BSF, MF, *Chinese Economic Trees* (Shanghai, 1921)

Clapp, Anne de Coursey, *Wen Cheng-ming: The Ming Artist and Antiquity*, Artibus Asiae Supplementum 34 (Ascona, 1975)

– *The Painting of T'ang Yin* (Chicago, 1991)

Clunas, Craig, *Superfluous Things: Material Culture and Social Status in Early Modern China* (Cambridge, 1991)

– 'Some Literary evidence for Gold and Silver Vessels in the Ming Period (1368–1644)', in Michael Vickers and Julian Raby, eds, *Pots and Pans: A Colloquium on Precious Metals and Ceramics*, Oxford Studies in Islamic Art 3 (Oxford, 1987), pp. 83–7

– 'Ideal and Reality in the Ming Garden', in Erik de Jong and Leslie Tjon Sie Fat, eds, *The Authentic Garden* (Amsterdam, 1991), pp. 197–205

– 'Regulation of Consumption and the Institution of Correct Morality by the Ming State', in Chün-chieh Huang and Erik Zürcher, eds, *Norms and the State in China*, Sinica Leidensia 28 (Leiden, New York and Cologne, 1993), pp. 39–49

– review of Rolf A. Stein, *The World in Miniature*, in *Journal of the Economic and Social history of the Orient*, xxxv (1993), pp. 370–72

Coffin, David R., *The Villa in the Life of Renaissance Rome* (Princeton, 1979)

– 'The "Lex Hortorum" and Access to Gardens of Latium During the Renaissance', *Journal of Garden History*, 11/3 (1982), pp. 210–32

Cosgrove, Denis, *The Palladian Landscape* (University Park, PA, 1993)

Currie, Christopher K., 'Fishponds as Garden Features, c. 1550–1750', *Garden History*, Journal of the Garden History Society, xviii (1990), pp. 22–46

Dan Shiyuan, *Mingdai jianzhu dashi nianbiao* (Chronology of Major Architectural Events of the Ming Period), photographic reprint of original *Zhongguo yingzao xueshe* edn of 1926 (Taibei, 1976)

Dardess, John W., 'Settlement, Land Use, Labor and Estheticism in T'ai-ho County, Kiangsi', *Harvard Journal of Asiatic Studies*, 1L/2 (1990), pp. 295–364

De Certeau, Michel, *The Practice of Everyday Life*, trans. Steven Rendell (Berkeley, Los Angeles and London, 1984)

Dennerline, Jerry, *The Chia-ting Loyalists: Confucian Leadership and Social Change in Seventeenth-century China* (New Haven and London, 1981)

D'Elia, Pasquale M., SJ, ed., *Fonti Ricciane . . .*, 3 vols (Rome, 1942)

Du Shiran, 'Mingdai shuxue ji qi shehui beijing' (Ming mathematics and its social background), *Ziran kexueshi yanjiu*, viii/1 (1989), pp. 9–16

Du Lianzhe, *Mingdai zizhuan wenchao* (Selected Autobiographical Writings of the Ming Period) (Taibei, 1977)

Ebrey, Patricia Buckley, *Chu Hsi's Family Rituals: A Twelfth-century Chinese Manual for the Performance of Cappings, Weddings, Funerals and Ancestral Rites*, trans., with annotation and introduction, by Patricia Buckley Ebrey, Princeton Library of Asian Translations Series (Princeton, 1991)

– *Confucianism and Family Ritual in China: A Social History of Writing about Rites* (Princeton, 1991)

Edwards, Richard, *The Field of Stones: A Study of the Art of Shen Chou (1427–1509)*, Smithsonian Institution, Freer Gallery of Art Oriental Studies no. 5 (Washington, DC, 1962)

– *The Art of Wen Cheng-ming (1470–1559)*, with an essay by Anne De Coursey Clapp, and special contributions by Ling-yun Shih Liu, Steven D. Owyoung, James Robinson and other seminar members, 1974–75 (Ann Arbor, 1976)

Eight Dynasties of Chinese Painting: The Collections of the Nelson–Atkins Museum of Art, Kansas City, and the Cleveland Museum of Art, with essays by Wai-kan Ho, Sherman E. Lee, Laurence Sickman and Marc F. Wilson (Cleveland, 1980)

Everett, Thomas H., *The New York Botanical Garden Illustrated Encyclopaedia of Horticulture*, 10 vols (New York and London, 1981)

Fan Wei, 'Village *Fengshui* Principles', in Roland G. Knapp, ed., *Chinese Landscapes: The Village as Place* (Honolulu, 1992), pp. 35–45

Ferguson, John C., 'Wang Ch'uan', *Ostasiatische Zeitschrift*, iii (1914–15), pp. 51–60

Feuchtwang, Stephen D. R., *An Anthropological Analysis of Chinese Geomancy* (Vientiane, 1974, reprinted Taibei 1982)

Foucault, Michel, *The Archaeology of Knowledge*, trans. A. M. Sheridan-Smith (New York, 1972)

– *The Order of Things: An Archaeology of the Human Sciences*, trans. Alan Sheridan-Smith (London, 1989)

– 'Of Other Spaces', *Diacritics*, xvi (Spring 1981), pp. 22–27

Frankel, Hans H., 'The Contemplation of the Past in T'ang Poetry', in Arthur F. Wright and Denis Twitchett, eds, *Perspectives on the T'ang* (New Haven and London, 1973), pp. 345–66

Fu Shanyi and Liu Shanghua, eds, *Panjing yishu zhanlan* (An Exhibition of the Art of Panjing) (Beijing, 1979)

Gao Yongyuan, 'Gudai Suzhou chengshi jingguan de lishi dili toushi' (A historical geography perspective on the urban landscape of early Suzhou), *Lishi dili*, VII (1990), pp. 62–71

Gao Jin, ed., *Nan xun sheng dian* (Imperial Digest of the Southern Tours), preface dated 1771, 120 *juan* edn

Goepper, Roger, *The Essence of Chinese Painting*, trans. M. Bullock (London, 1963)

Goodrich, L. Carrington and Chaoying Fang, eds, *Dictionary of Ming Biography*, 2 vols (New York and London, 1976)

Goody, Jack, *The Culture of Flowers* (Cambridge, 1993)

Graham, Dorothy, *Chinese Gardens: Gardens of the Contemporary Scene, an Account of their Design and Symbolism* (New York, 1938)

Gu Qiyuan, *Ke zuo zhui yu* (Idle Chatter on Sitting with my Guests), Yuan Ming shiliao biji congkan edn (Beijing, 1987)

Hai Rui, *Hai Rui ji* (Works of Hai Rui), 2 vols (Beijing, 1962)

Hamashima Atsutoshi, 'The Organization of Water Control in the Kiangnan Delta in the Ming Period', *Acta Asiatica*, XXXVIII (1980), pp. 69–92

Handlin Smith, Joanna F., 'Gardens in Ch'i Piao-chia's Social World: Wealth and Values in Late Ming Kiangnan', *Journal of Asian Studies*, LI (1992), pp. 55–81

Hargett, James M., 'Huizong's Magic Marchmount: The Genyue Pleasure Park of Kaifeng', *Monumenta Serica*, XXXVIII (1989–90), pp. 1–48

Harrist, Robert E., 'Site Names and their Meaning in the Garden of Solitary Enjoyment', *Journal of Garden History*, XIII (1993), pp. 199–212

Hase, Patrick H. and Lee Man-yip, 'Sheung Wo Hang Village, Hong Kong: A Village Shaped by *Fengshui*', in Roland G. Knapp, ed., *Chinese Landscapes: The Village as Place* (Honolulu, 1992), pp. 79–94

Hay, A. J., *Huang Kung-wang's 'Dwelling in the Fu-ch'un Mountains': Dimensions of a Landscape*, unpublished PhD diss., Princeton University, 1978

– *Kernels of Energy, Bones of Earth: The Rock in Chinese Art*, China Institute in America (New York, 1985)

– 'Structure and Aesthetic Criteria in Chinese Rocks and Art', *Res*, XIII (Spring 1987), pp. 6–22

Jean Claude Philippe Isidore Hedde, *Déscription méthodique des produits divers réceuillis dans un voyage en Chine* (St Etienne, 1848)

Henderson, John B., *The Development and Decline of Chinese Cosmology* (New York, 1984)

Ho Peng Yoke, *Li, Qi and Shu: An Introduction to Science and Civilisation in China* (Seattle and London, 1985)

– 'Chinese Science: the Traditional Chinese View', *Bulletin of the School of Oriental and African Studies*, LIV/3 (1991), pp. 506–19

Ho Ping-ti, 'The Introduction of American Food Plants into China', *American Anthropologist*, LVII (1955), pp. 191–201

Hong Kong Museum of Art, *Anthology of Chinese Art: Min Chiu Society Silver Jubilee Exhibition* (Hong Kong, 1985)

Hornby, Joan, 'China', in Bente Dam-Mikkelsen and Torben Lundbaek, eds, *Ethnographic Objects in the Royal Danish Kunstkammer*, Nationalmuseets skrifter Etnografisk raekke vol. 17 (Copenhagen, 1980), pp. 155–219

Hou Renzhi, ed., *Beijing lishi dituji* (Historical Atlas of Beijing) (Beijing, 1985)

Huang, Ray, *Taxation and Governmental Finance in Sixteenth-century Ming China*, Cambridge Studies in Chinese History, Literature and Institutions (Cambridge, 1974)

– _1587, A Year of No Significance: The Ming Dynasty in Decline_ (New Haven and London, 1981)

Huang Xingzeng, _Wu feng lu_ (A Record of the Customs of Wu), 1 _juan_, Xue hai lei bian, Han fen lou reprint edn (Shanghai, 1920)

Huangfu Fang, ed., _Changzhou xian zhi_ (Gazetteer of Changzhou County), 14 _juan_, preface dated 1571, published 1598

Hucker, Charles O., _The Censorial System of Ming China_, Stanford Studies in the Civilizations of Eastern Asia (Stanford, 1966)

– _A Dictionary of Official Titles in Imperial China_ (Stanford, 1985)

Hummel, Arthur W., _Eminent Chinese of the Ch'ing Period_, Ch'eng Wen Publishing Company reprint edn (Taipei, 1970)

Hunt, John Dixon, _Gardens and the Picturesque: Studies in the History of Landscape Architecture_ (Cambridge, MA, 1992)

Hyland, Alice R. M., _Deities, Emperors, Ladies and Literati: Figure Paintings of the Ming and Qing Dynasties_ (Seattle and London, 1987)

– 'Colophons Written by Wen Jia (1501–1583)', _Oriental Art_, n.s. xxxviii/3 (1992), pp. 134–44

Inden, Ronald, _Imagining India_ (Oxford, 1990)

Ip, Benjamin Wai-Bun, 'The Expression of Nature in Traditional Su Zhou Gardens', _Journal of Garden History_, vi/2 (1986), pp. 125–40

Jackson, John Brinckerhoff, _The Necessity for Ruins, and Other Topics_ (Amherst, 1980)

Ji Cheng, _The Craft of Gardens_, trans. Alison Hardie, photographs by Zhong Ming, with a foreword by Maggie Keswick (New Haven and London, 1988)

Jiang Zhaoshen, _Wen Zhengming yu Suzhou huatan_ (Wen Zhengming and the Suzhou Painting World), Gu gong congkan jiazhong (Taibei, 1977)

Jin Xuezhi, _Zhongguo yuanlin meixue_ (Chinese Garden Aesthetics) (Nanjing, 1990)

Karson, Robin, _Fletcher Steele, Landscape Architect: An Account of the Gardenmaker's Life, 1885–1971_ (New York, 1989)

Keirstead, Thomas, _The Geography of Power in Medieval Japan_ (Princeton, 1992)

– 'Gardens and Estates: Medievality and Space', _Positions: East Asia Cultures Critique_, 1 (1993), pp. 289–320

Kerby, Kate, _An Old Chinese Garden: A Three-fold Masterpiece of Poetry, Calligraphy and Painting, by Wen Chen Ming, Famous Landscape Artist of the Ming Dynasty. Studies Written by Kate Kerby, Translations by Mo Zung Chung_, Chung Hwa Book Company (Shanghai, 1922)

Keswick, Maggie, _The Chinese Garden: History, Art and Architecture_ (London, 1978)

Kline, S. L., _Colonial Culhuacan, 1580–1600: A Social History of an Aztec Town_ (Albuquerque, 1986)

Kong Xu, ed., _Zhongguo guosho zaipei xue_ (The Cultivation of Chinese Fruit Trees) (Beijing, 1978)

Kong Zhen, 'Liao yi hua tu xie qing ju – Tan yuanlin, tingyuan wei ticai de Wumen huihua' (Simple pictures of pure dwellings – On Wu school paintings of gardens and estates), _Gugong bowuyuan yuankan_, xlix (1990.3), pp. 87–91

Laing, Ellen Johnston, 'Wen Tien and Chin Chün-ming', _Journal of the Institute of Chinese Studies of the Chinese University of Hong Kong_, viii/2 (1976), pp. 411–22

– 'Qiu Ying's Depiction of Sima Guang's Duluo [sic] Yuan and the View from the Chinese Garden', _Oriental Art_, n.s., xxxiii (1987), pp. 375–80

– 'Ch'iu Ying's Two Garden Paintings Belonging to the Chion-in, Kyoto', _Proceedings of the International Colloquium on Chinese Art History: Painting and Calligraphy_, 2 vols, National Palace Museum (Taipei, 1992), i, pp. 331–58

Lang Ying, *Qi xiu lei gao* (A Categorized Draft Seven Times Revised), Dushu jian ji congkan dierji edn, 2 vols (Taibei, 1984)

Laufer, Berthold, 'The Wang Ch'uan T'u, a Landscape of Wang Wei', *Ostasiatische Zeitschrift*, I (1912–13), pp. 28–55

Li Wenxin, 'Quanguo wenwu gongzuozhe tuanjieqilai, zai dang de qizhi xia fencui youpai fenzi de jingong – su Chen Mengjia deng de miulun' (Cultural relics workers of the whole nation unite, and under the banner of the Party smash the attack of rightist elements – refuting the slanders of Chen Mengjia and others), *Wenwu cankao ziliao* (1956.8), pp. 1–2

Liang Hongzhi, 'Zhuo zheng yuan ji' (A record of the Garden of the Unsuccessful Administrator), *Gu jin*, XII/I (1942), pp. 460–61

Lazzaro, Claudia, *The Italian Renaissance Garden: From the Conventions of Planting, Design and Ornament to the Grand Gardens of Sixteenth-century Central Italy* (New Haven and London, 1990)

Ledderose, Lothar, 'Subject Matter in Early Chinese Painting Criticism', *Oriental Art*, n.s., XIX (1973), pp. 1–15

Lee, Peter H., *A Korean Storyteller's Miscellany: The 'P'aegwan chapki' of Ŏ Sukkwŏn*, Princeton Library of Asian Translations (Princeton, 1989)

Leeming, Frank, 'Official Landscapes in Traditional China', *Journal of the Economic and Social History of the Orient*, XXIII (1980), pp. 153–204

Li, Chu-tsing, and James C. Y. Watt, eds, *The Chinese Scholar's Studio: Artistic Life in the Late Ming Period* (New York, 1987)

Liscomb, Kathlyn, 'The Eight Views of Beijing: Politics in Literati Art', *Artibus Asiae*, IL (1988–89), pp. 127–52

Liu Ce, *Zhongguo gudai yuan you* (Ancient Chinese Garden Parks) (Ningxia, 1979)

Liu Dunzhen, *Suzhou gu jianzhu diaocha ji* (An Investigation of the Ancient Buildings of Suzhou), Zhongguo yingzao xueshe (Beiping, 1936)

– *Suzhou gudian yuanlin* (Classic Gardens of Suzhou), Zhongguo jianzhu chubanshe (n.p., 1979)

– 'The Traditional Gardens of Suzhou (*Su zhou gu dian yuan lin*), an abridged translation by Frances Wood, *Garden History*, Journal of the Garden History Society, X/2 (1982), pp. 108–41

Liu Jiuan, 'Wumen huajia zhi biehaotu ji jian bie ju li' ('The By-name Pictures of the Wu School Painters, with some Examples of their Connoisseurship'), *Gugong bowuyuan yuankan*, XLIX (1990.3), pp. 54–61

Liu Tong and Yu Yizheng, *Di jing jing wu lüe* (Resume of the Sights and Affairs of the Imperial Capital), preface dated 1635, Beijing guji chubanshe edn (Beijing, 1980)

Liu Ts'un-yan, 'The Penetration of Taoism into the Ming Neo-Confucian Elite', *T'oung Pao*, LVII (1971), pp. 31–102

Liu Zongzhou, [*Zeng ding*] *Ren pu lei ji* (An Augmented Categorized Record of the Chart of Humanity), Shanghai Daxing tushu gongsi edn (Shanghai, 1935)

Loudon, J. C., *An Encyclopaedia of Gardening: Comprising the Theory and Practice of Horticulture, Floriculture, Arboriculture and Landscape Gardening, Including all the Latest Improvements; A General History of Gardening in all Countries; and a Statistical View of its Present State, with Suggestions for its Future Progress in the British Isles*, A New Edition, Considerably Improved and Enlarged (London, 1834)

McDermott, Joseph P., 'Bondservants in the T'ai-hu Basin During the Late Ming: A Case of Mistaken Indentities', *Journal of Asian Studies*, XL (1981), pp. 675–701

– 'The Making of a Chinese Mountain, Huangshan: Politics and Wealth in Chinese Art', *Art and Power in Japan and China*, special number of *Asian*

Cultural Studies, International Christian University Publications III-A (Tokyo, 1989), pp. 145–76

– review of Ji Cheng, *The Craft of Gardens*, trans. Alison Hardie, in *Garden History*, Journal of the Garden History Society, XVIII/1 (1990), pp. 70–74

McPherson, C. B., *The Political Theory of Possessive Individualism* (Oxford, 1962)

Marmé, Michael, 'Population and Possibility in Ming (1368–1644) Suzhou: A Quantified Model', *Ming Studies*, XII (Spring 1981), pp. 29–64

March, Andrew, 'An Appreciation of Chinese Geomancy', *Journal of Asian Studies*, XXVII (1968), pp. 253–67

March, Benjamin, 'Linear Perspective in Chinese Painting', *Eastern Art: An Annual Published for the CAA*, III (1931), pp. 113–39

Meyer, Jeffery E., *The Dragons of Tiananmen: Beijing as a Sacred City* (Columbia, SC, 1991)

Miller, Mara, 'Gardens as Works of Art: The Problem of Uniqueness', *British Journal of Aesthetics*, XXVI (1986), pp. 252–6

Mingren zhuanji ziliao suoyin (Index to Ming Biographical Materials), Zhonghua shuju reprint edn (Beijing, 1987)

Mori Masao, 'The Gentry in the Ming – An Outline of the Relations Between the *Shih-ta-fu* and Local Society', *Acta Asiatica*, XXXVIII (1980), pp. 31–53

Mote, F. W., 'The Transformation of Nanking, 1350–1400', in G. William Skinner, ed., *The City in Late Imperial China* (Stanford, 1977), pp. 101–53

– 'A Millenium of Chinese Urban History: Form, Time and Space Concepts in Soochow', *Rice University Studies*, LIX/4 (1973), pp. 35–65

– and Dennis Twitchett, eds, *The Cambridge History of China*, vol. 7 *The Ming Dynasty, 1368–1644: Part I* (Cambridge, 1988)

Munakata, Kiyohiko, 'Mysterious Heavens and Chinese Classical Gardens', *Res*, XV (1988), pp. 61–88

Nance, F. R., *Soochow, The Garden City*, Kelly & Walsh Ltd (Shanghai, 1936)

Needham, Joseph, with the collaboration of Wang Ling, *Science and Civilization in China. Volume 3: Mathematics and the Sciences of the Heavens and the Earth* (Cambridge, 1959)

– with the collaboration of Lu Gwei-djen and a special contribution by Huang Hsing-tsung, *Science and Civilization in China. Volume 6: Biology and Biological Technology, Part I: Botany* (Cambridge, 1986)

Nienhauser, William, H., Jr., ed., *The Indiana Companion to Traditional Chinese Literature* (Bloomington, 1986)

Niu Ruolin and Wang Huanru, eds, *Wu xian zhi* (Gazetteer of Wu County), preface dated 1642, 54 *juan* plus 1 *juan* of illustrations

Olalquiaga, Celeste, *Megalopolis: Contemporary Cultural Sensibilities* (Minneapolis and Oxford, 1992)

Potter, Jack M., 'Cantonese Shamanism', in Arthur P. Wolf, ed., *Religion and Ritual in Chinese Society* (Stanford, 1974), pp. 207–31

Pugh, Simon, ed., *Reading Landscape: Country – City – Capital*, Cultural Politics (Manchester and New York, 1990)

– 'Introduction: Stepping out into the open', in *Reading Landscape*, Simon Pugh ed., pp. 1–6

Qian Yun, ed, *Classical Chinese Gardens*, Joint Publishing Company (Hong Kong and Beijing, 1982)

Qian Yong, *Lü yuan cong hua* (General Talk from the Garden of Clogs), Qingdai shiliao biji congkan edn, 2 vols (Beijing, 1979)

Ruitenbeek, Klaas, *Carpentry and Building in Late Imperial China: A Study of the Fifteenth-century Carpenter's Manual, Lu Ban Jing*, Sinica Leidensia 23 (Leiden, New York and Cologne, 1993)

Said, Edward, *Culture and Imperialism* (New York, 1993)

Sawada, Masahiro, 'Mindai Soshū Bun-shi no inseki. Gochū bun-en kōsatsu e no tekakari' (The Matrimonial Relations of the Wens in Su Chou in the Ming Dynasty), *Daitō bunka daigaku kiyō (jimbun kagaku)*, XXII (1984.3), pp. 55–71

Schafer, Edward H., *Tu Wan's Stone Catalogue of Cloudy Forest* (Berkeley and Los Angeles, 1961)

– 'Hunting Parks and Animal Enclosures in Ancient China', *Journal of the Economic and Social History of the Orient*, XI (1968), pp. 318–43

Schinz, Alfred, *Cities in China: Urbanization of the Earth/Urbanisierung der Erde*, ed. Wolf Tietze (Berlin and Stuttgart, 1989)

Schoppa, R. Keith, *Xiang Lake: Nine Centuries of Chinese Life* (New Haven and London, 1989)

Schurman, H. F., 'Traditional Property Concepts in China', *Far Eastern Quarterly*, XV/4 (1956), pp. 507–16

Shen Defu, *Wanli ye huo bian* (Random Gatherings of the Wanli Era, preface dated 1606), Yuan Ming shiliao biji congkan, 2nd edn, 3 vols (Beijing, 1980)

Shen Shixing, *Da Ming Huidian* (Collected Statutes of the Great Ming), Zhonghua shuju edn (Beijing, 1989)

Shuzo Shiga, 'Family Property and the Law of Inheritance in Traditional China', in David C. Buxbaum, ed., *Chinese Family Law and Social Change in Historical and Comparative Perspective* (Seattle and London, 1978), pp. 109–50

Siggstedt, Mette, 'Forms of Fate: An Investigation of the Relationship Between Formal Portraiture, Especially Ancestral Portraits, and Physiognomy (*xiangshu*) in China', *Proceedings of the International Colloquium on Chinese Art History: Painting and Calligraphy*, 2 vols, National Palace Museum (Taipei, 1992), II, pp. 713–48

Sirén, Osvald, *Gardens of China* (New York, 1949)

Smith, Richard J, *Fortune Tellers and Philosophers: Divination in Traditional Chinese Society* (Boulder, San Francisco and Oxford, 1991)

Steele, Fletcher, 'China Teaches: Ideas and Moods from Landscape of the Celestrial Empire', *Landscape Architecture*, XXXVII (1946–47), pp. 88–93

– *Gardens and People* (Boston, 1964)

Stein, Rolf A., *The World in Miniature: Container Gardens and Dwellings in Far Eastern Religious Thought*, trans. Phyllis Brooks, with a new foreword by Edward H. Schafer (Stanford, 1990)

Stewart, Susan, *On Longing: Narratives of the Miniature, the Gigantic, the Souvenir, the Collection* (Durham, NC, and London, 1993)

Stuart, Jan, 'Ming Dynasty Gardens Reconstructed in Words and Images', *Journal of Garden History*, X (1990), pp. 162–72

– review of Ji Cheng, *The Craft of Gardens*, trans. Alison Hardie, in *Journal of the Society of Architectural Historians*, XLIX (1990), pp. 213–14

Sun Yuinwei, ed., *Zhongguo guoshu shi yu guoshu ziyuan* (The History of Origins of Fruiting Trees in China) (Shanghai, 1983)

Suzhou shi wenwu baoquan weiyuanhui, *Suzhou Huqiu ta chutu wenwu* (Cultural Relics Excavated at Tiger Hill Pagoda, Suzhou) (Beijing, 1958)

Suzhou yuanlin bowuguan, *Suzhou yuanlin bowuguan jian guan jinian* (A Souvenir of the Opening of the Suzhou Garden Museum) (Suzhou, 1992)

– *Suzhou yuanlin bowuguan jian guan ziliao huibian* (Collected Materials on the Opening of the Suzhou Garden Museum) (Suzhou, 1992)

Swetz, Frank J., *The Sea Island Mathematical Manual: Surveying and Mathematics in Ancient China* (University Park, PA, 1992)

Tao Fuhai, 'Shanxi Xiangfen Dingcun minju' (Vernacular dwellings in Dingcun, Xiangfen county, Shanxi province), *Wenwu* (1992.6), pp. 53–62

Taylor, Romeyn, 'Official and Popular Religion and the Political Organization of Chinese Society in the Ming', in Kwang-ching Liu, ed., *Orthodoxy in Late Imperial China*, Studies on China 10 (Berkeley, Los Angeles and Oxford, 1990), pp. 126–57

Thomas, Nicholas, *Entangled Objects: Exchange, Material Culture and Colonialism in the Pacific* (Cambridge, MA, and London, 1991)

Tian shui bing shan lu (A Record of the Waters of Heaven Melting the Iceberg), preface dated 1562, in *Ming Wuzong wai ji*, Zhongguo lishi yanjiu ziliao congshu edn, reprint of 1951 Shanghai Shenzhou guoguang she edn (Shanghai, 1982)

Tong Bingya, *Guoshu shihua* (The History of Fruit Trees) (Beijing, 1983)

Tong Jun, *Jiangnan yuanlin kao* (A Study of the Gardens of Jiangnan), 2nd edn (Beijing, 1984)

Tribe, Keith, *Land, Labour and Economic Discourse* (London, Henley and Boston, 1978)

Tsu, Frances Ya-sing (Zhu Ya-xin), *Landscape Design in Chinese Gardens* (New York, 1988)

Tuan, Yi-fu, 'Language and the Making of Place: A Narrative-Descriptive Approach', *Annals of the Association of American Geographers*, LXXXI/4 (1991), pp. 684–96

Van Erp-Houtepen, Ann, 'The Etymological Origin of the Garden', *Journal of Garden History*, VI (1986), pp. 227–31

Vermeer, Eduard B., 'The Decline of Hsing-hua Prefecture in the Early Ch'ing', in E. B. Vermeer, ed., *Development and Decline of Fukien Province in the 17th and 18th Centuries*, Sinica Leidensia 22 (Leiden, 1990)

Vinograd, Richard, 'Family Properties: Personal Context and Cultural Pattern in Wang Meng's *Pien Mountains* of 1366', *Ars Orientalis*, XIII (1982), pp. 1–29

Wakeman Jr., Frederic, *The Great Enterprise: The Manchu Reconstruction of Order in Seventeenth Century China*, 2 vols (Berkeley, Los Angeles and London, 1985)

Wang Ao, ed., *Gusu zhi* (Gazetteer of Gusu [Suzhou], preface dated 1506, Zhongguo shixue congshu facsimile edn (Taibei, 1956)

Wang Chongmin, *Zhongguo shanben shu tiyao* (Essentials of Chinese Rare Books) (Shanghai, 1983)

Wang Dongfeng, ed., *Jianming Zhongguo pengren cidian* (A Short Dictionary of Chinese Cookery) (Taiyuan, 1987)

Wang Jiacheng, 'Wen Zhengming ji qing yuanlin de xinlu licheng' (How Wen Cheng-ming Found Comfort in Gardens), *Proceedings of the International Colloquium on Chinese Art History: Painting and Calligraphy*, 2 vols, National Palace Museum (Taipei, 1992), I, pp. 359–76

Wang Jian, 'Wen Zhengming "Zhen shang zhai tu"' (Wen Zhengming's painting of 'The Studio of True Connoisseurship'), *Wenwu* (1978.6), pp. 89–90

Wang Juyuan, 'Suzhou Ming Qing zhai yuan fenge de fenxi' (An Analysis of Stylistic Change in Suzhou Gardens of the Ming and Qing) *Yuanyi xuebao/ Acta Horticulturalia*, 11/2 (May 1963), pp. 177–94

Wang Qi, *Yu yuan za ji* (Scattered Records from the Yu Garden), preface dated 1500), Yuan Ming biji shiliao congkan edn (Beijing, 1984)

Wang Shiqing, 'Dong Qichang de jiaoyou' (The Circle of Dong Qichang), in Wai-kam Ho and Judith G. Smith, eds, *The Century of Tung Ch'i-ch'ang 1555–1636*, 2 vols (Seattle and London, 1992), II, pp. 461–83

Wang Shiren, ' 'Shao yuan xiu xi tu' zhong suo jian de yixie Zhongguo tingyuan buzhi shoufa' (Some Compositional Devices of Chinese Gardens as Seen in the Picture 'The Rebuilding of the Dipper Garden'), *Wenwu cankao ziliao* (1957.6), pp. 20–24

Wang Yaoting, 'Tao hua yuan yu Hua xi yu yin' (*The Land of Peach Blossoms* and *A Recluse Angling on a Flowering Stream*), *Proceedings of the International Colloquium on Chinese Art History: Painting and Calligraphy*, 2 vols, National Palace Museum (Taipei, 1992), I, pp. 279–305

Wang Yuhu, *Zhongguo nongxue shulu* ('A Bibliography of Chinese Works on Agronomy'), 2nd edn (Beijing, 1979)

Wang Zhen, *Nong shu* (The Book of Agriculture), Zhonghua shuju edn (Beijing, 1956)

Wei Qingyuan, *Mingdai huang ce zhidu* (The Yellow Registers System of the Ming Dynasty) (Beijing, 1961)

Wen Han, *Wen shi zu pu* (Genealogy of the Wen Family), 1 juan, Qu shi congshu edn (Suzhou, n.d.)

Wen Zhaozhi, ed., *Wen shi wu jia ji* (Collected Works by Five Masters of the Wen Family), 4 juan, Qinding si ku quan shu zhen ben chu ji edn (Shanghai, 1934–5)

– *Huqiu shan zhi* (Gazetteer of Tiger Hill), 5 juan, preface dated 1578

Wen Zhengming, *Futian ji* (Works of Wen Zhengming), Mingdai yishujia ji huikan, 2 vols (Taibei, 1968)

– *Wen Zhengming ji* (Works of Wen Zhengming), ed. Zhou Daozhen, Shanghai guji chubanshe edn, 2 vols (Shanghai, 1987)

Wen Zhenheng, *Zhang wu zhi jiao zhu* (Annotated and Collated 'Treaties on Superfluous Things'), Jiangsu kexue chubanshe edn, annotations by Chen Zhi, Yang Zhaobo, ed. (Nanjing, 1984)

West, Stephen H., 'Cilia, Scale and Bristle: The Consumption of Fish and Shellfish in the Eastern Capital of the Northern Song', *Harvard Journal of Asiatic Studies*, XLVII (1990), pp. 595–634

Westcoatt, James, 'Landscapes of Transformation: Lessons from the Earliest Mughal Gardens in India, 1526–1530 AD', *Landscape Journal*, X (1991), pp. 105–14

Whitfield, Roderick, with an Addendum by Wen Fong, *In Pursuit of Antiquity: Chinese Paintings of the Ming and Ch'ing Dynasties from the Collection of Mr and Mrs Earl Morse*, The Art Museum, Princeton University (Rutland, VT, and Tokyo, 1969)

Wilhelm, Hellmut, 'Shih Ch'ung and His Chin-ku Yüan', *Monumenta Serica*, XVIII (1959), pp. 314–27

Williams, Robert, 'Rural Economy and the Antique in the English Landscape Garden', *Journal of Garden History*, VII/1 (1987), pp. 73–96

Wilson, Marc F., and Kwan S. Wong, *Friends of Wen Cheng-ming: A View from the Crawford Collection*, China House Gallery (New York, 1974)

Wright, Arthur F., 'The Cosmology of the Chinese City', in G. William Skinner, ed., *The City in Late Imperial China* (Stanford, 1977)

Wu Changyuan, *Chen yuan zhi lüe* (A Brief Gazetteer of the Imperial Capital), preface dated 1788, Beijing guji chubanshe edn (Beijing, 1981)

Wu, Pei-yi, *The Confucian's Progress: Autobiographical Writings in Traditional China* (Princeton, 1990)

Wu pai hua jiushi nian ping/Ninety Years of Wu School Painting, Guoli Gu gong bowuyuan (Taibei, 1975)

Xie Guozhen, ed., *Mingdai shehui jingji shiliao xuanbian* (Selected Materials on the Social and Economic History of the Ming Period), 3 vols (Fuzhou, 1980–81)

Xie Zhaozhe, *Wu za zu* (Five Collected Offerings), Guoxue Zhenben wenku edn, 1st series, no. 13, 2 vols (Shanghai, 1935)

Xu Guangqi, *Nong zheng quan shu jiao zhu* (Annotated and Collated 'Complete Book of the Administration of Agriculture'), commentary by Shi Shenghan, ed. Xibei nongxueyuan gu nongxue yanjiushi, 3 vols (Shanghai, 1983)

Xu Zhongling, 'Du Qiong he tade liang fu shanshui hua' (Du Qiong and two of his landscape paintings), *Wenwu* (1991.9), pp. 74–77

Yang, C. K., *Religion in Chinese Society: A Study of Contemporary Social Functions of Religion and Some of their Historical Factors* (Berkeley and Los Angeles, 1967)

Ye Jingyuan, *Zhongguo nongxue yichan xuan ji, jia lei di shisi zhong: Gan ju I* (Selections from China's Agricultural Heritage, 1.14: Citrus Fruits 1) (Beijing, 1958)

Yee, Cordell D. K., 'A Cartography of Introspection: Chinese Maps as Other then European', *Asian Art*, v/4 (1992), pp. 29–47

Yu Zongben, *Zhong shu shu* (The Book of Planting Trees), 1 *juan*, in *Ge zhi cong shui, han* 19, *ce* 103

Yuan Hongdao, *Yuan Zhonglang quan ji* (Complete works of Yuan Zhonglang [Yuan Hongdao], Guang zhi shuju edn (Hong Kong, n.d.)

– *Pilgrim of the Clouds: Poems and Essays from Ming China*, trans. Jonathan Chaves (New York and Tokyo, 1978)

Yuan Shu, 'Zhuo zheng yuan ji' (A Record of the Garden of the Unsuccessful Administrator), *Gu jin*, xiv/1 (1943), pp. 536–42

Zeitlin, Judith, 'The Petrified Heart: Obsession in Chinese Literature, Art, and Medicine', *Late Imperial China*, xii/1 (1991), pp. 1–26

Zhang Haipeng and Wang Yanyuan, eds, *Ming Qing Anhui shang ziliao xuan bian* (Selected Materials on Anhui Merchants in the Ming and Qing) Hefei, 1985)

Zhang Jiaji, *Zhongguo zao yuan shi* (A History of Chinese Gardens) (Taibei, 1990)

Zhang Jianhua, *Ming Qing Jiangsu wen ren nian biao* (A Chronology of Jiangsu Scholars of the Ming and Qing) (Shanghai, 1986)

Zhang Tingyu, ed., *Ming Shi* (The Ming History), Zhonghua shuju edn, 28 vols (Beijing, 1974)

Zhao Gang, 'Ming Qing diji yanjiu' (Land registers of the Ming and Qing), *Zhongyang yanjiuyuan jindaishi yanjiusuo jikan*, xix (1980), pp. 37–59

Zhongguo cong shu zong lu (General Index to Chinese Collectanea), revised edn, 3 vols (Shanghai, 1982)

Zhongguo shehui kexueyuan lishi yanjiusuo Ming shi shi, ed., *Ming shi shiliao congkan* (Collected Materials on Ming History), 1 (Nanjing, 1981)

Zhu Wenjie, 'Wuxi xin faxian Mingdai Gao Panlong shou shu jia xin' (Family letters in the handwriting of Gao Panlong newly discovered in Wuxi), *Wenwu* (1986.4), pp. 75–6

Zurndorfer, Harriet T., *Change and Continuity in Chinese Local History: The Development of Hui-chou Prefecture 800 to 1800*, Sinica Leidensia 20 (Leiden, 1989)

Index